TRAGEDY AFTER NIETZSCHE:

RAPTUROUS SUPERABUNDANCE

PAUL GORDON

Tragedy
after Nietzsche

Rapturous

Superabundance

UNIVERSITY OF ILLINOIS PRESS

URBANA AND CHICAGO

Library of Congress Cataloging-in-Publication Data
Gordon, Paul, 1951–
Tragedy after Nietzsche : rapturous superabundance /
Paul Gordon.
    p.   cm.
Includes bibliographical references and index.
ISBN 0-252-02574-1 (alk. paper)
    1. Tragic, The. 2. Nietzsche, Friedrich Wilhelm, 1844–
1900. Geburt der Tragödie. I. Title.
BH301.T7G67   2001
128—dc21   99-050656

What do *Oedipus Rex, Oedipus at Colonus, Medea, Hamlet, Phèdre, Hedda Gabler* . . . have in common? It seems that there cannot be a true theory of tragedy, for underlying every theory of tragedy is the assumption that tragedy has a set of necessary and sufficient properties.

—"Tragedy," *Encyclopedia of Philosophy*

The extent to which I therewith discovered the concept "tragic," the knowledge at last attained of what the psychology of tragedy is, I most recently expressed in the *Twilight of the Idols:* "Affirmation of life even in its strangest and sternest problems; the will to life rejoicing in its own inexhaustibility [*Unerschöpflichkeit*] through the *sacrifice* of its highest types—that is what I called Dionysian. . . . That which takes in hand the greatest of all tasks . . . will again make possible on earth that *superfluity of life* [*Zuviel*] out of which the Dionysian condition must again proceed. I promise a *tragic age.*

—Nietzsche, *Ecce Homo*

Contents

Introduction

> According to Nietzsche it has never been understood
> that the tragic = the joyful. This is another way of put-
> ting the great equation: to will = to create. We have not
> understood that the tragic is pure and multiple positivi-
> ty, dynamic gaiety. Affirmation is tragic because it
> affirms chance and the necessity of chance; because it
> affirms multiplicity and the unity of multiplicity. The
> dicethrow is tragic.
>
> —Deleuze, *Nietzsche and Philosophy*

Ouden pros ton Dionyson—"Nothing to do with Dionysus"—
is the ancient complaint concerning the separation of tragedy from its
undisputed Dionysian origins.[1] Not surprisingly, this *decapitation,* which
is itself part of Dionysian ritual, is also reflected in the first critical (*kri-
nein:* to separate) attempt to analyze art and the specific genre of tragedy.[2] For the *Poetics,* which operates largely by a process of exclusion and
valorization,[3] mandates the sort of rational boundaries that are overrun,
if not overturned, by the many examples of Dionysian excess[4] that Aristotle's work seeks to avoid.

For example, the late-fourth-century *Poetics* largely disregards the
choral ode, denies the value of music, and demeans the value of metaphor within a schema that declares that the true value of tragedy lies in
the causal concatenation of its plot and so can even be derived from a
private reading.[5] Not that we should reject Aristotle's observations on the
grounds that they are insensitive to the nuances of poetic expression or
that they ignore the spectatorial power of actually seeing a stage production, for Aristotle himself established such terms as the "vividness of
actually seeing" (*pro ton ommaton*) that we would be attempting to

marshal against him. Instead, I would argue that Aristotle's teleological reliance on *terms, definitions,* and *ends* reenacts the tragic conflict with tragedy's more irrational, disruptive elements, with the *rapture* and *rupture* that, I shall argue, is the essential force in tragedy and all "great" (in Longinus's sense) works of art.

In seeking to emphasize "rapturous overabundance" and the Dionysian that have been largely excluded, *exō tou dramatos,* from discussions of tragedy "before Nietzsche," the present work is *not,* then, an anti-*Poetics.* For the *Poetics* deconstructs itself in attending to such illogical, disruptive elements as metaphor ("by far the greatest thing"[6]) and the ironic *peripeteia* that, like metaphor, denies the causal logic of which it is a part. Aristotle's banishment of the "obscene" act that is also the focus of the drama, the exclusion and/or devalorization of the illogical but necessary components of music, metaphor, the choral ode, and so forth, are variations on the variant myths of Dionysus's desired denial,[7] which are in turn derived from the "fraternal union" of rapturous overabundance and the creation of rational, Apollonian boundaries.[8] As the personification of rapturous forces of excess of which, as Dodds wisely points out,[9] intoxication is merely the most obvious manifestation, Dionysus is created by the selfsame rationalizing, civilizing, teleological tendencies that serve to deny him.

No wonder, then, that Aristotle ends up recreating the role of Oedipus in the *Poetics* by asserting his mastery over tragedy and the mastery of tragedy and the tragic plot over the rest of literature only to end up blinded by an enigma whose solution was its greatest riddle. But, again, one cannot be anti-Aristotle any more than one can be (pace Deleuze and Guattari) anti-Oedipus, for to do so would be to ignore the fact that such assertions of mastery are themselves derived from the selfsame forces of Dionysian excess to which they are opposed. That is why Nietzsche insists that tragic heroes such as Oedipus, Pentheus, Creon, and others who are all determined to stamp out the plague of an ever encroaching Dionysianism are themselves surrogates of Dionysus,[10] just as metaphor—the rapturous, overabundant, enigmatic contamination of logical discourse—creates as well as undermines its antithesis, the causally determined plot. (It is Aristotle who insisted that plot and metaphor are both the "most important" elements within their respective halves of the *Poetics*'s six-part schema.)

The aim of this book, then, is to return to a Dionysian, rapturously excessive understanding of tragedy and tragic art in general (as Nietzsche argued, all great art is tragic [*Birth of Tragedy* xxi, 131]) that has never really been missing, that itself informs the rationalistic, moralistic understanding of art—and, especially, of tragedy—that has dominated Western civilization up to the time of Nietzsche. The deliberately ambiguous title *Tragedy after Nietzsche* thus refers not only to the aftereffects of Nietzsche's reappraisal of tragedy but also allows for discussion of earlier works like Longinus's "On the Sublime" that subversively celebrate the Dionysian forces of rapturous overabundance which create the very civilization that denies them.[11]

"Seriousness" (Aristotle), the ethical "conflict of two rights" (Hegel), and, in general, the instructive *moral* value to be derived from tragedy's "cautionary tales" continue to inform our understanding of the "greatest" of literary genres, as Martha Nussbaum reminds us:

> But the tragedies also show us, and dwell upon, . . . the situation of "tragic conflict." In such cases we see a wrong action committed without any direct physical compulsion and in full knowledge of its nature, by a person whose ethical character or commitments would otherwise dispose him to reject the act. The constraint comes from the presence of circumstances that prevent the adequate fulfillment of two valid ethical claims. *Tragedy tends, on the whole, to take such situations very seriously.* It treats them as real cases of wrong-doing that are of relevance for an assessment of the agent's ethical life. *Tragedy also seems to think it valuable to dwell upon these situations, exploring them in many ways, asking repeatedly what personal goodness, in such alarming complications, is.*[12]

Such moral/ethical interpretations of tragedy in general and of specific tragedies (Nussbaum's indebtedness to Hegel is plainly evident here) have dominated and for the most part continue to dominate our understanding of tragedy before and after Nietzsche.[13] The tenacity of this understanding is no accident. Understanding tragedy in terms of understanding, whether such knowledge be, as argued by Aristotle, merely the formal recognition (*anagnorisis*) provided by the play's many examples of logical closure (preeminently that provided by the plot) or by knowledge of a more uplifting kind, such as the lesson to be learned from Oedipus's hubristic disregard of fate, is to be expected from a tradition which requires that, if art is to have any meaning or value, it must be rational or moral. This is helped by the fact just mentioned that tragedy, which came to prominence in the same century and in the same place as Socratic philosophy, itself reflects this rationalizing tendency without necessarily being subsumed by it: "But whoever tries to trace the tragic effect *solely* to these moral sources, as has been the custom among estheticians for so long, need not think that he is doing art a service. Art must insist on interpretations that are germane to its essence. In examining the peculiar delight arising from tragedy, we must look for it in the esthetic sphere, without trespassing on the areas of pity, terror, or moral grandeur" (Nietzsche, *Birth of Tragedy* xxiv, 142).

Alongside Nietzsche's statement, one should mention Freud's comparable view that *Oedipus Tyrannus* "fundamentally . . . is an amoral work. It absolves men from moral responsibility, exhibits the gods as promoters of crime and shows the impotence of the moral impulses of men. . . . The difficulty is overcome by the pious sophistry that to bow to the will of the gods is the highest morality even when it promotes crime. *I cannot think that this morality is a strong point of the play*."[14] Freud and Nietzsche both contend that Sophocles' play is not to be "solely" understood logically or morally. In Freud's case, the true meaning of *Oedipus Tyrannus* concerns the audience's gratification of its own unconscious, incestuous desires and not the conscious mind's repression of those desires in the form of the play's message about adherence to a higher law that all must obey.[15] Similarly, Nietzsche rejects praise of the play's moralistic interpretations as well as its sophisticated plot as "negative sunspots" that rise to the surface of the play's darker, more abysmal meaning: "And now we see that the poet's entire conception was nothing more nor less than the luminous afterimage which kind nature provides our eyes after a look into the abyss. . . . we may conclude that incest is the necessary antecedent; for how should man force nature to yield up her secrets but by successfully resisting her, that is to say, by unnatural acts?" (*Birth of Tragedy* ix, 61).

But if it is granted that tragedy is to be freed from the expectation of moral and/or logical closure (the famous motto of tragedy that Euripides affixed to the end of many of his plays[16] that we "expect the unexpected" needs to be rethought in less rationalistically ironic terms), how is one to understand tragedy in terms of rapture? It was in seeking an answer to the pleasure afforded by tragedy's spectacles of destruction and despair that Nietzsche formulated the notion of tragic joy or rapture (*Rausch*[17]) that underlies his philosophy of tragedy and his entire tragic philosophy:[18]

> How are we to account for the fact that the hero's sufferings, his most painful dilemmas—all the ugly, discordant things which support the wisdom of Silenus—are depicted again and again with such relish, and all this during the Greeks' most prosperous and vigorous period. . . . How can ugliness and disharmony, which are the content of tragic myth, inspire an esthetic delight?

At this point we must take a leap into the metaphysics of art by reiterating our earlier contention that this world can be justified only as an esthetic phenomenon. On this view, tragic myth has convinced us that even the ugly and discordant are merely *an esthetic game which the will, in its utter exuberance [der ewige Fülle seiner Lust], plays with itself.* . . . That primal Dionysiac delight, experienced even in the presence of pain, is the source common to both music and tragic myth. (*Birth of Tragedy* xxiv, 142–43 [emphasis added])

Nietzsche's famous notion of tragedy as the "justification of the world in esthetic terms" (*Birth of Tragedy* v, 9 and passim) involves a reconciliation with the world that is not moral or logical but rather esthetic. Life is made bearable, as with the creation of the exuberant Olympian deities, through the creation of delightful illusions whose falseness is only such when judged from the standpoint of an "anti-life system of ideas and values" (v, 10). On the other hand, tragedy returns us to Silenus's "worst possible world" that is not worth living[19] because the creation of such delightful illusions has its origin in—is *born* from—an abysmal, "dissonant" loss of meaning that, unlike "weak pessimism," turns its despair into revelrous abandonment. Rapture (*Rausch*) is thus the key to tragedy; for without it, one would not understand the wisdom of the archsatyr Silenus, the father of tragedy, which is that delightful artistic illusions such as tragedy are born from a rapturous *overabundance* (*Fülle*) of spirit that can and will affirm the worst that life has to offer. The seemingly contrary notions that "life is not worth living" and "life is most worth living" are thus strangely compatible in Nietzsche's tragic worldview, which is that artistic creation results from a rapturous overfullness (the two terms are synonymous) that no longer needs to hide the most horrible aspects of life.

The array of chapters assembled in this book is as arbitrary as it is necessary. "Arbitrary" because tragedy in the Nietzschean sense is synonymous with all "great" works of art (*Birth of Tragedy* xxi, 131) and, as such, encompasses essential works and issues in aesthetics that are every bit as important as those discussed here. "Necessary" in that each of these chapters applies Nietzsche's theory of tragedy as rapturous overabundance to works that raise the question of tragic rapture in a particularly compelling way. This includes Nietzsche himself, whose perplexing doctrine of "the eternal return of the same" must be read as the "return of the same" theory of tragedy proffered in Nietzsche's first book (chapter 8, "The Birth of Zarathustra from the Spirit of Tragedy").

The opening chapter on *The Birth of Tragedy* argues for the centrality of Nietzsche's notion of rapturous overabundance as "the basic aesthetic state."[20] Nietzsche's definition of tragedy as a "game which the will, *in the eternal superabundance of its pleasure,* plays with itself" ("Spiel . . . welches der Wille, in der ewigen Fülle seiner Lust, mit sich selbst spielt" [*Birth of Tragedy* xxiv, 143, 131) is understood as the power of rapture to overcome the "reality principle" of preserving life at all costs while affirming the value of life in its "eternal," superabundant fullness. Oedipus, who is for Nietzsche as for others the model of the tragic hero, is heroic precisely because of the excessive hubristic spirit that informs his character as well as his crimes and not in spite of it or them.

Longinus's *On the Sublime,* as one commentator has recently written,[21] is a sort of "shadow-*Poetics*" that has only recently come into its own as an alternative to Aristotle's formalist treatise. Sublimity (*to hypsos*), according to Longinus, is the capacity of "great art" to exceed what is usual or customary and thus to invoke our sense of wonder ("But on such matters I would only say this: that which is useful and indeed necessary is cheap enough; it is always the unusual which wins our wonder"[22]). As such, the Longinian sublime is not limited to a particular media or genre and even includes figures and tropes such as metaphor, which also "invokes wonder" in refiguring common language in new and unusual ways. In "Fulgurations: Tragedy, Figuration, and the Sublime" (chapter 2), I contend that the sublime as the "presentation of the nonpresentable" (Lyotard) is synonymous with Nietzsche's definition of tragedy as the rapturous confrontation between the human and those forces that exceed it. It is also argued that Kant's notion of the sublime as the artistic rendering of the metaphysical supersensible is the equivalent of Nietzsche's notion of the relationship between the Apollonian *"principium individuationis"* and the Dionysian *"Ding-an-sich."*

Nietzsche's direct and indirect influence on Yeats's tragic vision (chapter 3) of "gaiety transforming all that dread" ("Lapis Lazuli") is as evident in the poet's earliest Celtic poems and essays as it is in his later works. Analysis of the former will show that Nietzsche's (and the Greeks') satyrs have here become Druids and faeries that represent the Irish equivalent of a Dionysian "worship of the abundance of nature" where "unearthly ecstasy" unites passion and beauty with destruction.[23] Yeats's vision of the beauty of tragedy and the tragedy of beauty will provide the key to understanding the luxuriant Dionysian dismemberment of Celtic heroes like Fergus as well as the later unleashings of creativity and chaos in poems like "The Second Coming" and "Lapis Lazuli."

Freud's later writings, particularly *Civilization and Its Discontents* and *Beyond the Pleasure Principle,* amended his famous "pleasure principle" to include a "death drive" that is more powerful, and pleasurable, than the former in exceeding the limits of life itself: "The dominating tendency of mental life, and perhaps of nervous life in general, is the effort to reduce, to keep constant or to remove internal tension due to stimuli (the 'Nirvana principle,' . . .)—a tendency which finds expression in the pleasure principle; *and our recognition of that fact is one of our strongest reasons for believing in the existence of death instincts.*"[24]

In "Tragedy and Psychoanalysis: 'Beyond the Pleasure Principle'" (chapter 4), it is argued that the relation between the pleasure principle and the death drive is the same as the relationship between the Apollonian and the Dionysian described by Nietzsche in *The Birth of Tragedy.* There, too, we find two related but different forms of pleasure; there, too, the latter, the Dionysian death drive, is described as more powerful in overcoming the pleasurable Apollonian *principium individuationis* and the other rational, civilizing laws of the conscious mind:

> Tremendous awe seizes man when he suddenly begins to doubt the cognitive modes of experience, in other words, when in a given instance the law of causation seems to suspend itself. If we add to this awe the glorious transport [*Verzückung*] which arises in man, even from the very depths of nature, at the shattering of the *principium individuationis,* then we are in a position to apprehend the essence of Dionysian rapture [*Rausch*], whose closest analogy is furnished by physical intoxication. . . . So stirred, the individual forgets himself completely. (i, 22)

If it is granted that the relationship between the Freudian model of Conscious/Unconscious (with the latter being taken over, in the later works, by the death drive) is analogous to or even synonymous with the Apollonian/Dionysian, then psychoanalysis becomes a theory of the tragic desire to overcome the boundaries—the cathexes—of life itself.

Writers on the blues have often wondered "how is it that we gain definite pleasure by identifying with the singer's sadness? . . . A clarification of this problem is essential if we are to understand how and why we enjoy the blues."[25] "'Nietzsche Sings the Blues': Tragedy and the Blues" (chapter 6) attempts to answer this question by applying Nietzsche's theory of tragic rapture to the distinctly American musical genre. Nietzsche's theory, one will recall, is based on a theory of music (the complete title of *The Birth of Tragedy* is *The Birth of Tragedy from the Spirit of Music*) as the most Dionysian medium insofar as it lacks the more objective, spatiotemporal boundaries of the other Apollonian art forms. As such, "music alone allows us to understand the delight felt at the annihilation of the individual" (*Birth of Tragedy* xvi, 101), for music is closest of all the arts in expressing the rapturous overabundance of the will. Through Nietzsche, we come to understand the blues' perennial plaint in tragic, Silenian terms as the expression of a supreme joy that delights in expressing the sufferings of the "worst possible world."

While some would argue that there could be no better example of tragedy than the Holocaust, others such as Theodor Adorno contend that civilization "after Auschwitz"[26] has lost anything but a "negative" relation to the meaningful structures of the past. The Holocaust, following Richard Rorty's more optimistic argument, is part of a modern reduction to "contingency" wherein "the Truth" has been replaced by *truths* that can only be relied on if one is smart enough not to rely on them too much. "On the Kindness of Strangers: Tragedy, Contingency, and the Holocaust" (chapter 7) argues that both these views actually support a reading of the Holocaust as tragedy, for Adorno's end of meaning and Rorty's reduction to contingency signal a return to tragedy's requisite confrontation with the abyss of meaninglessness that more optimistic epochs had hoped to avoid. Moreover, it is precisely because of the enormity of the tragedy of the Holocaust that it best exemplifies Nietzsche's notion of tragedy's requisite destruction of civilization and its most fundamental values. If this is, for Nietzsche, ultimately life affirming, it is only so to the extent to which we have the courage to face the enormity of the horror of the Holocaust.

Despite Nietzsche's bold prediction of a "rebirth of tragedy" and the Dionysian in modern times (*Birth of Tragedy* xvi, 96),[27] the general consensus of the twentieth century is that there is no "tragedy after Nietzsche" and that tragedy actually perished long before: "at the touch of Hume and Voltaire the noble or hideous visitations which had haunted the mind since Agamemnon's blood cried out for vengeance, disappeared altogether or took tawdry refuge among the gaslights of melodrama."[28] George Steiner's influential argument of *The Death of Tragedy* was anticipated by Robbe-Grillet's essay on "Nature, Humanism, Tragedy,"[29] which also rejects tragedy as too idealistic in recuperating meaninglessness, too anthropomorphic in projecting a visage onto the forces that exceed human control and understanding. Both arguments are themselves the product of the Hegelian notion that modernism is defined by a process of increasing rationalism and individualization that would preclude the fundamental loss of objectivity, of grounding in reality, with which all tragedy is concerned.

"The Life of Tragedy: Tragedy after Nietzsche" (chapter 5) rejects the arguments of Steiner, Robbe-Grillet, and others on the grounds that, if anything, the twentieth century has increased our sense of a fundamental loss of meaning, of a confrontation with the abyss with which all tragedy is concerned. It is naive and self-contradictory to suggest that one can simply abandon the notion of meaning, that modernity is in the position to reject the possibility of meaningfulness to avoid the "tragic sense of life."[30] Indeed, it is the purpose of all the chapters of this book to counter this notion of the death of tragedy with Nietzsche's declaration that as the product of rapturous overabundance, the "highest manifestation of the will," our greatest works of art all attest to the eternal rebirth of a tragic spirit that must exceed the very boundaries that it needs to exist.

1 Nietzsche's Double Vision of Tragedy

> How can ugliness and disharmony, which are the
> content of tragic myth, inspire an aesthetic delight? . . .
> of all the strange effects of tragedy this double claim—
> the need to look and at the same time to go beyond that
> look—is the most peculiar.
> —Nietzsche, *The Birth of Tragedy*

The Birth of Tragedy is Nietzsche's most difficult and archae-
ologically bewildering book.[1] It will probably never be clear, for example, whether Nietzsche interprets Wagner from the standpoint of Greek
drama or vice versa; whether Nietzsche's Apollonian/Dionysian distinction derives ultimately from Schopenhauer or is merely confirmed there;[2]
or whether Nietzsche's totally unascertainable and seemingly implausi-
ble notions of Greek music have anything or everything to do with Greek
tragedy.[3] But questions of historical anteriority such as these pale before
the real concern of Nietzsche's work, which is to fathom how such a thing
as tragedy—the aesthetic celebration of destruction—can come to be, can
be "born."

The essential question is how tragic art can exist at all. For if one
accepts that the goal of art is to provide us with "metaphysical solace"
for the rigors of life,[4] how can tragedy produce art when it appears to deny
the possibility of such solace? If "life can only be justified in aesthetic
terms" ("dass nur als ein ästhetisches Phänomen das Dasein und die Welt
gerechtfertigt erscheint"), then how can tragedy justify itself in justifying life when it seems to be doing just the opposite?

There is no need to defer answering this question, since it is under-standing the question posed by the answer that requires an immense, even infinite deferral. Nietzsche's first book explains the origin—the "birth"—of tragedy from a state of rapturous superabundance, viewing it as a "game which the will, *in the eternal abundance of its pleasure,* plays with it-self" [*Birth of Tragedy* xxiv, 143].[5] In addition to the obvious influence of Schopenhauer's doctrine of the will,[6] the German text reveals that crucial Nietzschean notions like the "will-to-power" (*Wille zur Macht*), the "eternal return" (*ewige Widerkehr*[7]), and a superabundant "fullness" (*Fülle*) to overflowing[8] are all already part of Nietzsche's tragic vision, thus confirming Heidegger's notions that "the experience of the tragic and the contemplation of its origin and being belong to the ground of Nietzsche's thinking."[9] Such compactness of thought warns us against the kind of hasty acceptance or dismissal that has often characterized the reception of Nietzsche's *Birth of Tragedy*[10] and cautions us to proceed carefully in uncovering the crucial relation between the "eternal fullness" of the will—*rapture*—and tragedy.

It is important, then, to begin this book with a discussion of how rapture assumes for Nietzsche its role as the key formative concept of art and how, moreover, this concept explains the creation and existence of tragic works of art. Although this approach to tragedy (and, specifical-ly, Nietzsche's theory of tragedy) as a theory of rapture is new,[11] it is in-formed—and, at the outset, explicitly guided by—Heidegger's monumen-tal two volumes on *Nietzsche,*[12] particularly the sections 12–17 in volume 1 devoted to rapture as an "aesthetic state" and "form-engendering force." Although Heidegger does not, in these particular sections of his work, talk explicitly about tragedy, his analysis of "rapturously engendered form" (*der Rausch as formschaffende*) is clearly as relevant to Nietzsche's no-tion of tragedy in particular as it is to his theory of art in general.

The first part of this chapter shall follow Heidegger's lead in analyz-ing the way Nietzsche's writings on rapture demonstrate how the will's "going beyond itself" (*hinübergehen*) engenders artistic form in general as a result of rapture exceeding its own limits and the limits of the "ob-jects" it would describe. The second part of this chapter will approach this general aesthetic notion from the other direction, as it were, in dem-onstrating how tragic scenarios of nihilistic destruction such as that of Oedipus return us to the origin of art as products of the rapturous will's overcoming all boundaries. It is necessary to move in these two directions because of Nietzsche's contention that the origin of tragedy lies in a Di-onysian state of rapturous superabundance that is essential to all "great" works of art (*Birth of Tragedy* xxi, 131)[13] and belies the supposed pessimism that continues to plague interpretations of plays such as *Oedipus Tyrannus.*

Nietzsche's will-to-power, as Heidegger describes it, is a paradoxical formulation, a force that, unlike "resolve" or "striving," "wills itself outside itself" (*über-sich-hinaus-wollen*). Through the will-to-power, "we know ourselves as out beyond ourselves; we sense a mastery-over somehow achieved; a thrill of pleasure announces to us the power attained, a power that enhances itself."[14] As such, the excessiveness of the will-to-power is identified with rapture (*Rausch*) as an "overfull, teeming will," which manifests itself not only during "feasts, sexual arousal, springtime," and so forth, but also in works of art:

> If there is to be art, if there is to be any aesthetic doing and observing, one *physiological precondition* is indispensable: *rapture.* . . . All the variously conditioned forms of rapture have the requisite force: above all, the rapture of sexual arousal, the oldest and most original form of rapture. In addition, the rapture that comes as a consequence of all great desires, all strong affects; the rapture of the feast; contest, feat of daring, victory; all extreme movement; the rapture of cruelty; rapture in destruction; rapture under certain meteorological influences, for example, the rapture of springtime; or under the influence of narcotics; finally, the rapture of will, of an overfull and teeming will.[15]

Heidegger notes that in 1888, the same year as this seemingly straightforward enunciation of rapture as "the basic aesthetic state without qualification," Nietzsche writes in *The Will to Power* of the Apollonian and Dionysian as the "*two* states in which art emerges as a force of nature in man."[16] These two states, as also described in *The Birth of Tragedy,* are dream (identified with the Apollonian) and rapture (identified with the Dionysian). What, Heidegger wonders, causes Nietzsche to speak of the two states (rapture and dream, the Dionysian and the Apollonian) as one (Dionysian rapture) and of the one as two?[17] This categorical confusion is itself repeated chronologically, for Nietzsche writes, in the three texts cited, of first one, then the other, and then, again, the first possibility: "In Dionysian rapture there is sexuality and voluptuousness: in the Apollonian they are not lacking." And if that is not enough confusion, Heidegger also cites Nietzsche's own self-questioning in *Twilight of the Idols:* "What is the meaning of the conceptual opposition, which I introduced into aesthetics, of the Apollonian and the Dionysian, *both conceived as kinds of rapture* [*beide als Arten des Rausches begriffen*]?"[18]

Following Heidegger in sorting out the function of the rapturous will (which, as we have seen, is for Nietzsche a redundancy) as both the essential precondition of art *and* as merely one of two artistic states (with the Apollonian) will help clarify the relationship between rapture and the creation of artistic forms such as tragedy. Although the focus has moved, in the later work, more toward the rapturous will as such, there is much to suggest that Nietzsche still has in mind his earlier discussion of the Dionysian and the Apollonian in *The Birth of Tragedy.*[19] Indeed, although the latter stands at the beginning of his career, it is even possible to claim that the passages Heidegger cites from the later works are in a sense earlier than those of the earlier work. For in *The Will to Power* and elsewhere, the abstractions, personifications, and pseudohistorical arguments have been replaced by a more focused analysis of the forces represented by Dionysus and Apollo. Thus it is possible to understand the notoriously complex relationship between Dionysus and Apollo as if the later discussion of rapture preceded *The Birth of Tragedy*—or, at any rate, as if it is contemporary with it.

To understand the causal connection between rapture and art, one must rethink such basic aesthetic notions as form and idealization, for such notions wrongly imply a mere delimiting of, if not a defense against, actual content that hopelessly distorts their fundamental connection to rapture's superabundance:

> By "form" Nietzsche never understands the merely "formal," that is to say, what stands in need of content, what is only the external border of such content, circumscribing it but not influencing it. Such a border does not give bounds, it is itself the result of sheer cessation. It is only a fringe, not a component, not what lends consistency and pith by pervading the content and fixing it in such a way that its character as "contained" evanesces. Genuine form is the only true content.[20]

> But to idealize is not, as one might think, merely to omit, strike, or otherwise discount what is insignificant and ancillary. Idealization is not a defensive action.[21]

Rather than the traditional, "Platonic" view of form and idealization as separate from the artwork's content, its physical reality, the rapturous attack (versus "defensive action") that gives birth to artistic form

> is an emphasizing of major features, a seeing more simply and strongly.[22]

> Artists ought not to see what is, but more fully, simply, stronger: for which they must possess a kind of youth and spring-like quality, *a kind of habitual rapture.*[23]

The critical terms here, for the purpose of understanding the relationship of rapture to form, are the "outwardly mobile" *Heraustreiben* ("emphasize") and *Hauptzüge* ("major features"). We are thus reminded of Heidegger's definition of *Rausch*, the epitome of the will-to-power, as an *über-sich-hinaus-Steigen*. Corresponding, then, to the subjective "ascent beyond oneself" is the objective *Heraustreiben* of artistic form. In the "going outside oneself" of rapture, one also discovers that which is outside the ordinary objects of experience; one discovers, in other words, aesthetic objects and experiences. Rapture is thus not just a subjective state of feeling, for it also changes the way one views the "objective" world and can also change the very nature of that world.

Artistic form and idealization must, then, be rethought in terms of their origin in rapture's excessiveness of the will. Rapture engenders (gives birth to) form because out of (*hinaus*) the author's rapture there emerge (*heraustreibt*) forms that themselves emerge out of the objects of experience. The forms produced are "more fully, simply, stronger" than those of ordinary experience because of their origin in the artist's excessive will, "a kind of youth and spring-like quality, a kind of habitual rapture" without which such idealized forms would not emerge out of the mere objects lying there before us, separate from our will. As such, these aesthetic forms are never these mere objects. Rather, the aesthetic "object" requires the aforementioned "double vision" of looking beyond the object as such; it requires, in other words, the excess of rapture.

The rapturous moment that gives birth to art is, in the words of Rilke quoted by Heidegger, "a beginning of the terrible we but barely endure." Similarly, in art's *Hauptzüge* (main features), one finds "what we can but barely overcome."[24] For at the moment of the will's rapturous overabundance it can create an equally subjective and objective *trait* (or form) in which the subject is momentarily unable to recognize itself, but as a result of which its existence is ecstatically confirmed. The Platonic separation of form from content, however, leads aesthetic formalization to identify, wrongly, rapture with contextual subjectivity and form with formal objectivity: "We have only to call whatever is related to rapture 'subjective,' and whatever is related to beauty 'objective,' and in the same fashion understand creation as subjective behavior and form as objective law. The unknown variable would be the relation of the subjective to the objective: the subject-object relation. What could be more familiar than that?"[25]

The purpose of Heidegger's final, sarcastic statement is to show that such schematization hopelessly distorts the process that it purports to describe. The rapturous manifestation of the will-to-power as an *über-sich-hinaus-Steigen* is objective in going beyond the bounds of the subject and in seizing the distinctive features (*Hauptzüge*) of experience. The rapturous manifestation of beautiful form, however, is also subjective, insofar as it emphasizes (*heraustreibt*) features that can only be grasped by the rapturous will. If, Heidegger wryly observes, one uses the two terms "subjective" and "objective" at all, then one could as rightly label rapture objective and form subjective, "since there is no such thing as beauty in itself." But, in reality, "the two fundamental terms designate in the same way the whole aesthetic state, and that which in it is opened and persists."[26] In other words, the objectively beautiful Apollonian form is the Dionysian, although it has been momentarily detached from the Dionysian process of incessant change and overcoming that has engendered it.

This explanation of rapture's essential relation to artistic form is necessary for understanding the structure of all "great" works of art, including the "greatest" (Aristotle) genre of tragedy. Indeed, the use of the word "great" to refer to works of art (which it has now become fashionable to deride) should be understood as referring to all aesthetic, rapturous "objects" that inherently exceed themselves as such, just as they exceed the spectators who observe them.

Before turning, in the second part of this chapter, to the specific ways that tragedies reveal their origin in rapture, it is now possible to relate the preceding general discussion of rapture as a "form-engendering force" more explicitly to tragedy.

    1. In *The Will to Power*, Nietzsche writes of art as "the single superior counterforce against all will to negation of life . . . as anti-Nihilist *par excellence*" and of art as "the greatest *stimulans* of life."[27] And yet tragedy, by anyone's reckoning, seems to be the nihilistic genre of a *nein-Sagen* ("nay-saying") that takes perverse delight in bringing all its human hopes and aspirations to ruin "par excellence." Would it not be the case, then, that Nietzsche is here excluding tragedy from his later notion of art as rapturous and life-affirming?

Those familiar with the reception of Nietzsche and his works are aware that this possibility repeats the common tendency to label Nietzsche himself as a nihilist when the opposite is closer to the truth. Just as it would be wrong to label Nietzsche as a nihilist because of his mission of destroying what he sees as the desiccated and petrified values of Western culture (values that, according to Nietzsche, are themselves antilife), it would be equally wrong to label tragedy as nihilistic because of its inherent rebellion against the stabilizing forces of civilization (Prometheus's revolt against Zeus's dicastic hierarchy would be the archetype of this). There is, to be sure, a certain truth in labeling Nietzsche and tragedy as nihilistic, but not if one fails to underscore that for Nietzsche, art and tragedy are metaphysical activities that only destroy what exists to engage the originality of life more directly (this is precisely what Nietzsche means by his famous notion of the need for an "aesthetic justification of life"[28]).

The key to understanding art as the "metaphysical activity" of life is understanding the role of rapture as the essence of an aesthetic state ("If there is to be any art, rapture is indispensable") whose essence is the will-to-power ("Art is the most familiar and perspicuous configuration of the will-to-power").[29] This is because art and the artist do not concern themselves with things as they are but rather with things as they *may be* according to the rapturous will overcoming the artist. As such, the artist's activity is metaphysical because it creates anew out of the rapturous will what, as the epitome of the will-to-power, is closest to life itself. And tragedy is the essential art form (according to Nietzsche) because it is closest to life and most life-affirming and metaphysical in denying—as Nietzsche himself continually denies—the supposed reality of things as they are. As Heidegger notes: "Since the new valuation [of will-to-power in art] is a revaluation of the prior one, however, opposition and upheaval arise from art. . . . so it is that art affirms what the supposition of the ostensibly true world denies."[30]

2. "In what sense," Heidegger wonders, "is rapture *the* basic aesthetic state?" He continues:

> According to what we explained earlier, such enhancement of force [of the rapturous state] must be understood as the capacity to extend beyond oneself, as a relation to beings in which beings themselves are experienced as being more fully in being, richer, more perspicuous, more essential. Enhancement does not mean that an increase, an increment of force, "objectively" comes about. Enhancement is to be understood in terms of mood: to be caught up in elation—and to be borne along by our buoyancy as such. In the same way, the feeling of plenitude does not suggest an inexhaustible stockpile of inner events. It means above all an attunement which is so disposed that nothing is foreign to it, nothing too much for it, which is open to everything and ready to tackle anything—*the greatest enthusiasm and the supreme risk hard by one another.*[31]

"The greatest enthusiasm and the supreme risk hard by one another." As mentioned at the outset of this chapter, Heidegger does not explicitly relate his discussion of rapture as the key aesthetic concept in Nietzsche to tragedy. It remains to be done here, and passages such as this make such a connection easy, for Heidegger himself provides the key terms that are necessary to bridge the gap separating, on the one hand, rapture as a supreme feeling of joy and "buoyancy" and, on the other hand, tragedy's spectacles of suffering. First, one is told that the enhancement (*Steigerung*) of rapture causes one to "extend beyond oneself" and objects to be "experienced as more fully in being" ("richer, more perspicuous"). This corresponds, in tragedy, to the divinely "hubristic" extension of the tragic hero beyond himself or herself in the name of a plenitude of being (Antigone's heady rebelliousness, Agamemnon's pride, Clytemnestra's wrath, Oedipus's excessive temper and desires, and so forth) whose only impoverishment is a result of the conflict with civilization's human boundaries.[32] It is not that tragedy does not have a downside, but one misunderstands tragedy when one fails to acknowledge its fundamental connection to rapture and instead takes up society's antiaesthetic leanings by defending its "reality principle" against Dionysian joy and excess (a tendency that can be understood psychoanalytically—see chapter 4— as mirroring the archetypal plot of Greek tragedy, which is that of the civilized polis's rejection of Dionysus in the name of the father/law). Finally, it should also be noted how this passage clarifies the common characterization (since Aristotle) of tragedy as about royal personages (or, more generally, persons "greater than us")—a characterization that turns into a complaint by those intent on rejecting tragedy as irrelevant to the modern age. The notion that tragic rapture involves a "richer" "feeling of plenitude," of going "beyond oneself," and of beings experienced "more fully in being" requires only a richness or "nobility" of soul that is as evident in the proletarian heroes of Arthur Miller as it is in the fallen aristocrats of Chekhov.

"Enhancement does not mean that an increase in force 'objectively' comes about." Elsewhere, Nietzsche writes, somewhat surprisingly, that "artists are *not* men of great passion."[33] Both of these quotations refer to the fact that the rapture of art and artists—which, as we have seen, is the most powerful form of the rapturous will-to-power—exists as play (*Spiel*) and not as part of the real world. This is important to remember in terms of tragedy because it is a "*game* which the will plays"; in other words, *trag-oedy*, as the reference to song in its name suggests, is to be understood solely as an aesthetic phenomenon in which rapture denies the "reality principle" of the real world. Here, too, the problem of tragedy's many moralistic interpretations (e.g., Antigone's saintliness or Oedipus's damning temper) is evident, for tragedy is never, on close examination,[34] about role models or real-life situations of any sort (although comparisons with those can always be made).

The problem of tragic joy, of why we enjoy such spectacles of suffering, and, related to this, the problem of why tragedy—and not just comedy—is related to its patron deity Dionysus (which explicitly concerns Nietzsche in *The Birth of Tragedy*) are addressed in the second part of this passage. As a mood, "enhancement" (*die Steigerung*) is not a real condition of "stockpiling inner events" but rather of being "elated" and "buoyed" by this elation such that "nothing is foreign to it, nothing too much for it, which is open to everything and ready to tackle anything— the greatest enthusiasm and the supreme risk hard by one another."

Tragic suffering, then, is indeed another breed of suffering, sui generis. It is born out of a state of rapturous superabundance that brushes aside any obstacle and welcomes any risk with the "greatest enthusiasm." This must lead—or, at any rate, will often lead—to a destruction that is itself welcome to the sufferer insofar as he or she accepted such risks when buoyed by such elation. This is why Cavell's astute notion of tragedy as the "recognition" of who one is and what one has done[35] (Oedipus's identity, Phaedra's shameful "incest," Macbeth's regicide, and so forth) nonetheless must be placed within its larger context as the Apollonian counterpart to a Dionysian moment of rapturous nonrecognition that leads, only afterwards, to the recognition of who one is.

3. Finally, how does the process of "idealization" and "seeing more simply and strongly" that this study has followed Nietzsche and Heidegger in deriving from a state of "rapturous overabundance" relate explicitly to tragedy? One recalls that aesthetic form is to be understood precisely as it derives from rapture, that it is rapture that causes the artist to seize and to see things "more fully, simply, stronger." Art does not, then, ever see things as they are. The following statement from *Twilight of the Idols* will help to understand the connection between this "seizing" and tragedy: "From this feeling [rapturous overabundance] one bestows upon things, one compels them to take from us, one violates them. . . . this process is called idealization."[36] The form, the ideal, that the artist seizes is a gift ("bestowal") that "violates" both subject and object. That is because self and world are both overcome through the creation of a "third thing," the "aesthetic object," which is a gift in the fullest sense of having come freely and unexpectedly from elsewhere.

Why is this tragic? Because tragedy is the genre most explicitly about the way such a loss or "violation" produces an aesthetic object—the tragedy itself. And, at the actor's level, the tragic hero is always destroyed (whether actually, symbolically, or psychologically), but he or she is also idealized insofar as he or she exists doubly as both a transcendent figure of overcoming as well as an all-too-human figure that it is the purpose of the tragedy to deny. For example, Oedipus is not only a preeminent figure of rapturous transcendence and violation, but he is also recognized as an innocent, penitent king; Antigone, likewise, is not only a headstrong bacchante but also a pious, saintly martyr; Macbeth appears as a bloodthirsty usurper but also a preeminently admirable hero. The point being that tragedy, as the genre par excellence of rapturously engendered form, requires such a "double vision," requires the need to "look and go beyond the look."

In the second section, this chapter will demonstrate how tragedy's specific origin in Dionysian rapture[37] and its propensity for worst-case scenarios and a nihilistic worldview also lead us back to this view of rapturously engendered form. As Nietzsche writes:

> Both [music and tragic myth] have their origin in a realm of art which lies beyond the Apollonian; both shed their transfiguring light on [*ver-klären*] a region in whose *rapt harmony* dissonance and the horror of existence fade away in enchantment. *Confident of their supreme powers* [*überaus mächtigen Zauberkünsten*], *they both toy with the sting of displeasure, and by their toying* [*durch dieses Spiel*] *they both justify the existence of even the "worst possible world."* Thus the Dionysiac element, as against the Apollonian, proves itself to be the eternal and original power of art, since it calls into being the entire world of phenomena.[38] (*Birth of Tragedy* xxv, 145, [emphasis added])

The same experience of superabundant Dionysian rapture that produces Apollonian form as the highest expression of the will-to-power "toys with the sting of displeasure" and produces, through this "toying" (*Spiel*), tragic myths such as that of Oedipus. If, as we have seen, rapture only produces Apollonian form by exceeding the limits of the objective world (*über-sich-hinaus-wollen*), then the explanation for tragedy's so-called pessimism and dire scenarios of cataclysmic destruction may be decidedly different from the one frequently provided by the genre's many moralistic interpreters.[39] If, as we have seen in the first part of this chapter, we need to rethink artistic form in its essential relation to Dionysian rapture, the same rethinking will now allow us to reconsider the form of art that, according to Nietzsche, is closest to the Dionysian origin of all art.

Like Aristotle, Schelling and others, Nietzsche also bases his theory of tragedy on Sophocles' *Oedipus Tyrannus*. However, like Freud,[40] Nietzsche insists that the myth's real meaning is obfuscated or denied by critics' concerns with such abstract issues as fate versus free will (as though Oedipus's "free will" was not predestined, and his fate was not his own doing[41]), the polis versus the individual, and by the play's own apparent denial of Oedipus's crimes (incest, parricide, and attempted matricide).[42] But before further analyzing Nietzsche's reinterpretation of this paradigmatic myth in section nine of *The Birth of Tragedy*, certain preliminary notions discussed in the earlier parts of Nietzsche's book need to be clarified. Why, first of all, does Nietzsche repeatedly insist that the Dionysian spirit of tragedy is an experience of the "original Oneness" (*Ur-eine*) of life? And, second, why does this experience of original Oneness necessarily involve pain and suffering (*Ur-eine als das Ewig-Leidende*)?[43]

Responding to the second question first, this chapter has already mentioned that one must understand Dionysian suffering—tragic suffering[44]—as an emotion seen from the particular perspective of the Dionysian reveler and his or her rapture. That "ecstatic reality which takes no account of the individual and may even destroy him" (*Birth of Tragedy* ii, 24) does not separate joy from terror, as evident from the joyful terror of a god whose loss, in Dionysus's *sparagmos* (ritual dismemberment), is part of his ecstatic presence: "Yet the peculiar blending of emotions in the heart of the Dionysiac reveler—his ambiguity [*Doppelheit*], if you will—seems still to hark back to the days when the infliction of pain was experienced as joy while a sense of supreme triumph elicited cries of anguish from the heart. For now in every exuberant joy there is heard an undertone of terror, or else a wistful lament over an irrecoverable loss" (*Birth of Tragedy* ii, 27).

In answer to our first question, just as one must understand Dionysian suffering as a function of Dionysian rapture and its rupturing of the *principium individuationis*,[45] original Oneness must be understood as the necessary loss of boundaries that results from a Dionysian state of rapturous superabundance. In other words, it is the ecstatic loss of the *principium individuationis* and of other, related forms of objective reality that produces this experience of metaphysical suffering and Oneness. As Thomas Böning has argued, Nietzsche's frequent rejection of traditional metaphysical truth claims, including those of Schopenhauer, was never meant to preclude the very real possibility of humans creatively making such claims: "Sobald man das Ding-an-sich erkennen will, so ist es eben diese Welt" (As soon as one posits a thing-in-itself it is part of their world).[46]

The crucial passage in the third section of *The Birth of Tragedy* concerning Dionysus's mentor, the archsatyr Silenus (the figure who thus represents, in a very real sense, the "birth of tragedy"),[47] clarifies the curious relationship between "supreme triumph and anguish" that is of such paramount importance in tragedy:

> An old legend has it that King Midas hunted a long time in the woods for the wise Silenus, companion of Dionysos, without being able to catch him. When he had finally caught him the king asked him what he considered man's greatest good. The daemon remained sullen and uncommunicative until finally, forced by the king, he broke into a shrill laugh and spoke: "Ephemeral wretch, begotten by accident and toil, why do you force me to tell you what it would be your greatest boon not to hear? What would be best for you is quite beyond your reach: not to have been born, not to be, to be nothing. But the second best is to die soon." (*Birth of Tragedy* iii, 29)

Given the aforementioned "blending of emotions in the heart of the Dionysiac reveler," Silenus's gloomy reply to Midas must be understood as a continuation, rather than an interruption, of his usual mirthmaking. In the "Versuch einer Selbstkritik" of 1886, the important—even essential—introduction that Nietzsche added fourteen years after *The Birth of Tragedy*, Nietzsche coins the term "strong pessimism" (*Pessimismus der Stärke*) to explain this essential "ambiguity" (*Doppelheit*) that links Silenus's intrinsic love of life to his contempt for its preservation:

> Or is there such a thing as a **strong** pessimism? A penchant of the mind for what is hard, terrible, evil, dubious in existence, *arising from a plethora of health [aus überströmender Gesundheit], plenitude of being* [**Fülle des Daseins**]? *Could it be, perhaps, that the very feeling of superabundance* [*Überfülle*] *created its own kind of suffering:* a temerity of penetration, hankering for the enemy (the worth-while enemy) so as to prove its strength, to experience at last what it means to fear something? What meaning did the tragic myth have for the Greeks during the period of their greatest power and courage? And what of the Dionysiac spirit, so tremendous in its implications? What of the tragedy that grew out of that spirit? (*Birth of Tragedy* i, 4 [emphasis added; boldface is Nietzsche's emphasis])

The Greeks' strong pessimism is not to be confused with the defeatist mentality of which examples may be found among virtually every generation of the modern world, from Petronius through Voltaire and up to the present time. Indeed, strong pessimism is not really pessimism at all. The early Greeks' contempt for life is quite different; it arises, says Nietzsche, from a rapturous "feeling of superabundance" ("aus überströmender Gesundheit . . . [und] Fülle des Daseins") that experiences pain from the *principium individuationis* and objective human experience and that thus looks to worst-case, tragic scenarios to exceed the conventional limitations of life. Silenus's nihilism and the terror of tragedy are thus a result of the tremendous joy—the rapture—that takes the Dionysian reveler outside the self and into a state of "metaphysical Oneness" that can only occur with the destruction of boundaries imposed by the *principium individuationis*. Another way of hearing, then, Silenus's statement that "the best is never to have been born" would be as a joyous reminder that the Greek gods are immortals (*athanatoi*) who are not themselves constrained by the normal limitations of birth and death.

The key to the Silenus passage, then, is in understanding why the same satyr who himself represents a "plethora of health and a plenitude of being" should deliver such a devastating message of pessimistic despair. But it is precisely because Silenus represents such overwhelming vitality and strong pessimism that he can tolerate, and even welcome, the worst that life can offer. Achilles' view, which Nietzsche discusses in the same section, that "the worst is to die soon"[48] is actually synonymous with Silenus's statement, for, in a tragic state of rapturous superabundance, it is best and worst to "die soon" and thereby live life to the fullest, bereft of human boundaries.

The relation of strong pessimism to satyric joy help one understand the relationship between Shakespeare's Hamlet and the Greek satyr, two tragic figures whose dissimilarity is precisely what, in Nietzsche's theory of tragedy, joins them together. Although Hamlet's reflective world of "words words words" is representative of Apollonian reality, it is his disgust with such a world that marks him as a transitional, potentially satyric figure. Hamlet, who is usually lacking in the "enchantment" (*Verzauberung*) that Nietzsche sees as "essential to the drama"—"enchantment is the precondition of all dramatic art" (*Birth of Tragedy* viii, 56)—is nonetheless a powerful dramatic presence[49] precisely because he represents this lack so perfectly. As in the example of Silenus, the rejection of everyday, literal life as meaningless is but another way of affirming life as potentially superabundant and so exceeding all limitations. (Relevant to Hamlet is Freud's important analysis of melancholy as the rejection of conscious life and the unconscious desire for rapturous libidinal satisfaction.[50]) Thus, the essential nihilism of which Hamlet is only a more recent avatar must be rethought in terms of tragedy's Dionysian origin as a positive affirmation of superabundant excessiveness for which Hamlet's melancholy, Aristotle's "seriousness,"[51] and tragedy's countless scenarios of nihilistic destruction are just a means, not an end.

It is because of transitional figures like Hamlet that represent the "transfiguration"[52] of Dionysian into Apollonian forces that the history of aesthetics has so often, according to Nietzsche, been duped into believing that poetry is a product of Hamlet-like brooding rather than the result of the satyr's rapturous embrace of nature.[53] But, even so, the satyr represents more than just a sensual embrace of physicality. The "metaphysical solace" (*metaphysiche Trost*) that the satyr's art and tragedy provide is synonymous with the "eternal core of Being" (*das ewige Leben jenes Daseinskernes*) that is exposed after the phenomenal world is "looked beyond." As a repressed version of the satyr's Oneness (so beautifully expressed in the satyr's status as half-man, half-animal), Hamlet's melancholia also represents the true nature of tragedy, which is to mock all the conventional modes of civilized behavior.[54] As a repressed figure or "surrogate" (Nietzsche, *Birth of Tragedy* x, 66) of the Dionysian satyr, Shakespeare's hero resembles Oedipus—although, unlike Hamlet, Oedipus actually perpetrates the deeds over which Hamlet can only brood.

The extraordinary image of "negative sunspots" with which Nietzsche begins his brief discussion of Oedipus in section 9 of *The Birth of Tragedy* encapsulates his theory of tragedy as "double vision" and "rapturous superabundance":[55]

> Everything that rises to the surface in the Apollonian portion of Greek tragedy (in the dialogue) looks simple, transparent, beautiful. . . . However, once we abstract from [*absehen von*] the character of the hero as it rises to the surface and becomes visible (a character at bottom no more than a luminous shape projected onto a dark wall, that is to say, *appearance* [*Erscheinung*] through and through), and instead penetrate into the myth which is projected in these luminous reflections, we suddenly come up against a phenomenon which is the exact opposite of a familiar optical one. After an energetic attempt to focus on the sun, we have, by way of remedy almost, dark spots before our eyes when we turn away. Conversely, the luminous images of these Sophoclean heroes—those Apollonian masks—are the necessary productions of a deep look into the horror of nature [*eines Blickes ins Innere und Schreckliche der Natur*]; luminous spots, as it were, designed to cure an eye hurt by the ghastly night. Only in this way can we form an adequate notion of Greek "serenity." (ix, 60)

Francis Golfing's fine translation of *The Birth of Tragedy* nonetheless misleads the reader by denoting an "abstraction" where the very opposite notion is clearly at stake, for Nietzsche is here saying that we must "look away from" (*absehen von*), not "abstract from," the more pleasing parts of the play to see the "real story." Be that as it may, one might usefully compare this image to Nietzsche's reversal of the notion, traditional since Aristotle, that music is a mere accompaniment to the more primary plot;[56] it can also be compared to his use of Schopenhauer's example of the man resting in a gently rocking rowboat, quietly contemplating (*Birth of Tragedy* iv, 33). In all these cases, Greek "serenity" may allow us to appreciate the plot and to see and think about other such "whole and complete" objects of perception, but such knowledge is a soothing afterthought, or afterimage, that only comes about as a result of the more turbulent reality that creates it, whether it be the sun, the sea, or musical transport. Indeed, Nietzsche's entire critique of knowledge is contained in this metonymic image[57] of "negative sunspots" as the "truth" we see or know *après coup*, "after the fact" of the turbulent reality that creates it.

Such beautifully "serene" forms of Apollonian knowledge as the beatific Christ of Raphael's *Transfiguration*, although existing in opposition to or as an escape from Dionysian chaos, are also engendered by the very loss of such static forms or objects (thus resembling literal procreation) that occurs in the "energetic" state of Dionysian rapture (*Birth of Tragedy* iv, 33). Again, this "seeing more simply and strongly" of artistic form is a direct result of such an "energetic look" into the sun of rapturous overcoming. If, in this passage, Nietzsche seems to be privileging the Apollonian over the Dionysian, he more often reverses this in describing the rapturous joy of overcoming. Both are true because, as Nietzsche wisely cautions, "Greek serenity" is a direct result of, is *born* from, the excesses of Dionysian rapture.

Nietzsche's model for the "double vision of tragedy" and the turbulent "anti-knowledge" of Dionysian rapture is the same "know-nothing Oedipus" who figures prominently in the play's long-recognized excellence of form and plot.[58] In contradistinction to the luminous mastery of plot that most critics followed Aristotle in seeing as the supreme achievement of the play,[59] the "dark, religious message" of *Oedipus Tyrannus* is that "a man who is truly noble is incapable of sin; though every law, every natural order, indeed the entire canon of ethics, perish by his actions, those very actions will create a circle of higher consequences able to found a new world on the ruins of the old. This is the poet's message, insofar as he is at the same time a religious thinker" (*Birth of Tragedy* ix, 60).[60]

The notion put forth here is only vaguely related to more popular ideas about the "exceptional" individual who does not think that the laws apply to her or to him. Rather, the point of *Oedipus Tyrannus*, according to Nietzsche, is that the "truly noble" soul can and must do anything in overwhelming the ordinary limitations of society ("though the entire canon of ethics perish by his actions"). Sophocles' Antigone is another example of this idea of nobility, for she defies the obsessively legalistic Creon not just because she has a sense of duty to her fallen brother but, more importantly, because she will not be ordered about by someone who lacks her self-declared sense of nobility.[61]

Oedipus is not, then, canonized at Colonus (*Oedipus at Colonus*) because the gods have taken pity on his suffering; Nietzsche notwithstanding, this would be a terribly anachronistic misreading of the play. Rather, by violating "the entire canon of ethics," Oedipus has shown himself to be one with the Greek gods who, after all, commit Oedipus's particular two crimes remorselessly and unremittingly. Oedipus's suffering is only one part of a "divine dialectic" that links the chaotic turbulence of human sin and suffering with the radiant bliss of Oedipus's "canonization" at Colonus. The blind, sexually transgressive Oedipus at the end of Sophocles' play has joined his divine counterpart Tiresias in "suffering" a fate more than human and in "*not* having eyes / and therefore seeing."

When the Chorus of *Oedipus Tyrannus,* commenting on Oedipus's sorry fate, declares, "Oh generations of men, I reckon you as equal to those who live not at all!"[62] this merely repeats Silenus's tragic message that the "greatest boon" to humankind would be "never to have been born." Yet both statements of tragic nihilism are paradoxically life-affirming, for the tragic "game which the will, in its exuberance, plays with itself" is a satyric, Silenian game that plays with all boundaries and may even destroy them. Silenus's message and the Chorus's as well can thus be heard as rapturous invitations to "reckon ourselves as nothing at all."[63] As shown in the first part of this chapter, the creation of "great" works of art occurs as a function of the same rapturous overcoming of boundaries that produces the "double vision" of new aesthetic "objects" inherently contingent on the tragic destruction of the old:

> No handiwork of Callimachus
> . . . .
> . . . . stands;
> His long lamp chimney shaped like the stem
> Of a slender palm, stood but a day;
> All things fall and are built again
> And those that build them again are gay.[64]

2 Fulgurations: Tragedy, Figuration, and the Sublime

In one of the many books and essays marking the recent rebirth of interest in the sublime, Phillipe Lacoue-Labarthe makes two claims that will serve as guideposts to this study of tragedy as "rapturous superabundance" and the sublime. First, Lacoue-Labarthe maintains that, with respect to Heidegger, "curiously, he does not make the slightest allusion to the problematic of the sublime: 'sublime' is a word which does not belong to the Heideggerian lexicon, even if the concept—and the thing itself—are everywhere present (if only under the name of 'greatness')."[1]

Indeed, the absence in Heidegger's work of any explicit reference to the problematic of the sublime can betoken an even greater engagement with a concept whose very notion entails its own occlusion, or hiddenness:

> the sublime utterance is a divine utterance: it is a god who speaks. In both cases [the Kantian examples of Moses' proscription against imagery and the famous inscription on the veil of Isis[2]], however, this utterance is not really direct, despite grammatical appearances: it is not in his or her own voice that the god speaks; its speech is reported and inscribed (on tables, on the pediment or in the interior of the temple). Finally, in both cases, and in accordance with their common indirection, the utterance has to do with the nonrepresentation of the god. . . . *We are confronted, then, in Kantian terms (but also in pre-Kantian terms, for this has been said in any number of ways since Longinus), with the canonical definition of the sublime: the sublime is the presentation of the nonpresentable* or, more rigorously, to take up the formula of Lyotard, "the presentation (of this:) that there is the nonpresentable."[3]

If it is true that, in Heidegger, "it is in the thought of the sublime—a certain thought of the sublime—that the memory has been maintained, however vague or half-forgetful, of a comprehension of the beautiful which is more original than its Platonic interpretation in terms of the *eidos*-idea,"[4] it is even truer in the case of Nietzsche's work, which presents itself as a direct challenge to the usurpation of the Dionysian sublime by the Apollonian/Platonic *eidos* (*Schein*).

The second claim made in Lacoue-Labarthe's essay that will inform the present study is that the sublime is not really a limited category of art that is only present at certain times, in certain artworks, or in opposition to other aesthetic categories such as that of the beautiful. Adopting Longinus's expanded view of the sublime, which is not structured in opposition to any category of the "beautiful" and includes rhetoric, metaphor, and figuration in general ("the best figure seems . . . that figure which hides and which casts into oblivion its own existence,"[5] Lacoue-Labarthe insists that sublimity is intrinsic to all "great" works of art (greatness being part of the definition of sublimity) and to artistic imitation (*mimesis*) in general: "It is on the basis of such a mimetology that Longinus undertakes to treat of the sublime. But for this very reason his treatment of the sublime has an entirely different significance [than Aristotle's]: it is not simply the question of great art that is posed but, within the question of great art, the question of the possibility and essence of art."[6]

Although Lacoue-Labarthe mentions Nietzsche in passing in his essay, he does not relate Nietzsche's Dionysian aesthetic and corresponding theory of tragedy to an aesthetics of the sublime. This is unfortunate, because Nietzsche's lengthy elaboration of the relationship between the Apollonian and Dionysian in tragedy and other works of art[7] is important for an understanding of the relationship between *techne* and the sublime, which Lacoue-Labarthe's essay seeks to capture: "It is necessary to moderate the excess of the sublime. But this means that art, *techne* in the restricted sense, is capable only of assiduousness, the exactitude of perfectionism . . . and this defines and sums up the beautiful as aspect (*eidos*) in the mode of resemblance."[8] The present essay will try to remedy this omission in demonstrating the affinities between the sublime as the "presentation of the nonpresentable" and Nietzsche's insistence that because of the rapturous superabundance of tragedy, one must "look for the eternal delight of existence not in phenomena but behind them" (*Birth of Tragedy* xvii, 102).

While tragedy and the sublime both foreground a confrontation between the human and the forces that exceed it, the extent to which the supposed category of the sublime corresponds to the supposed genre of tragedy needs to be worked out with care. Are all tragedies sublime? Are all sublime works tragic? To decide whether certain differences prevail, or whether we are finally dealing with what Longinus, Schelling, Nietzsche, Lacoue-Labarthe, and others[9] consider the essential nature of all "great" works of art, this chapter will begin at the beginning with Longinus's treatise *On the Sublime* and then move to a discussion of the Kantian sublime to consider to what extent these two foremost theories of the sublime are compatible with tragedy and, specifically, with Nietzsche's theory of tragic rapture.

Longinus writes: "But on such matters I would only say this: that which is useful and indeed necessary is cheap enough; it is always the unusual which wins our wonder." However, as this statement would suggest—and as the rest of Longinus's tattered first-century treatise on the sublime confirms—such sublimity is also compatible with the formal mastery to be found in all "great" poetry or rhetoric. In fact, most of *On the Sublime* is given over to the kind of cataloging of tropes and figures one would expect from Quintilian, for Longinus makes clear from the outset of his discussion that "excellence of language" is the "bolt of lightning" that scatters the mundane from one's thoughts in all inspired works of literature. Longinus's discussion of style differs from those of Aristotle, Quintilian, and others insofar as he emphasizes rather than marginalizes the potential of such tropes and figures to transform the literal presentation of a message's content "into a passage of transcendent sublimity and emotion, giving it the power of conviction that lies in so strange and startling" an expression. "Figurative writing has a natural grandeur and metaphors make for sublimity" because successful poetry and rhetoric always "master our minds." In this sense, all the tropes and figures discussed by Longinus are tropes and figures of his discussion of the figure of *asyndeton,* whose "disconnected connectedness" paradoxically unites us with something other than that with which we are connected, "so that [the poet's] very order is disordered and equally his disorder implies a certain element of order."[10]

Later treatments of the subject in Burke, Kant, Hegel, and others that eliminate Longinus's emphasis on the formal aspect of artistic style nonetheless repeat his emphasis on the spectatorial effect of awe or "wonder for whatever is greater than ourselves." The sublime is "a moment of divine inspiration" or, in more secular terms, the "elevation" through poetry or rhetoric by which we are "transported outside ourselves" into the greater world of "Nature":

> and she [Nature] therefore from the first breathed into our hearts an unconquerable passion for whatever is great and more divine [*daimoniot- erou*] than ourselves. Thus within the scope of human enterprise there lie such powers of contemplation and thought that even the whole uni- verse cannot satisfy them, but our ideas often pass beyond the limits that enring us. Look at life from all sides and see how in all things the extraor- dinary, the great, the beautiful stand supreme, and you will soon realize the object of our creation [*pros ha gegonamen*]. So it is by some natural instinct that we admire, surely not the small streams, clear and useful as they are, but the Nile, the Danube, the Rhine, and far above all, the sea. The little fire we kindle for ourselves keeps clear and steady, yet we do not therefore regard it with more amazement than the fires of Heav- en, which are often darkened, or think it more wonderful than the cra- ters of Etna in eruption, hurling up rocks and whole hills from their depths and sometimes shooting forth rivers of that pure Titanic fire. But on all such matters I would only say this, that what is useful and indeed necessary is cheap enough; it is always the unusual which wins our wonder.[11]

This passage makes clear what Kant will call the metaphysical and Longinus, the "divine" or "Natural" impulse of the sublime.[12] The rap- turous emotion and excessive displays of power that inevitably spill over into scenarios of destruction are a function of the human drive to exceed the human and thereby enter the sub-liminal, meta-physical world of the gods and Nature. Nature (*physis*) is here identified more with the destruc- tive thunderbolt and lightning than with the flower or stream because the latter better expresses the "whole" entirety of Nature that as such cannot be circumscribed ("inviting us to some great gathering, into the whole universe, there to be spectators of all that she has made."[13] Like the volcano, the divine also expresses this sublime metaphysical power because, in whatever form, it always represents that which cannot be represented, that which exceeds the normal forms and modes of exis- tence.

These two defining characteristics of the Longinian sublime—artis- tic excellence and metaphysical wonder—lead us to the very essence of tragedy. As an expression of the sublime's "unconquerable passion for whatever is great and more divine than ourselves,"[14] tragedy consistent- ly devolves on divine, hubristic protagonists who must exceed their own limits and those of the society that surrounds them. But one is also able to understand better the connection between tragedy and figuration that is also suggested in Aristotle's and Nietzsche's treatises on tragedy (*Birth of Tragedy* vi, 46). For the destruction of the sublime, tragic hero repeats the destruction of every metaphor as the sublime expression of something other, something greater, than what is literally referred to in the figure (the so-called tenor).[15] As the artistic re-presentation of the world-as-other sublime, tragic figuration not only destroys the moral, literal boundaries of the known world (Oedipus's incest, Medea's infanticides, and so forth) but its own boundaries as well, leaving one forever pondering over the mystery of its basic meanings and intents: Why does Oedipus's antisocial behavior ultimately, as in *Oedipus at Colonus*, serve society's best interests? Why does Medea's brutality seem justified, and why does Phaedra's shameful desire appear noble? As a "game which" (paraphrasing Nietzsche's definition of tragedy[16]) "the *sublime*, in its eternal superabundance, plays with itself," art must be seen as a veil of figuration—a fulguration—that is undermined by its own meanings and intents, and tragedy must be seen as the ultimate manifestation of the sublime meaning of all art.

———

In a section of "The Analytic of the Sublime" entitled "The Capacities of the Mind [*Gemüts*] Which Constitute Genius," Kant illustrates his notion of the sublime with the example of "the veil of Isis." But, to understand the meaning of this note and its relevance to tragedy in general and Nietzsche's theory in particular, one must first examine other relevant passages and concepts from the Second Part of the Third Critique, beginning with the main text to which the footnote is added:

> So, for example, a certain poet says in his description of a beautiful morning: "The sun arose, as out of virtue rises peace." The consciousness of virtue, even where we put ourselves only in thought in the position of a man, diffuses in the mind a multitude of sublime and tranquilizing feelings, and gives a boundless outlook into a happy future, *such as no expression within the compass of a definite concept [bestimmten Begriffe] completely attains.* *
> *Perhaps there has never been a more sublime utterance, or a thought more sublimely expressed, than the well-known inscription upon the Temple of Isis (Mother *Nature*): "I am all that is, and that was, and that shall be, and no mortal hath raised the veil from before my face." *Segner* made use of this idea in a suggestive vignette on the frontispiece of his Natural Philosophy, in order to inspire his pupil at the threshold of that temple into which he was about to lead him with such a holy awe as would dispose his mind [*Gemüt*] to serious attention.[17]

Both the notion of the "supersensible" on which Kant bases his "Analytic of the Sublime" as well as the particular discussion here of figurative language as sublimely nonconceptual were already found (as we have seen) in Longinus's treatise. Whether in his treatment of the "mathematical" or "dynamic" sublime, Kant stresses the mind's (*Gemüts*) necessarily figurative—its veiled—representation of a "supersensible absolute," which, because it is "absolutely and not relatively great," exceeds any attempt to represent it and is represented by this very incomplete representation:

> The mind [*Gemüt*] feels itself set in motion in the representation of the sublime. . . . This movement, especially in its inception, may be compared with a vibration [*Erschütterung*], i.e. with a rapidly alternating repulsion and attraction produced by one and the same Object. The point of excess [*Das Überschwengliche*] for the imagination (towards which it is driven in the apprehension of the intuition) is like an abyss [*gleichsam ein Abgrund*] in which it fears to lose itself; yet again for the rational idea of the supersensible [*für die Idee der Vernunft vom Übersinnlichen*] it is not excessive [*überschwenglich*].[18]

Kant's use of the important term *überschwenglich* is stressed for two reasons: first, because the term is also used a number of times by Nietzsche in his discussion of tragic rapture in *The Birth of Tragedy*;[19] second, because it means more than is captured by the English "excessive"—indeed, one can say that the term, true to its meaning, exceeds itself. *Überschwenglich* also "spills over" into the subjective realm in referring to the exuberant rapture felt by the observer (without whom, Kant repeatedly states, the experience of a supersensible absolute would not exist), who is literally beside himself or herself in contemplating that which by definition exceeds the boundaries of one's thought even as one thinks it. In considering something such as God, which is "absolutely, and not merely relatively great" (94), there must be, according to Kant, a rapturous moment of excessiveness in which the mind (*Gemüt*) "violently vibrates" or "shutters" (*erschüttert*) in considering a supersensible that goes beyond the limits of the imagination that conceives it.[20]

Central to Kant's analytic is the notion that the spectator is simultaneously repelled by the experience of something that destroys his or her own particular, individual vantage point while at the same time attracted by the vision of something greater than that afforded by the limits of knowledge and its correlate, everyday, quotidian reality: "Hence charms are repugnant to it; and, since the mind is not simply attracted by the object, but is also *alternately repelled* thereby, the delight in the sublime does not so much involve positive pleasure as admiration or respect, i.e. *merits the name of a negative pleasure.*"[21] Just as Kant speaks of the fear necessarily invoked by the dynamic sublime's power over us ("the aesthetic judgment can only deem nature dynamically sublime in so far as it is looked upon as an object of fear"), Aristotle insists that tragedy "represents incidents arousing fear and pity."[22] Such fear, Aristotle goes on to explain, is due to the destruction of a "man like ourselves," neither so deserving nor undeserving of misfortune that one feels safe from his or her fate. Thus, in both Kant's theory of the greatness of the sublime and Aristotle's theory of tragedy, one encounters the same crucial element of fear for one's imminent destruction.

It can also be argued that the particular agency of destruction is the same in both cases. Like Longinus, Kant defines this agency as the greatness of Nature, which may not destroy us but nonetheless can at any moment ("the irresistibility of the might of nature forces upon us the recognition of our physical helplessness as beings of nature").[23] As Aristotle argues, tragic misfortune can never be the result of the protagonist's own misdeeds but is due, as in the case of Oedipus, to a confrontation with forces—such as the gods—beyond one's control. (Aristotle's famous and famously confusing doctrine of the "tragic flaw" [*hamartia*] can now be understood as demonstrating how individuals like Oedipus, Antigone, Phaedra, and Medea are caught in the grip of forces greater than themselves that are not only destructive but also synonymous with the elevation of these heroes "beyond ourselves"—hence the flaw in Aristotle's notion of the flaw.[24]) Thus, whether the forces beyond one's control are called "fate" or "Nature," tragedy and the sublime both involve us in the same destructive confrontation with a "supersensible" reality, which is by definition greater than ourselves and our understanding.

The "negative pleasure" that is derived from the destructive encounters of the sublime and tragedy is also the same. For Kant, the unpleasant confrontation with a mathematical or natural absolute that denies objective understanding (for example, the mind's paradoxical attempt to grasp mathematical infinity) is redeemed by reason's (*Vernunfts*) subjective grasp of what is unbounded. This is pleasurable because at the very moment that the mind fails to grasp the infinite, it is made aware of its own immortality by acknowledging (again, through the faculty of Reason) forces greater than itself.

In terms of tragedy, the pleasurable spectacle of individuals "greater than ourselves" coming to utter grief and ruin,[25] which is only suggested by Aristotle's celebrated but universally misunderstood notion of catharsis, should also be understood in Kantian terms as the sublime confrontation between one's mortal understanding (*Verstehen*) and immortal reasoning (*Vernunft*). The painful destruction of the greatest heroes is gratifying for the spectator because he or she is thereby reminded of forces greater than those of even the greatest individuals, such as those of fate and the gods, which, while making a mockery of human attempts at understanding (for example, Oedipus's futile attempts at logical reasoning[26]), elevate us beyond ourselves and into an immortal, acausal world. In other words, tragedy allows the mind to delight in its own destruction because it is thus reminded of an immortal world that exceeds mortal limitations, as evident, for example, in Medea's furious rejection of Jason's petty rationalizations or Antigone's destructive unwillingness to obey the behests of the polis.

Kant's theory of the aesthetic sublime as that which "contravenes the ends of our power of judgment to be ill-adapted to our faculty of presentation, and to be, as it were, an outrage on the imagination"[27] also corresponds specifically to Nietzsche's theory of tragedy as the opposition between the Apollonian *principium individuationis* (with its correlative powers of objective representation) and the Dionysian experience of "metaphysical Oneness," which is achieved by the destruction of Apollonian objects and understanding (*Verstehen*):

> It is vain to try to deduce the tragic spirit from the commonly accepted categories of art: illusion and beauty [*Kategorie des Scheines und der Schönheit*]. Music alone allows us to understand the delight felt at the annihilation of the individual. . . . Dionysiac art expresses the omnipotent will behind individuation, eternal life continuing beyond all appearance and in spite of destruction. The metaphysical delight in tragedy is a translation of instinctive Dionysiac wisdom into images. The hero, the highest manifestation of the will, is destroyed, and we assent, since he too is merely a phenomenon [*doch nur Erscheinung ist*], and the eternal life of the will remains unaffected. Tragedy cries, "we believe that life is eternal!" (*Birth of Tragedy* xvi, 92, 102)

In this passage Nietzsche distinguishes, in language that distinctly recalls Kant's *Third Critique*, between the pleasing appearance of the beautiful object (*Kategorie des Scheines und der Schönheit*) and the "metaphysical delight" in music and tragic scenarios of destruction. "The beautiful," writes Kant, "is a question of the form of the object, and this consists in limitation, whereas the sublime is to be found in an object even devoid of form."[28]

Kant and Nietzsche are thus united in their efforts to define a category of the aesthetic in opposition to the "sensible" (keeping in mind all the senses of this term), which devolves on the destruction of finite, limited objects in space and time and the presentiment of the supersensible infinite. Nietzsche calls this category of art the Dionysian (which includes tragedy and music, from which the former is "born"), Kant calls it the sublime; but the two are for all intents and purposes the same, despite the reluctance of the former to use a term that, by the end of the nineteenth century, had lost much of its metaphysical import—its sublimity, if you will.

Yet, one might object, what of the fact that Nietzsche identifies his version of the sublime with music, whereas Kant does not?[29] In the passage just quoted, Kant refers to the paradoxical need for a sensible representation of the supersensible: "But this idea of the supersensible . . . is awakened in us by an object the aesthetic estimating of which strains the imagination to its utmost, whether in respect of its extension (mathematical), or of its might over the mind (dynamical)."[30] This description of the almost imaginationless art of the sublime, I would maintain, is exactly what Nietzsche means by his definition of music as the art form closest to the eternal Dionysian. Although Kant himself joins the numerous failed attempts to link music with mathematics,[31] Nietzsche's understanding of music is based on the notion that, as the most nonverbal and nonobjective art form, music is actually closest to a sublime art of the supersensible in its movement beyond the ordinary, empirical categories of space and time. If, on the contrary, one tends to view music as anything but sublime and representative of the supersensible, that is because music is the "blind spot" of Western culture's rationalistic thinking and, as such, has largely eluded its proper status—and, what is worse, has eluded eluding its proper status.

Beyond the obvious fact of tragedy's musical, lyrical dimension (if not its "origin"), we know that actors of the fifth-century Greek plays always wore masks, a fact that is often acknowledged but seldom taken into account in attempts at understanding tragedy. As the sublime artwork par excellence, tragedy celebrates an "absolutely great" reality that is represented by the destruction of characters "greater than us." But the Aristotelian phrase must now be heard differently: it means, instead, that the tragic hero is superhuman, supersensible, and so destroyed as "one of us." The mask, then, is a sign that tragedy in its essence is not about "us" at all. Rather, tragedy is about something other relative to which the "human character" is merely a mask or a veil—a fact that is also confirmed by the lyrical/musical dimension of the genre.

We can now return to another masked figure, the "most sublime" masked figure of Isis. Recall that, in Kant's famous footnote to his discussion of "The Powers of the Mind Which Constitute Genius," it is seemingly not the temple or even the veiled sculpture that is sublime (as in the texts of Schiller, Novalis, and others) but the inscription and that, moreover, this inscription is in the form of a first-person statement by means of which the temple or statue speaks to its beholder directly: "Perhaps there has never been a more sublime utterance, or a thought more sublimely expressed, than the well-known inscription upon the Temple of *Isis* (Mother *Nature*): 'I am all that is, and that was, and that shall be, and no mortal hath raised the veil from before my face.'"

The inscription and its context distinctly recall the example of Jehovah's sublime divinity mentioned by Kant, Hegel, and others; they present both the all-encompassing "I am who is" and also the Judaic proscription against attempting to represent God's infinite greatness.[32] But Kant singles out the example of Isis for his highest praise because the inscription adds the reference to mortality's veiling, humanity's paradoxical status of looking at things in time, which must veil the greater, eternal truth of which they are a part (recalling the earlier discussion of a synecdoche that is also an asyndeton). One must then add to Kant's admiration for the inscription an admiration for the entire temple/statue, which refers to the truth of all other artworks as veiled representations of an eternal truth that it represents precisely because it does not represent it more clearly. The veiled Isis and its inscription would thus stand as an emblem/epigraph to all the visual arts that are beautiful (*schöne*) to the extent that one admires their appearance (*Schein*) but sublime to the extent that the beauty one admires is only a veiled representation of sublime "greatness"—"greatness" that is "eternal" in that it "goes beyond" whatever one sees or understands objectively.

The veiled, figurative stone statue of Isis is thus as much about music as it is about the sublime; and thus it is also about the tragic nature of all art. For although music is the only art not contained in the "multimedia" statue/temple of Isis, which has both verbal and visual components, this is precisely because music is the only one of the "sister" arts that does not exist in space or time and so is already eternal. Obviously, music is not a visual object that exists in space. The score, if it exists at all, is not the artwork (the musical artwork consists in the music being performed); also, a musical note does not have the objective definition of a word in a story or a poem. But music also does not exist in time because it cannot be assigned any one of the three temporal modes as defined in the statue's inscription: it does not even fit into the present—which, unlike the hic et nunc of temporal consciousness, is always already the past as one experiences it and the future as it leads to what is about to be. Thus, music is always more sublime than beautiful, although we frequently err is using the term, for it lifts the veil of our quotidian, spatiotemporal consciousness by blinding us to the reality that surrounds us.

At the conclusion of the passage from *The Birth of Tragedy* quoted above (xvi), Nietzsche addresses the sublimity of tragedy and the tragedy of sublimity while referring, like Kant in his footnote on Isis, to the "Original Mother" of appearances:

> The metaphysical delight in tragedy is a translation of instinctive Diony-siac wisdom into images. The hero, the highest manifestation of the will, is destroyed, and we assent, since he too is merely a phenomenon, and the eternal life of the will remains unaffected. . . . That same nature [which underlies but is veiled in Apollonian art] addresses us through Dionysiac art and its tragic symbolism with its true, undisguised voice: "Be like me, the Original Mother, who finds eternal satisfaction in the ceaseless changing of appearances [*Erscheinungen*], in the eternally cre-ative, eternally bringing into existence." (xvi, 102, 93)

The objective appearance of Apollonian art allows the spectator to retain his or her own identity and the identity of the object (hence, Nietzsche's emphasis throughout *The Birth of Tragedy* on the Apollonian *principi-um individuationis*), whereas music, as just discussed, destroys such objectivity as the listener loses himself or herself within the "suffering" (*Leiden*) of music (*Lieder*). Tragedy, then, destroys the tragic hero "out of the spirit of music" just as, in Nietzsche's complete title, music is defined as the origin from which all Apollonian appearances in tragedy are born.

Yet, as Nietzsche's use of "eternity" in this passage to describe *both* Apollonian visual art and Dionysian music suggests, the two "poles" of art are not really opposed. "That same nature" that is veiled or "glossed away" in the beautiful Apollo Belvedere, or in the upper half of Rapha-el's *Transfiguration* (as discussed by Nietzsche in *The Birth of Tragedy* [iv]) addresses us "in its true voice" in tragedy; there the voices of Isis and the "Urmutter" speak directly, urging us to rejoice in the sublime, oce-anic "Oneness" that is the underlying truth of the nonempirical appear-ances (*Erscheinungen*) of art. It is thus that Nietzsche, like Kant in his invocation of "Isis (Mother *Nature*)," here invokes the "Original Moth-er": she who, as the eternal, creative matrix of everything, revels in the tragic destruction, the "fulguration," of individual, veiled forms that, as such, block the flow of eternity. However, the Apollonian "veil" of beau-tiful artworks is also sublime and tragic in its contingency and depen-dence on the Absolute, which is its underlying reality.[33] The veil of Isis, the Apollonian object of formal beauty, is beautiful precisely because, as Longinus understood as well as Nietzsche, all "great art" is ultimately sublime, and tragic.

3 "Troubled Ecstasy": Yeats's Tragic Vision

There is no laughter too bitter, no irony too harsh for utterance, no passion too terrible to be set before the
minds of men. The Greeks knew that. Only in this way
can mankind be understood, only when we have put
ourselves in all the possible positions of life, from the
most miserable to those that are so lofty that we can
only speak of them in symbols and in mysteries, will entire wisdom be possible.

—Yeats, *First Principles*

It is a general point of consensus among Yeats scholars that
the poet's vision of life and poetry is fundamentally tragic: "For Yeats,
tragedy is the privileged genre, bearer of heroic ethics into the twentieth
century. Above other aesthetic types, he says with almost monotonous
frequency, tragedy can simulate and so stimulate the heroic. His favor-
ite generic rule is that 'tragedy is a joy to the man who dies.'"[1]

This consensus immediately collapses, however, under the weight
of numerous questions concerning Yeats's tragic vision: How does Yeats
define tragedy and/or the tragic?[2] Whose definitions, from the commonplace to the esoteric, from the Greeks through Nietzsche, influenced that
conception? And, finally, how did that conception change as Yeats's sen-
sibilities evolved from the early phase of the "Celtic Twilight" to the
later, "modern" phase of the mask?[3] These questions, when added to the
perennial problem of defining tragedy from its "birth" in ancient Greece
to its so-called death in the twentieth century,[4] seem to turn any gener-

al agreement about Yeats and tragedy into a more vexing problem than if there had been no consensus at all.

However tempting it might be to jettison such generic considerations, it is clear that tragedy is a, if not the, central concern from Yeats's early poems through such later works as the verse drama *Purgatory* and "Lapis Lazuli." The plan of the present chapter is to focus on examples from the poems and essays before 1900 to establish the fundamental importance of tragedy for Yeats and, then, to demonstrate the continued importance of Yeats's tragic vision in the later writings. Yeats's idea of tragic "gaiety," as will be shown, is both implicitly and explicitly related to Nietzsche's notion of tragic rapture; indeed, it would not be an overstatement to claim that the two major advocates of tragedy during the modern era share the same "affirmative" view of tragedy as a form of rapturous overabundance that is synonymous with artistic creation in general.[5] Nor is it an overstatement to claim that Yeats's Nietzschean notion of tragic "gaiety" is essential to understanding the works of one of the twentieth century's greatest poets.

———————

Larry Brunner's *Tragic Victory* vitiates its own admirable thesis concerning the essentially tragic nature of Yeats's vision of human experience by adopting the widespread but erroneous belief that Yeats's early lyrics are inferior to, or at least not as important as, his later works.[6] Such slighting of Yeats's early work is a sure indication that the essence of Yeats's tragic vision has not been fully grasped, for the tragic philosophy that informs the later poems is already fully evident in such early poems as "The Rose of the World":

> Who dreamed that beauty passes like a dream?
> For those red lips, with all their mournful pride,
> Mournful that no new wonder may betide,
> Troy passed away in one high funeral gleam,
> And Usna's children died.

> We and the labouring world are passing by:
> Amid men's souls, that waver and give place
> Like the pale waters in their wintry race,
> Under the passing stars, foam of the sky,
> Lives on this lonely face.

> Bow down, archangels, in your dim abode:
> Before you were, or any hearts to beat,
> Weary and kind one lingered by His seat;
> He made the world to be a grassy road
> Before her wandering feet.[7]

Like the much later "Lapis Lazuli" (1938), where Yeats explicitly rejects the "reality principle" of politics for the "pleasure principle" of aesthetic gaiety, this early poem, published in 1892, begins with scornful disregard for those who would deem beauty, not the "real world," as passing: "Who dreamed that beauty passes like a dream?" Rather than the traditional view of beauty as an ephemeral phenomenon that leaves its admirers mournful of its passing, Yeats here defines beauty as eternal and thus predating the creation of the world ("Before you were, or any hearts to beat"). Moreover, Yeats says specifically that the world passes away because of beauty, not the reverse: "For those red lips, . . . / . . . / Troy passed away . . . / And Usna's children died."

Nonetheless, our perception of beauty, Yeats would have to agree, is always momentary and "passing," even if its essence is not. That being said, the poem's perceiver, who "dreams that beauty passes like a dream," is right in assessing the subtle peculiarities of beauty's being: "we can dream beauty," to paraphrase a well-known statement by Yeats, "we cannot know it."[8] Such a dream of beauty reveals at once a profound awareness of the truth about beauty as well as a profound mistake in failing to observe that it is not beauty that is passing, but humanity that is in flux. Moreover, since "passing" is another word for tropes such as metaphor (*meta-pherein* means to "carry across"), one might extrapolate a theory of figurative language from this argument that would hold that the supposedly evanescent troping of metaphor is the language of what Yeats calls the eternally unchanging. But what is important for the purpose of this analysis is that the truth about beauty's unchanging essence is tied to the truth about its passing; that, tragically, beauty only exists through its constructive disintegration—its de-con-struction—as a result of a metaphysical overabundance whose temporal embodiment affirms what it denies and denies what it affirms.

According to Yeats's Neoplatonic belief,[9] there is from the first a realm of eternal, overabundant beauty that can only be reflected in the passing, or troping, of those same objects ("Like the pale waters in their wintry race") whose stability, or literalness, deludes one into thinking that it is the world, and not beauty, that is eternal. As a symbol of this eternal beauty, the ephemeral rose is for Yeats as much the red lips of Helen as it is a flower, both of which represent the eternity of their own tragic passing or troping.

The final stanza of "The Rose of the World" anticipates the violent overthrowing of the Judeo-Christian God in favor of the pagan beauty of the rose, which is also encountered in later poems like "The Second Coming": "Bow down, archangels, in your dim abode." Yeats clearly establishes beauty and the love that attaches to it as the divine power that stands above the world and causes it to "rise"[10] and, in its inherent struggle to attain the unattainable eternal beauty, fall. The reference to beauty as "weary" refers us back to the first stanza, where Helen is "Mournful that no new wonder may betide." As will be shown in other examples in the poetry as well as from numerous statements in the essay "The Celtic Element in Literature," it is impossible for Yeats to conceive of beauty except as weary, mournful, and tragic, for the world can only endlessly repeat the rise and fall of trying to capture love's eternal, overabundant beauty.

> *The Sorrow of Love*
>
> The brawling of a sparrow in the eaves,
> The brilliant moon and all the milky sky,
> And all that famous harmony of leaves,
> Had blotted out man's image and his cry.
>
> A girl arose that had red mournful lips
> And seemed the greatness of the world in tears,
> Doomed like Odysseus and the labouring ships
> And proud as Priam murdered with his peers;
>
> Arose, and on the instant clamorous eaves,
> A climbing moon upon an empty sky,
> And all that lamentation of the leaves,
> Could but compose man's image and his cry.[11]

One is reminded here of Paul de Man's deconstructive reading of the linguistic, emblematic sign's importance over the naturalistic, romantic symbol in Yeats's poems.[12] For the romantic symbolism referred to in the first stanza ("all that famous harmony of leaves . . . / . . . blotted out man's image and his cry"), which is traditionally seen as transcending the merely human world, is replaced in the second stanza by an emblematic relationship between Helen and her associates (Odysseus and Priam) and in the third stanza by "man's image and his cry." De Man's argument for emblematicity in Yeats also seems to be well supported by the Helen/ rose figure ("A girl *arose*") of the second stanza, which is not an ineffable symbol but (among other things) the traditional emblem of love, passion, beauty, and violence.

The essential moment of the poem occurs in the third stanza, with the phrase "on the instant." For "on the instant" that the "girl arose"— a girl who, as has just been stated, is an emblem of beauty, passion, and destruction—the natural, symbolic world, the world of the "clamorous eaves," the "climbing moon upon an empty sky," and the "lamentation of the leaves" is lost. As in "The Rose of the World," this poem restates the position that "He made the world to be a grassy road / Before her wandering feet"—in other words, the eternal beauty of the rose antedates and effaces the natural world. The "could but" is thus essential as a qualification to "compose" in the final line: it is not that these naturalistic elements themselves symbolize Helen's beauty but that, because of the overwhelming nature of her power, they have ceased to blot out man's image and cry as they had in the earlier stanza. It is important to note, in this regard, the ambiguity of the final stanza: "Could but compose man's image and his cry" can also mean—and I would argue it must mean—that the eaves, the moon, and the leaves have ceased to signify anything, for they have been occluded—"blotted out"—by the emblematic middle stanza and its significant grammatical extension onto the final stanza.

The tragedy here is that the "greatness" of Helen's rapturous beauty is identified by Yeats with destruction in general as well as with the massacre and destruction at Troy. Beyond the traditional view of Helen as "the face that launched a thousand ships," both of Yeats's poems posit a tragic vision of beauty as inherently destructive: Helen is always mourning, she is always the "greatness of the world in tears," always Odysseus's ten-year return journey home after ten long years of battle. As we shall argue throughout this chapter, Yeats's notions of beauty and tragedy, and of tragedy and beauty, are synonymous: there is no "joy of love" to balance "The Sorrow of Love" (there is, significantly, "The Pity of Love") because the Celtic poet consistently views beauty and love as the product of a state of rapturous overabundance that destroys temporality with eternity.

Among the best of Yeats's critics, two stand out as having bucked the tendency to dismiss or subordinate Yeats's early lyrics. Harold Bloom speaks of the "remarkable number of lasting poems" to be found among Yeats's earliest work and rejects the constant "undervaluing" of collections like *Crossways* and *The Rose*.[13] William Empson, while not as interested as Bloom in defending Yeats's place in the poetic tradition, is nonetheless in complete agreement with him about the value of the early poems, which he discusses brilliantly in *Seven Types of Ambiguity*. Although neither Bloom nor Empson discusses what I see as the essential tragic component of these works, my reading relies on their careful attention to these early poems.

Whatever one might think about some of the unfortunate implications of Yeats's notions of aristocracy,[14] the fact is that kings rarely, if ever, fare badly in Yeats's poems. Goll, Cuchulain, Fergus, and even Lear are

all guaranteed a higher level of esteem than even the Greeks and Eliza-
bethans were prepared to grant their kings. This will be important to
remember when one considers the debate, carried on by Bloom and Empson, over whether King Fergus, the titular hero of two of Yeats's most
important early poems, is to be viewed as triumphant or a failure. "Fergus and the Druid" tells of how the fabled king renounced his throne to
learn the occult wisdom of the Druid:

> Fergus: This whole day have I followed in the rocks,
>   And you have changed and flowed from shape to shape,
>   First as a raven on whose ancient wings
>   Scarcely a feather lingered, then you seemed
>   A weasel moving on from stone to stone,
>   And now at least you wear a human shape,
>   A thin grey man half lost in gathering night.
> Druid: What would you, king of the proud Red Branch kings?
> Fergus: This would I say, most wise of living souls:
>   Young subtle Conchubar sat close by me
>   When I gave judgment, and his words were wise,
>   And what to me was burden without end,
>   To him seemed easy, so I laid the crown
>   Upon his head to cast away my sorrow.
> Druid: What would you, king of the proud Red Branch kings?
> Fergus: A king and proud! and that is my despair,
>   I feast amid my people on the hill,
>   And pace the woods, and drive my chariot-wheels
>   In the white border of the murmuring sea;
>   And still I feel the crown upon my head.
> Druid: What would you, Fergus?
> Fergus: Be no more a king,
>   But learn the dreaming wisdom that is yours.
> Druid: Look on my thin grey hair and hollow cheeks
>   And on these hands that may not lift the sword,
>   This body trembling like a wind-blown reed.
>   No woman's loved me, no man sought my help.
>   (Because I be not the things I dream.)
> Fergus: A king is but a foolish labourer
>   Who wastes his blood to be another's dream.
> Druid: Take, if you must, this little bag of dreams;
>   Unloose the cord, and they will wrap you round.

Fergus: I see my life go drifting like a river
From change to change; I have been many things—
A green drop in the surge, a gleam of light
Upon a sword, a fir-tree on a hill,
An old slave grinding at a heavy quern,
A king sitting upon a chair of gold—
And all these things were wonderful and great;
But now I have grown nothing, knowing all.
Ah! Druid, Druid, how great webs of sorrow
Lay hidden in the small slate-coloured thing![15]

Bloom, whose own interest in occult systems of thought makes him especially tolerant in unraveling some of Yeats's most abstruse mystical writings, sees Fergus's encounter with the Druid as foreshadowing Yeats's own later attempts to learn, through Theosophy and elsewhere, the "dreaming wisdom" of the world. But, unfortunately, this does not mitigate Bloom's judgment of Fergus's encounter with the Druid as a failure.[16] Yeats's dreaming Druid is, to be sure, a decidedly brooding presence; but as this poem ultimately reveals and the contemporary prose essays in *Ideas of Good and Evil* confirm, such brooding is synonymous with tragic overabundance for Yeats: "Men did not mourn merely because their beloved was married to another . . . but because they had been born and must die with their great thirst unslaked."[17] If there is a "failure" here at all, it is the failure Fergus feels in terms of his civic responsibility as king. The crucial final speech, with Fergus having "grown nothing, knowing all," should not, then, be construed negatively but rather as the celebration of Fergus's rapturous "tragic victory"[18] at having "grown nothing, knowing *all*."

Comparisons between Yeats's Fergus and Nietzsche's story of King Midas (*Birth of Tragedy* iii, 29), as well as a brief look at Yeats's contemporary essay on "The Celtic Element in Literature," will help to resolve this paradox of greatness and destruction, of rapture and suffering, which are conjoined in the final stanza of "Fergus and the Druid." In *The Birth of Tragedy,* Nietzsche tells the story of how Midas finally caught the archsatyr Silenus (Dionysus's companion and tutor) and asked him to name mankind's greatest boon. With a "shrill laugh," Silenus answers with the Greeks' commonplace notion of tragic meaninglessness: "The greatest thing of all for mankind would be never to have been born; the next best, to die as quickly as possible" (iii, 29). The Druid, along with the rest of Yeats's decidedly sinister faery world,[19] compares well with the Greeks' own woodland deity. Moreover, as a king eager to learn the

Druid's "dreaming wisdom," Fergus closely parallels King Midas's desire to gain Silenus's wisdom. But beyond these obvious points of comparison, a more important point of agreement with Nietzsche's anecdote will enable us to return Yeats's poem to its proper tragic context.

As we saw in the first chapter, the fundamental project of Nietzsche's *Birth of Tragedy* was to fathom why the joyful, "gay" vitality of the satyr would give voice to such a damning utterance as Silenus's and to tragic works of art in general.[20] Nietzsche resolved this paradox with his notion of "tragic superabundance," the idea that superabundant joy—gaiety—leads the satyr to acknowledge all the suffering of existence even as he overcomes it: "Tragedy has convinced us that even the ugly and discordant are merely an esthetic game which the will, in its utter exuberance [*in der ewigen Fülle seiner Lust*], plays with itself" (xxiv, 64). Nietzsche goes on to insist, in his discussion of Silenus, that the satyr's statement is actually the logical extension of Achilles' statement that "the worst of all would be *never* to have been born," for both statements express the notion of life as that which exceeds itself and so conjoins, like Achilles' short but illustrious career, life's highest fulfillment with destruction. Tragedy's horrid spectacles of destruction, then, must be reconsidered as expressions of a satyric exuberance that embraces destruction precisely because it embraces life to the fullest.

When the chorus of Sophocles' *Oedipus Tyrannus* utters its own version of Silenus's statement—"Oh generations of mankind, how I reckon you as equal to those who live not at all!"[21]—this must now be reheard as more than just a pessimistic evaluation of Oedipus's (and all humanity's) suffering. In the same way that Silenus's statement can be heard as the satyr's exuberant condemnation of "ordinary" human experience, the chorus's words can also refer to a moment of "tragic victory" when mankind has gone beyond the limits of mortal existence and become divine ("live not at all"). Similarly, when Fergus laments that he has "grown nothing, knowing all," one has not just to do with "failure" (pace Bloom) but, more importantly, with tragic superabundance, which triumphantly overcomes the boundaries of mere human experience.

The title of Yeat's collection of essays written during the same early period of his career, *Ideas of Good and Evil*, is not the only suggestion of a strong Nietzschean current that runs through Yeats's thought in even his earliest works.[22] For example:

An Elizabethan writer describes extravagant sorrow by calling it "to weep Irish"; and Oisin and Leyrach Hen are, I think, a little nearer even to us modern Irish than they are to most people. That is why our poetry and much of our thought is melancholy. "The same man," writes Dr. Hyde in the beautiful prose which he first writes in Gaelic, "who will to-day be dancing, sporting, drinking, and shouting, will be soliloquizing by himself to-morrow, heavy and sick and sad in his own lonely little hut, making a croon over departed hopes, lost life, the vanity of this world, and the coming of death."[23]

If we take Yeats at his word, the key of "The Celtic Element in Literature" is melancholy brooding.[24] Indeed, it would not be extending Yeats's comments in his essay too far to say that the key element in all of Yeats's early poems is such melancholy brooding and that without an explanation of such brooding, beginning with that offered by Yeats himself in "The Celtic Element in Literature," it is impossible to understand these poems. It is clear from the passage just quoted that Celtic melancholy, like the Greek version of Silenian brooding, is a function of excessive joy: "'The same man . . . who will to-day be dancing, sporting, drinking, and shouting, will be soliloquizing by himself to-morrow, heavy and sick and sad in his own lonely little hut.'" Yet, psychological or psychoanalytic explanations of mania/depression disorders aside,[25] why is it the case that excessive joy—overjoy—should lead to brooding? Yeats writes:

> From this "mistaking dreams," which are perhaps essences, for "realities," which are perhaps accidents, from this "passionate, turbulent reaction against the despotism of fact," comes, it may be, that melancholy which made all ancient peoples delight in tales that end in death and parting, as modern peoples delight in tales that end in marriage bells; and made all ancient peoples, who like the old Irish had a nature more lyrical than dramatic, delight in wild and beautiful lamentations. Life was so weighed down by the emptiness of the great forests and by the mystery of all things, and by the greatness of its own desires, and, as I think, by the loneliness of much beauty; and seemed so little and so fragile and so brief, that nothing could be more sweet in the memory than a tale that ended in death and parting, and than a wild and beautiful lamentation. Men did not mourn merely because their beloved was married to another, or because learning was bitter in the mouth, for such mourning believes that life might be happy were it different, and is therefore the less mourning; but because they had been born and must die with their great thirst unslaked. And so it is that all the august sorrowful persons of literature, Cassandra and Helen and Deirdre, and Lear and Tristan, have come out of legends and are indeed but the images of the primitive imagination mirrored in the little looking-glass of the modern and classic imagination.[26]

Like Nietzsche, Yeats refers to a lyric origin for tragic, melancholy beauty: "all ancient peoples . . . like the old Irish had a nature more lyrical than dramatic." The lyrical beauty Yeats is referring to is melancholic and bound to end tragically in "death and parting" and "wild and beautiful lamentation" because it is inherently at odds with the reality principle of the real world, where the "despotism of fact" prevails. The "greatness of [one's] own desires" causes a particular delight in "tales that end in death and parting" because the "excess which is abundantly excessive" cannot be satisfied and so can only be satisfied in not being satisfied.[27] As we just saw with Fergus and Silenus, superabundant joy culminates in tragedy not by default but because it wills more than anything that can satisfy it: "Life was so weighed down by the emptiness of the great forests and by the mystery of all things, and by the greatness of its own desires, and, as I think, by the loneliness of much beauty; and seemed so little and so fragile and so brief, that nothing could be more sweet in the memory than a tale that ended in death and parting, and than a wild and beautiful lamentation." Silenus, the reader will recall, advocated the shortest possible life not because of the harshness of the "reality principle" (something of little concern to a satyr anyway) but because of an overabundant joy and vitality that, in embracing life to the fullest, embraces death as well.

One last passage from "The Celtic Element in Literature" will make the connection between the world of the Greek satyr and the realm of the Celtic faery even clearer:

> Men who lived in a world where anything might flow and change, and become any other thing; and among great gods whose passions were in the flaming sunset and in the thunder and the thunder-shower, had not our thoughts of weight and measure. *They worshipped nature and the abundance of nature, and had always, as it seems, for a supreme ritual that tumultuous dance among the hills or in the depths of the woods, where unearthly ecstasy fell upon the dancers, until they seemed the gods or the godlike beasts, and felt their souls overtopping the moon; and, as some think, imagined for the first time in the world the blessed country of the gods and of the happy dead.* They had imaginative passions because they did not live within our own strait limits, and were nearer to ancient chaos, every man's desire, and had immortal models about them. The hare that ran by among the dew might have sat upon his haunches when the first man was made, and the poor bunch of rushes under their feet might have been a goddess laughing among the stars; and with but a little magic, a little waving of the hands, a little murmuring of the lips, they too could become a hare or a bunch of rushes, and know immortal love and immortal hatred.[28]

The Dionysian ecstasy of the Celtic dancers—who, like the satyrs, "worshipped nature and *the abundance of nature* . . . where unearthly ecstasy fell upon the dancers, until they seemed the gods or the godlike beasts"—is only a "failure" if it is not understood in terms of the Celtic sensibility that Yeats has carefully explained. The end of the first Fergus poem is a fairly literal transcription of what Yeats describes here as "a world where anything might flow and change, and become any other thing." What Bloom fails to realize is that the tragic, destructive aspect of Fergus's transformation is part of an ecstatic embrace of the "abundance of nature" that leaves behind all the ordinary cares and concerns of the everyday world. For "melancholy . . . made all ancient peoples delight in tales that end in death and parting" because it is only in such tragedies that the greatness of life is fulfilled, that the limits of "the despotism of fact" are overcome.

The titular question of "Who Goes with Fergus?" might be applied to readers and critics confused about the curious placement of this second Fergus poem. How is one to follow Fergus from the first to the second poem when, although "Who Goes with Fergus?" follows "Fergus and the Druid" in the volume *The Rose* (there are intervening poems), the action of the second poem may or may not follow that of the first?[29] In "Who Goes with Fergus?" we encounter one who might still be a king (he "rules the shadows of the woods") and drives his chariots through woods and along the strand in ways that could either precede or follow the final transformation of "Fergus and the Druid":

> Who will go drive with Fergus now,
> And pierce the deep wood's woven shade
> And dance upon the level shore?
> Young man, lift up your russet brow,
> And lift your tender eyelids, maid,
> And brood on hopes and fear no more.
>
> And no more turn aside and brood
> Upon love's bitter mystery;
> For Fergus rules the brazen cars,
> And rules the shadows of the wood,
> And the white breast of the dim sea
> And all dishevelled wandering stars.[30]

Bloom neatly avoids problems concerning the order of the two poems by choosing to focus on "Who Goes with Fergus?" as a poem of victory ("This is not the defeated Fergus of 'Fergus and the Druid'") without considering any chronological relation to the other Fergus poem.[31] In other words, Bloom chooses to read the poems synchronically rather than diachronically, a decision that, given the problematic status of the ordering of poems in this or any collection, is certainly justified. Nonetheless, Bloom's own uncertainty as to whether the two poems are both about "poetic failure" belies his certainty about the thematic relation between the two poems, thus reopening the question of a diachronic relationship. Empson, however, makes the questions raised by the ambiguous ordering of the two poems the basis of his interpretation of "Who Goes with Fergus?" in *Seven Types of Ambiguity:*

> ["Who Goes with Fergus?"], of course, assumes this story, but *now* may mean before or after the transformation. If after, the first line means: "Now that the awful example of Fergus is in front of you, surely you will not be so unwise as to brood?" . . . if before, so that the force of *now* is: "There is still time to drive with Fergus, as he is still a king in the world," or "there is still time to give a warning, as the fatal thing has not yet happened"; then the first line gives: "Who will come out with the great figures of the Court, and join in their sensible out-of-door pleasures?"[32]

Empson's brief treatment of the two Fergus poems is a marvel of New Critical sensitivity to textual nuance and precision; indeed, Empson's few pages may be among the very best ever written on Yeats. Yet, as concerned as Empson is to follow Fergus from one poem to the next, his close reading is vitiated by a technique that compels him to consider the two poems together but not the context of other poems by Yeats from this and other collections. One cannot insist, as Empson does, that the second poem, "of course, assumes" the first without also considering the play in which the second poem first appeared (preceding, in fact, *both* Fergus poems) as well as the rest of Yeats's poetry, where one must also "go with Fergus" if contexts are to be "assumed."

"Who Goes with Fergus?" belongs among a large group of what one might call "invitation poems" that encompasses all of Yeats's so-called phases: poems that involve an invitation proffered to a central, mortal character that asks him to leave one realm—usually earthly—to enter another—usually supernatural or immortal. "Sailing to Byzantium," for example, might be compared not only to "Who Goes with Fergus?" but also to "The Stolen Child" of Yeats's early collection *Crossways,* where the faeries repeatedly invite the mortal child: *"Come away, O human child! / To the waters and the wild / With a faery, hand in hand."*[33] Taken together, such invitations are always strangely ambiguous, for the human is invited to a superhuman realm, which, while clearly desirable in certain ways, is also decidedly sinister in others. The faeries of "The Stolen Child" want to steal the human child from a cozy domestic world to a place where "flapping herons wake / The drowsy water-rats;" where "we've hid our faery vats / Full of berries / And of reddest stolen cherries."[34] The old man of "Sailing to Byzantium" longs to leave a world of joyous youthful sensuality to one where he might become a mechanical bird "Of hammered gold and gold enamelling / To keep a drowsy Emperor awake."[35] Other poems, such as Yeats's famous "The Lake Isle of Innisfree," proffer similarly troubling invitations.

With this pattern in mind, it is possible to approach what is arguably the most invitational of all of Yeats's poems with the wariness proper to its "genre." Even if one reads the first line of "Who Goes with Fergus?" without assuming "now" to refer to "Fergus and the Druid," there is enough in the poem to suggest that Fergus's situation in the second poem is not an altogether happy one. Coupled with the call to "dance upon the level shore" is the rather violent offer to "*pierce* the deep wood's woven shade." And what, one must ask, is lost as well as gained if one agrees to leave behind "love's bitter mystery"? Before accepting such an invitation, one would do well to consider just how wonderful it would be to join the ruler of the "white *breast* of the dim sea / And all *dishevelled* wandering stars."[36]

What Fergus does offer here is a world of tragic beauty such as that described in these poems and in the essays on Celtic literature discussed earlier. There, as was shown, melancholic "brood[ing] / Upon love's bitter mystery" was described as a staple of Celtic art, but, as such, it needed to be understood, not in terms of the "weights and measures" of love lost or love gained, but in terms of the very nature of love's excessive passion, its tragic longing for more, which inevitably leads to the destructiveness described in "The Sorrow of Love" and "The Rose of the World." True, Yeats here seems to be describing an alternative to the Celtic world of "moody brooding," for the young lovers are urged to raise up their downcast eyes and to cease brooding on love. But, as Empson points out, this is because the world we are being invited to is a world of even greater brooding ("'Do not brood in this [the lovers'] comparatively trivial fashion but go and drive with Fergus, who will teach you to brood about everything").[37] The lovers here are described in terms that are, for Yeats, distinctly patronizing; they can be likened to other condescending references in the early poems to the ordinary world of domesticity, such as that described in "The Stolen Child." Their concerns appear "so little and so fragile and so brief" compared to a life such as Fergus's, which is "weighed down by the emptiness of the great forests and by the mystery of all things, and by the greatness of its own desires." The "deep wood's woven shade" and "dishevelled wandering stars" offered up here as an alternative to the lovers' all-too-human concerns are no refuge but, quite the contrary, a world of even deeper mystery and greatness such that it "empties" itself of ordinary human experience. The forest world of "Who Goes with Fergus?" is thus neither earlier nor later than but simultaneous with the world of the Druid in the earlier poem; in both cases, it is a tragic world of emptiness and greatness. As will be shown in the following discussion, this tragic vision of life as destroyed by the "greatness of its own desires" is by no means limited to Yeats's early, Celtic writings but is the central message of the later works as well.

> Turning and turning in the widening gyre
> The falcon cannot hear the falconer;
> Things fall apart; the centre cannot hold;
> Mere anarchy is loosed upon the world . . .[38]

It is not at all surprising that the meaning of this troubling work, like the falcon described in the opening lines, swirls out of the reach of critical understanding while, at the same time, the poem is almost universally viewed as Yeats's most important. What is surprising is that a number of Yeats's most prominent critics are able to ridicule the poem at the same time as they praise its greatness. Bloom, for example, makes many incisive comments about the work but nonetheless raises a number of surprisingly petty objections to the "misleading and illegitimate" aspects of the poem: "Is it legitimate to use 'born' for what would be a demonic epiphany? . . . 'Mere anarchy' does not always bring a revelation. . . . Why does the falconer's loss of control over the falcon betoken a lapse in the maintaining of ritual?" Clearly, despite its enormous popularity, the poem's meaning is not "at hand." Yet, by placing "The Second Coming" within the larger context of Yeats's tragic vision one may hopefully avoid the part of Bloom's reading that ends with the wistful prayer that "If the good time yet comes, [may] 'The Second Coming' impress the common reader rather less than it does now."[39]

There is indeed much to brood on, much to be horrified by in "The Second Coming": war, the loss of cultural refinements, and the supplanting of Christian love and innocence by bestial intensity, to mention but a few of the poem's horrors. But what troubles critics most, I believe, is that it seems to waver between the gaiety of "Lapis Lazuli," where the chaos of destruction is explicitly overcome by artistic joy and a more sober assessment of the horrific results of such a catastrophe. Bloom, like Ivor Winters, "hears in the poem exultation on the speaker's part";[40] this may exaggerate somewhat the tone of "The Second Coming," but it accurately portrays the poem's air of excited apprehension. Empson would likely say that the poem is decidedly ambiguous in this regard and that the "speaker's part" is not as easily defined as Bloom would have it.

Reading "The Second Coming" in the context of the present study, one encounters the same combination of awesome sorrow and sinister delight as in the two Fergus poems and in the two rose poems discussed earlier. Had Bloom listened to Yeats a little more and to Blake and Shelley a little less, he might have realized the impossibility of the speaker's "exulting" in a poem where "the worst / Are full of passionate intensity."[41] "The Second Coming" is a great poem precisely because it celebrates greatness inclusive of the world's catastrophes. Yeats's tragic vision allows him to see clearly that great beauty, far from being incompatible with destruction, always leaves destruction in its wake: "For those red lips, with all their mournful pride, / . . . / Troy passed away . . . / And Usna's children died." The only difference between this and other poems such as "Leda and the Swan" and "Lapis Lazuli" is that here the notion that destruction leads to beauty (rather than the converse) is emphasized. It is wrong, then, to think that one must choose between the relatively bestial cycle of Egyptian art and the romantic (in Hegel's use of the term), humanistic art of Christianity. The reference to Egypt is here merely meant to underscore the fact that great art—be it Egyptian or Greek, Christian or Chinese—is always, as Longinus argued centuries before, a sublime, tragic art that "transcends the human."[42]

Although Yeats uses the term "tragic" throughout his writings,[43] and although references to "gaiety" stretch back all the way to his earliest verse,[44] the two terms are nowhere used more often or more emphatically than in the late "Lapis Lazuli":

> I have heard that hysterical women say
> They are sick of the palette and fiddle-bow,
> Of poets that are always gay. . . .
> . . . .
> There, on the mountain and the sky,
> On all the tragic scene they stare.
> One asks for mournful melodies;
> Accomplished fingers begin to play.
> Their eyes mid many wrinkles, their eyes,
> Their ancient, glittering eyes, are gay.[45]

Leaving aside the critical terms "gay" and "tragic" for the moment and beginning at the beginning, what does it mean for Yeats to have named his poem after a semiprecious stone? One could argue that the title merely refers to the carved piece of lapis referred to in the poem; but most, two-thirds, of the poem is not about this but about the relationship between the ephemeral fantasies of art and the harsh reality of the real world. And so the question remains: what does the idea of "tragic joy," which everyone seems to agree is the point of the poem, have to do with the idea of the poem-as-stone?

Yeats marked the following aphorism (#541) in his English translation of Nietzsche's *Dawn of Day:* "How we turn to stone. By slowly, very slowly growing hard like precious stones, and at last lie still; a joy to all eternity." The transformation of a person into stone described here helps one to understand the metamorphosis of a poem into stone.[46] To become hard, cold, and indifferent, while sure to trouble those who, like Bloom, feel the need to defend human values of compassion, pity, and so forth,[47] is to be elevated above the temporal, naturalistic sphere and to become "a joy to all eternity." This, one might add, is also the point of the poet's desired transformation into a mechanical bird in "Sailing to Byzantium." The poem becomes "Lapis Lazuli" by turning a deaf ear to the all-too-human voices of the opening stanza and being reborn as stone; it is thus like the description of the indifferent Chinese who are, quite literally, born out of the stone sculpture and whose jewel-like eyes convey the final meaning of the poem.[48] But the Chinese are not only indifferent—they are "gay." How, then, does one reconcile the transformation into stone with the notion of gaiety?

In a letter from Yeats to Dorothy Wellesley, the poet explains his use of the term "gay." Much of this letter is directly relevant here:

> I think that the true poetic movement of our time is towards some heroic discipline. People much occupied with morality always lose heroic ecstasy. Those who have it most often are those Dowson has described (I cannot find the poem but the lines run like this or something like this)
>
> > Wine, women and song
> > To us they belong
> > To us the bitter and gay.
>
> "Bitter and gay," that is the heroic mood. When there is despair, public or private, when settled order seems lost, people look for strength within or without. . . . The lasting expression of our time is not this obvious choice but in a sense of something steel-like and cold within the will, something passionate and cold.[49]

Greater familiarity with the famous Nietzschean use of "gay" (in, for example, *Fröhliche Wissenschaft*) would have led Brunner to sharpen his sense of gaiety in this letter beyond that of "stoic fortitude" and the "*reward* for withstanding despair."[50] The gaiety of the "Chinamen" of "Lapis Lazuli," of Nietzsche's satyrs or Dowson's insouciant chevaliers, is not a "reward" for "stoic fortitude"; rather, as Yeats's letter makes clear, it is the result of "heroic ecstasy," which, intoxicated by its own super-abundant power, disdains all everyday mortal or moral concerns. Recall the satyr Silenus who, likewise reveling in the gaiety of "Wine, women and song," also insists that the best life is the life *not* worth living. Poetic figures like Fergus and the other inhabitants of Yeats's Celtic faery world,[51] the speaker of "The Second Coming," and other Yeatsian heroes are all gay because, like the Chinese of "Lapis Lazuli," they exist (if that is the right word for it) in a playful space outside the naturalistic concerns of the so-called real world. From Yeats's earliest Celtic poems to this, the greatest of his later works, Yeats's tragic vision is consistent and clear: if "there is no laughter too bitter, no irony too harsh for utterance, no passion too terrible to be set before the minds of men," it is because the "tragic song," *trag-ody*, is indifferent to the cares of the real world. "The Greeks knew that."

4 Tragedy and Psychoanalysis: "Beyond the Pleasure Principle"

> It is remarkable that the genitals themselves, the sight
> of which is always exciting, are hardly ever regarded as
> beautiful; the quality of beauty seems, on the other
> hand, to attach to certain secondary sexual characters.
> —Freud, *Civilization and Its Discontents*

If the index to the *Standard Edition* of the collected writings
is correct, there is only one significant reference to tragedy in all of Freud's
works.[1] Given psychoanalysis's well-known reliance on tragedies like
Oedipus Tyrannus, only Freud's oft-declared dilettantish approach to art
could explain such an omission, which has led to a subsequent disregard
for the importance of the literary genre within the entire psychoanalytic
field. For, as will be shown, Freud's theory of the inherent conflict between
unconscious gratification and the socially determined "reality-principle"
of consciousness clarifies and is clarified by Nietzsche's theory of tragedy as rapturous delight (*Rausch*) in worst-case scenarios of death and destruction. In particular, it will be shown that Freud's theory of civilization as tragically conflicted between the libidinal id's "death wish" and
the societal individual's life-preserving ego corresponds exactly to Nietzsche's theory of the conflict between Dionysian and Apollonian drives.

Greek tragedy is dominated by the conflict between the civilized rule
of the polis (as represented by its male leader, the *tyrannus*) and more natural, older forces (frequently associated with women[2]) that threaten to

destroy society and its forces of law and order. Occasionally this schema is modified, but in such cases, the modifications ultimately serve to confirm rather than undermine this general model. In the case of *Oedipus Tyrannus,* for example, the conflict is not so much the obvious opposition between male and female that occurs in plays like the Oresteia trilogy, *Hippolytus, Antigone,* and *Medea* as it is a more fundamental opposition between Athenian culture—which was, of course, dominated by males—and the uncivilized, unconscious forces of Oedipus's incestuous and parricidal past. Seen this way, Oedipus's famous confrontation with the hybrid but female Sphinx, which initiates his later problems at Thebes, mirrors his subsequent encounter with his mother-wife Jocasta, which also begins as a victorious celebration but ultimately proves equally disastrous.

Euripides' *Bacchae,* while disparaged by Aristotle, Nietzsche, and others as a late entry onto the stage of fifth-century Athenian drama, is nonetheless in many ways a model tragedy—perhaps even the model tragedy—insofar as it is the only extant play about the god of tragedy, Dionysus.[3] Indeed, Freud's and especially Nietzsche's theories of libidinal, Dionysian psychology were deprived of considerable support and substantiation because of the general acceptance of the "evolutionary" view of Sophocles'—and, to a lesser extent, Aeschylus's—preeminence and the supposed degeneration of Euripidean drama.[4] Resembling earlier dramas like *Agamemnon, Antigone,* and *Hippolytus,* the *Bacchae* also pits a male *tyrannus,* who represents the proper rule and order of the state, against "free-running women,"[5] who threaten his attempt to govern the state. But unlike these earlier plays, the real antagonist of the drama is not these women or even passionate excess—such as that of Oedipus and his children—in general but their god Dionysus, the androgynous (Freud would say bisexual) god of libidinal gratification for whom this and all tragedies were performed.[6]

Freud's *Civilization and Its Discontents* might well be the subtitle of all the Greek tragedies just discussed (if not the subtitle of art in general).[7] As Freud defines it, civilization is tragic insofar as it is marked by an ambiguous "conflict of two rights"[8] between the individual's inherent and ineradicable need for her or his own happiness and society's inherent need to curtail the individual as such. The tragic dilemma results from the fact, as Freud points out, that attempts at ethically streamlining the individual's disruptive behavior are often the cause of even more violence as the individual rebels against a life without pleasure: "In commanding and prohibiting with such severity it [the ethical superego] troubles too little about the happiness of the ego, and it fails to take into ac-

count sufficiently the difficulties in the way of obeying it—the strength
of instinctual cravings in the id. . . . *What an overwhelming obstacle to
civilization aggression must be if the defense against it can cause as
much misery as aggression itself!"*⁹ (77–78 [emphasis added]).

This ambivalence regarding the mollifying tendencies of civilization,
which, in destroying destruction, also destroy the libido's most immedi-
ate forms of anarchical gratification as well as the primordial death wish,
leads Freud to consider the ambivalence with which society regards its
superheroes or superegos:

> The super-ego of any given epoch of civilization originates in the same
> way as that of an individual; it is based on the impression left behind
> them by great leading personalities, men of outstanding force of mind,
> or men in whom some one human tendency has developed in unusual
> strength and purity, often for that reason very dis-proportionately. In
> many instances the analogy goes still further, in that during their lives—
> often enough, even if not always—such personas are ridiculed by others,
> ill-used or even cruelly done to death, just as happened with the primal
> father who also rose again to become a deity long after his death by vio-
> lence. The most striking example of this double fate is the figure of Jesus
> Christ, if indeed it does not itself belong to the realms of mythology
> which called it into being out of a dim memory of that primordial event.¹⁰

The mention of Jesus Christ leads, a few pages later, to a discussion
of "the most recent of the cultural super-ego's demands . . . the command-
ment to love one's neighbour as oneself."¹¹ This "golden rule" epitomizes
society's need to regulate the individual's narcissistic need for gratification, the contrary aim of which is to love one's neighbor only if doing so
enhances one's own happiness.¹² Because he attempted to limit humanity's "pleasure principle" Christ's "super-ego," like Freud's "primal father," who imposed a similar law prohibiting incest, is simultaneously
hated and revered, destroyed and recreated.

Freud's theory of the tragic dilemma of the superego confirms our
earlier statements about tragedy's relation to such civilizing tendencies.
It has already been noted that tragic heroes like Oedipus, Agamemnon,
Creon, Jason, Theseus, Pentheus, and others fit a typology that pits them,
as rulers of the polis, against the unlawful forces of Clytemnestra, Antigone, Phaedra, Medea, and, of course, Dionysus himself. Such "great leading personalities, men of outstanding force of mind" as Oedipus and the
others are all destroyed, according to Freud, because their audience condemns as well as celebrates their Apollonian contributions of dominating chaos and thus bringing law and order to the city (e.g., Agamemnon's
triumph over Troy, Pentheus's attempt to curb Dionysianism, Oedipus's

confrontation with the Sphinx, Creon's ascension after the civil wars of Thebes, and so forth. As Freud noted, the ethical forces that serve as welcome therapeutic remedies to Dionysian chaos and destruction are nonetheless also despised for inhibiting the individual's need to satisfy its own craving for pleasure and power.[13] If Nietzsche seems to contradict this in referring to the ethical tragic hero (the male *tyrannus*) as a surrogate of Dionysus, it is not because he misunderstands the aforementioned typology but because he is aware that the figure of the *tyrannus* in tragedy is always destroyed by the greater Dionysian forces to which he stands in necessary opposition.[14]

The familiar presence of anxiety in tragedy, beginning with the watchman's famous foreboding in the first lines of *Agamemnon,* is indicative of the inherent conflict between the ego's—or superego's—desire to control and repress illicit pleasure and the even stronger desire to experience the very pleasures one seeks to repress. As is the case with its cousin guilt,[15] such anxiety must not be misunderstood merely as unhappiness or a lack of pleasure but rather as the relation of consciousness to unconscious pleasure or gratification. Understood thus, *Agamemnon*'s greatness lies as much in its satisfaction over the vengeance exacted on a righteous, patriarchal king whose sense of guilt led to the sacrifice of his own daughter as in the sense of justice (*dikē*) that the audience is supposed to believe is the meaning of the play.[16] Indeed, the traditional interpretation of the Oresteia as concerning justice and the evolution of the judicial system corresponds perfectly to what Freud says about consciousness and guilt, with the destructive power of the play leading to greater emphasis on the play's constructive ethical signification. Likewise, Phaedra's ethically powerful sense of guilt, piety, and injustice are only significant insofar as they stand in relation to her still greater "incestuous" (Racine's word) desires to have sex with her stepson. Phaedra's sense of guilt, Oedipus's paranoia about everyone being "out to get him," and the general sense of anxiety that pervades tragedy should all be understood from the Freudian perspective as resistances to the contrary erotic/aggressive instincts that are omnipresent throughout these plays: "the thwarting of the erotic gratification provokes an access of aggressiveness against the person who interfered with the gratification, and then this tendency to aggression in its turn has itself to be suppressed. So then it is, after all, only the aggression which is changed into guilt, by being suppressed and made over to the super-ego."[17]

Freud's theory not only allows us to understand the destruction of the tragic hero who tries to override the very repressed, erotic forces on which the plays are based; it also enables us to understand why critics of these plays, and the authors themselves, often subordinate this resentment and elevate the hero and the ethical significance of the play in opposition to the plays' repressed, sensual content. We are also in a position to understand why we should experience aesthetic delight when confronted with the horrible spectacles of tragic suffering. The audience enjoys these plays because they are not about the hero's suffering and the moral message that this suffering is thought to support. When, as Nietzsche urges his readers to do, we "look and go beyond the look" at tragedy, we see the powerful libidinal instincts of Clytemnestra (ten years without a husband), Medea (in a jealous rage), Pentheus (a closet bacchante), Oedipus (married to his mother), Phaedra (in love with her stepson), all of which it is the very nature of consciousness to enjoy and to enjoy repressing.

The Freudian formula for tragedy as laid out in *Civilization and Its Discontents* results, then, in a curiously convoluted schema whereby the repression of erotic—or Dionysian—gratification is itself repressed, leading to the satisfactory synthesis for the consciousness and unconscious of the spectator of both agencies. And yet the omnipresence of death and destruction in tragedy is not just to be understood negatively as the repression of the libido and of the civilizing forces that would control it. The libido is also expressed positively as a "death-drive," which is at once a more primitive desire than the erotic as well as the latter's conscious repression. Turning now to Freud's later, revised theory, which attempts to account positively for the desire for death, we will come to understand how tragedy, in playing out the drama of "civilization and its discontents," also goes beyond that opposition in expressing the primordial delight in death.

———————

Freud's confidence in the value of the revisionist *eros/thanatos* dichotomy ("they have won such a hold over me that I can no longer think in any other way") is belied by the notorious confusion created by the new opposition, especially when it is related to other fundamental psychoanalytical oppositions such as those between the ego and the id and between the individual and society.[18] In this chapter I will try to shed some light on this confusion by comparing it to tragedy, where the same problem arises concerning the relation of aesthetic pleasure to the genre's well-known propensity for worst-case scenarios of death and destruction. Specifically, is tragedy understandable in terms of sadomasochism, and is Nietzsche's theory of tragic rapture as the will's delight in overcoming itself understandable in terms of Freud's theory of a sadomasochistic death-drive (and vice versa)? Is the pronouncement of the satyr Silenus as retold by Nietzsche in *The Birth of Tragedy*—that "the best in life would be never to have been born, the next best to die soon" (iii, 29)—actually a confirmation of Freud's theory of "primary masochism" and the death-drive?

In *Beyond the Pleasure Principle*, Freud modifies his earlier theory of sadomasochism to include the possibility that "there might be such a thing as primary masochism."[19] Stated briefly, sadism and masochism take pleasure in the destruction of the love-object and the ego respectively. In the former case, the sadist takes pleasure in suffering imposed on her or his beloved because of the desire for possession or control of the love-object. Masochism is actually a mirror image of the former in that being humiliated, dominated, or even destroyed by the love-object also brings the ego and the love-object together, although this time it is the ego that is destroyed. In his earlier writings, Freud considered sadomasochism as one among a number of sexual "perversions" (along with autoerotism, fetishism, scopophilia, and so forth) that are opposed to the societally acceptable "sexuality for the purpose of reproduction."[20] But in *Beyond the Pleasure Principle*, the primacy of such destructive perversions is now seen as evidence of a "death-drive" that stands in opposition to *eros*—the "pleasure principle"—and "sexuality for the purpose of reproduction."

True, there is an obvious component of pleasure in all the examples of the destructive death-drive that Freud adduces in *Beyond the Pleasure Principle*, such as in the repetition-compulsion of trauma patients and the famous *fort-da* game of Freud's nephew, just as there is an obvious component of destruction in *eros*. This is particularly true of sadomasochism, which is Freud's main example of a death instinct here and in *Civilization and Its Discontents*. But Freud himself acknowledges both the necessity as well as the inadequacy of such fundamental oppositions as that "between ego-instincts and sexual instincts" while admitting at the same time that such dualisms are "figurative" and that "psychoanalysis has not enabled us hitherto to point to any [ego] instincts other than the libidinal ones."[21]

One must, then, view the life-death opposition as a sort of dance where "one group of instincts rushes forward so as to reach the final aim of life as swiftly as possible; but when a particular stage in the advance has been reached, the other group jerks back to a certain point to make a fresh start and so prolong the journey." That is, when the instinct toward death ("the aim of all life") finds the desired end of desire in sleep, in erotic fulfillment, in the structures of society and culture in general, which serve as a "safe shelter" from the "stimuli of the external world," it allows the contrary life-drive, the instinctual need for stimuli, to reemerge (and vice versa). Thus, the death-drive is the life-drive, just as the life-drive is the death-drive. It is because of this that the example of primary masochism (or, if one prefers, sadomasochism) just discussed can be "an example of a death instinct" as well as exemplifying the opposing "self-preservative sexual instincts."[22] The primary goal of an end to stimulus and a return to an earlier inanimate state, because it can be partly successful in destroying either the desired object or the ego, allows one to experience momentary pleasure before the pursuit of the real goal, total satisfaction or death, is renewed, as it must be in life. Indeed, it is possible to follow Freud's lead in defining all pleasure as the momentary, objective equivalent of a deeper satisfaction that can only be achieved in death.[23]

Returning to the notion of sadomasochism as the key to understanding tragic pleasure, one can now state that, although the desire to return to an inanimate state—the death-drive—is opposed to the pleasure principle, that does not mean that pleasure (for example, aesthetic pleasure) is not be involved in its pursuit. It is also now possible to return to Nietzsche, whose equally complicated theory of opposing Dionysian and Apollonian "drives" closely parallels Freud's theory of the two opposing principles of *thanatos* and *eros* respectively. Silenus's statement that life is not worth living and that one would be better off dead is only one of the ways that Nietzsche's theory of tragedy coincides with Freud's notion of a death-drive that goes "beyond the pleasure principle."

Nietzsche's/Silenus's statement conveys more than just world-weary resignation. Even if the archsatyr were capable of such "weak pessimism,"[24] it is doubtful whether even the most intense disappointment with life's hardships would lead to such a pronouncement. The satyr's statement is understandable, however, from the psychoanalytical perspective of a powerful underlying death-drive that is the basis of the more limited pleasures to be enjoyed in life. As a marginalized, even criminal figure who stands in clear opposition to civilization, the Dionysian satyr of early Greek culture (as Nietzsche points out) is a very different figure from the playful "nature sprite" he was later to become (*Birth of Tragedy* viii, 52–53). From a psychoanalytic point of view, Silenus's statement is actually a rejection of all the defenses against death established by the repressive forces of culture, law, and civilization.

But what about the satyr's association not with death and tragedy but with sexuality and the pleasure principle in general? The satyr's association with *eros* and the phallus must be considered with the strange fact that their leader Dionysus is a surprisingly asexual being.[25] Unlike Heracles, Zeus, and the other Olympians, there are surprisingly few early myths recounting the dalliances of a sexual Dionysus. This can now be understood in terms of the association between Dionysianism and the death-drive. For the erotic sexual-drive, as Freud describes it in *Beyond the Pleasure Principle*, is actually a defense against unbound cathexes and, like culture in general, is object oriented and "conservative" insofar as it preserves the transitory individual against destruction:

> The instincts which watch over the destinies of these elementary organisms that survive the whole individual, *which provide them with a safe shelter while they are defenseless against the stimuli of the external world*, which bring about their meeting with other germ-cells, and so on—these constitute the group of sexual instincts. They are conservative in the same sense as the other instincts in that they bring back earlier states of living substance; but they are conservative to a higher degree in that they are peculiarly resistant to external influences; and they are conservative too in another sense in that they preserve life itself for a comparatively long period. (*Yet it is to them alone that we can attribute an internal impulse towards "progress" and towards higher development!*) *They are the true life instincts.*[26]

The surprising opposition between satyric Dionysianism and sexuality becomes understandable in terms of Freud's equally surprising equation here of sexuality with society and the "internal impulse towards 'progress' and towards higher development." The latter is the result of the erotic "instinct towards preservation" moving even further away from the unconscious libido and attaching itself to nonsexual objects (Freud's theory of sublimation as the redirection of the erotic libido). Opposed to all this is the satyr's sexual energy, the lower goatlike part of the satyr that contains the phallus: the unconscious libido (also equated with the Dionysian state of destructive frenzy and drunkenness) that is destructive of all things conscious, of all things human. It is worth recalling, in this regard, that the very word "tragedy" refers back to the Dionysian "goat song" that is the ritual marker of humanity's connection to a lower world that it purports to deny.

There are numerous passages in Nietzsche's first book that connect tragedy with Freud's theory of a "death-drive" that is opposed to sexuality, civilization, and the preservation of the ego. The Apollonian *principium individuationis* referred to throughout *The Birth of Tragedy* can be easily identified with the erotic pleasure principle, the conservative tendency toward reproduction (iv, 34), the ego insofar as it binds the unconscious individual together and joins it collectively with the larger community or culture and, finally, with civilization's defining "desire for perfection" (iv, 35–36). In opposition to this Apollonian pleasure principle, there are also numerous passages in *The Birth of Tragedy* that connect the tragic Dionysian desire for "rapturous superabundance" and "metaphysical Oneness" to the Freudian death-drive.

Nietzsche's *principium individuationis* stands as a desirable—and pleasurable—bulwark against the surrounding surge of forces that would dissolve all separate entities into one:

> one might say of Apollo what Schopenhauer says, in the first part of *The World as Will and Idea*, of man caught in the veil of Maya: "Even as on an immense, raging sea, assailed by huge wave crests, a man sits in a little rowboat trusting his frail craft, so, amidst the furious torments of this, the individual sits tranquilly, supported by the *principium individuationis* and relying on it." . . . *Apollo himself may be regarded as the marvelous divine image of the principium individuationis, whose looks and gestures radiate the full delight, wisdom, and beauty of "illusion."*
> In the same context Schopenhauer has described for us the tremendous awe which seizes man when he suddenly begins to doubt the cognitive modes of experience, in other words, when in a given instance the law of causation seems to suspend itself. If we add to this awe the glorious transport [*Verzükung*] which arises in man, even from the very depths of nature, at the shattering of the *principium individuationis*, then we are in a position to apprehend the essence of Dionysian rapture, whose closest analogy is furnished by physical intoxication [*Rausch*]. . . . So stirred, the individual forgets himself completely. (*Birth of Tragedy* i, 22)

The "sapient tranquillity of the plastic god" Apollo (i, 21) is compared to Schopenhauer's image of the *principium individuationis* as a small rowboat in a storm because the boat provides stability, solace, and a way of rescuing the self from its surrounding tumult. In other words, the creation of an object—which is to say, the creation of some *thing* with limits—is the common denominator that unites the objectification of the self (the *principium individuationis*) with the objective world, a world of objects that are always (as Protagoras had already argued) true.[27] Apollo, "who is etymologically the 'lucent' one," is thus for Nietzsche the god of truth insofar as the truth is defined, as it usually is in our Western "Socratic" culture, as an object whose limits allow it to appear. But it must also be pointed out that Nietzsche relegates this comforting belief (this "deep and happy delight") in the truth of appearances to the status of dream and fictive illusion (*Birth of Tragedy* i, 21). That is, the belief in humanity's existence as individuals and in the "objective world," like the belief in the rowboat's ability to withstand the storm, is an illusion:[28]

"Row, row, row your boat, gently down the stream. / Merrily, merrily, merrily, merrily, life is but a dream."

The Apollonian *principium individuationis* is associated with the pleasure of appearances, appearances that include entrancing objects of beauty as well as laws (the limitations on experience) and the "law of identity" that redeems us from the surrounding infinitude of experience. Although Nietzsche does not himself say so, it follows from his theory that the beautiful Apollonian object of appearance (for example, the love-object) also preserves the individual from destruction in being joined to it through the desire for reproduction. Similarly, Freud's pleasure principle preserves the individual from destruction by "binding it" to itself, to objects, and to others and is thus also associated with *eros* and the desire for reproduction:

> The instincts which watch over the destinies of these elementary organisms that survive the whole individual, which provide them with a safe shelter while they are defenseless against the stimuli of the external world, which bring about their meeting with other germ-cells, and so on—these constitute the group of the sexual instincts. They are conservative in the same sense as the other instincts in that they bring back earlier states of living substance; but they are conservative to a higher degree in that they are peculiarly resistant to external influences; and they are conservative too in another sense in that they preserve life itself for a comparatively long period. They are the true life instincts. They operate against the purpose of the other instincts, which lead, by reason of their function, to death.[29]

In a passage remarkably similar to the passage just quoted from *The Birth of Tragedy*, Freud here contrasts the conservative pleasure principle, whereby the individual delights in his or her own existence and that of objects in general, which preserve it from destruction, with the contrary death-drive, which functions as the Dionysian death-drive does in the earlier passage. Both the Apollonian *principium individuationis* and the Freudian pleasure principle work to preserve the individual from destruction by binding it to objects of perception, and both are synonymous with *eros* and the desire for reproduction.

One might add, in this regard, Nietzsche's reference in the passage just discussed to the "law of causality" as a function of Apollonian objectivity; that is, the delight in appearances and the related belief in the identity of objects and the self are necessarily related to that cardinal law of logic, which makes the existence of all these objects possible. Similarly, in a passage from *Beyond the Pleasure Principle* (and elsewhere in his writings), Freud refers to Kant's "theorem that time and space are necessary forms of thought" as a function of the way consciousness, as opposed to the "timeless" processes of the unconscious, preserves the individual from too much stimulus.[30] Moreover, Freud defines this "system cs."—consciousness—as part of the pleasure principle that preserves the individual by limiting the field of experience through its organization into time, space, and so forth.

Still other parallels can be observed between the Apollonian *principium individuationis* and the psychoanalytic pleasure principle. As has been shown, the sense of identity or individuation with which the self protects itself against its chaotic surrounding ("It is Apollo who tranquilizes the individual *by drawing boundary lines* and who, by enjoining again and again the practice of self-knowledge, reminds him of the holy, universal norms" [*Birth of Tragedy* ix, 65 (emphasis added)]) resembles the Freudian pleasure principle insofar as the latter also replaces pleasure per se with what one might call "pleasure-for-me," a pleasure that works within the confines of the reality-principle to preserve the ego:

> We know that the pleasure principle is proper to a primary method of working on the part of the mental apparatus, but that, *from the point of view of the self-preservation of the organism among the difficulties of the external world,* it is from the very outset inefficient and even highly dangerous. Under the influence of the ego's instincts of self-preservation, the pleasure principle is replaced by the reality-principle. This latter principle does not abandon the intention of ultimately obtaining pleasure, but it nevertheless demands and carries into effect the postponement of satisfaction.[31]

Following this process whereby the primary pleasure principle becomes a corollary of the reality principle, civilization and the general notion of individual perfection are then also linked together with the pleasure principle (*Birth of Tragedy* xviii, 110–12). For Nietzsche, too, it is clear that civilization, far from being opposed to the *principium individuationis*, is actually the result of the Apollonian process of individuation whereby the subject "draws boundary lines" for itself and the world of objects that exist for it: "Apollo, the founder of states, is also the genius of the *principium individuationis*, and neither commonwealth nor patriotism can subsist without an affirmation of individuality" (xxi, 125).

This statement by Nietzsche is followed by another that also has its parallel in Freud's *Beyond the Pleasure Principle:* "The only path from orgiastic rites, for a nation, leads to Buddhism, which, given its desire for Nirvana, requires those rare moments of paroxysm that lift man beyond the confines of space, time and individuation" (*Birth of Tragedy* xxi, 125).

Here, Nietzsche is referring to the contrary, anti-Apollonian, Dionysian principle that informs such deindividuating tendencies as the Buddhistic desire for Nirvana. Similarly, Freud speaks in *Beyond the Pleasure Principle* of the "Nirvana principle" as a function of the death-drive: "The dominating tendency of mental life, and perhaps of nervous life in general, is the effort to reduce, to keep constant or to remove internal tension due to stimuli (the 'Nirvana principle' . . .)—a tendency which finds expression in the pleasure principle; *and our recognition of that fact is one of our strongest reasons for believing in the existence of death instincts.*"[32] For both Freud and Nietzsche, the "Nirvana principle" represents the death-drive's movement toward the elimination of all moral, epistemological, and spatiotemporal limitations. Comparing the two references, it is also interesting to note that both writers tend to denigrate this tendency (Nietzsche more explicitly than Freud) as failing to realize the full tragic implications of this loss of individuation and the spatiotemporal world that it inhabits.

Nietzsche's notion of the Dionysian is exemplified by a passage quoted earlier: "at the shattering of the *principium individuationis,* then we are in a position to apprehend the essence of Dionysian rapture, whose closest analogy is furnished by physical intoxication. . . . So stirred, the individual forgets himself completely." We have already observed numerous examples of the parallels between Freud's life/death opposition and Nietzsche's Apollonian/Dionysian opposition. But is it not the case that, in emphasizing the "rapturous" quality of the Dionysian, Nietzsche departs from Freud, who opposes the death-drive to the pleasure principle? On the contrary; it will become quickly apparent that the differences between death and the Dionysian will actually serve, on closer examination, to bring the two terms closer together.

It has been shown how Nietzsche frequently uses more moderate terms for "delight" and "pleasure" (*freudiges Behagen, schön, geniessen, angenehme und freudliche Bilder,* etc.) in reference to the Apollonian. In referring to the Dionysian, Nietzsche prefers terms such as those used here: rapture, tumult, passion, ecstasy, enchantment, and so forth (*Rausch, Gewühl, Leidenschaft, Urschmerz, ungeheure Grausen, wonnevolle Verzückung, Verzauberung,* etc.). The common denominator of these terms is that they all refer to the experience, which Nietzsche mentions at the end of the passage just quoted, of the self forgetting itself and its objectifications or of the imminent threat of this fundamental loss.

Two passages, one from Nietzsche and one from Freud, will demonstrate the extent to which the ecstatic Dionysian and the death-drive are actually synonymous and serve to explain each other. First, Nietzsche repeatedly speaks of the "primordial pain and suffering" that the Dionysian inflicts on its participant:

> Music alone allows us to understand the delight felt at the annihilation of the individual. Each single instance of such annihilation will clarify for us the abiding phenomenon of Dionysiac art, which expresses the omnipotent will behind individuation, eternal life continuing beyond all appearance and in spite of destruction. The metaphysical delight in tragedy is a translation of *instinctive unconscious Dionysiac wisdom* [*instinktiv unbewussten Dionysischen Weisheit*] into images. The hero, the highest manifestation of the will, is destroyed, and we assent, since he too is merely a phenomenon, and the eternal life of the will remains unaffected. Tragedy cries, "We believe that life is eternal!" and music is the direct expression of that life. . . .
>
> Dionysiac art, too [like the Apollonian], wishes to convince us of the eternal delight of existence, but it insists that we look for this delight not in the phenomena but behind them. *It makes us realize that everything that is generated must be prepared to face its painful dissolution.* It forces us to gaze into the horror of individual existence, yet without being turned to stone by the vision: a metaphysical solace momentarily lifts us above the whirl of shifting phenomena. For a brief moment we become, ourselves, the primal Being, and we experience its insatiable hunger for existence. Now we see the struggle, the pain, the destruction of appearances as necessary because of the constant proliferation of forms pushing into life, because of the *extravagant fecundity* of the world will. We feel the furious prodding of this travail in the very moment in which we become one with the immense lust for life and are made aware of the eternity and indestructibility of that lust. Pity and terror notwithstanding, we realize our great good fortune in having life—not as individuals, but as part of the life force with whose procreative lust we have become one. (*Birth of Tragedy* xvi, 101–2 [emphasis added])

The myth of the sirens' song, which is usually seen as an aberration from the true function of music, is here seen as emblematic not only of music but of all great, tragic art (xxi, 131). This is because music releases us from the time and space, and the objects that inhabit them, of our quotidian reality; we enjoy music because we enjoy being transported out of ourselves from the temporal world into an "eternal" world that is relatively unbounded. We also learn from this passage that examples of the death-drive are more numerous than Freud had thought, for one need look no further than the "ecstatic delight felt at the annihilation of the individual" that occurs whenever the joy of music is felt.[33] More importantly for this study's purposes, the passage defines tragedy as an expression of the individual human's desire to return to "eternal life," "the omnipotent will behind individuation"; tragedy exists because of the death-drive, because of our desire to be rid of the "horror of individual existence" altogether.

Nietzsche's description of tragedy, however, tells us even more about the death-drive, just as Freud's description of the death-drive tells us more than we would otherwise know about tragedy. "Instinctive unconscious Dionysian wisdom" (*instinktiv unbewussten Dionysischen Weisheit*), which is synonymous with the instinctive unconscious of the Freudian death-drive, is our unconscious affiliation with the original, procreative force that lies "behind" things (hence Nietzsche's repeated, affirmative use of the term "metaphysical" here, which he otherwise avoided[34]) rather than with individual things themselves. Such is the ultimate manifestation of the will that, in always seeking to "go beyond itself" (*hin-über-gehen*), finds its ultimate confirmation in the destruction of all abiding phenomenon. Thus Nietzsche refers to the necessary destruction of the tragic hero, whose power represents "the highest manifestation of the will," as a joyous celebration of our desire to overcome all individual experience. Like Freud, Nietzsche too adheres to the notion that "the goal of all life is death," but he expands on the Freudian notion here by describing the death-drive in more distinctly positive terms as the return of the will to the procreative force that underlies—and creates—itself and all individual existence.

One must also consider the numerous times Nietzsche refers here (and throughout his book) to the derivation of the Apollonian *principium individuationis* from the Dionysian death-drive. Tragic nihilism, the ultimate manifestation of the will's desire to "go beyond itself" and return to the "eternal" origin of life (an origin that, as the complete title of Nietzsche's work also reveals, is musical in its exemption from objective, spatiotemporal reality), is also a return to the creative origin of life. Appearance, the "organ" of objectivity and the *principium individuationis*, emerges out of the death-drive's destruction of appearance ("Be like me, the Original Mother who, constantly creating, finds satisfaction in the turbulent flux of appearances" [*Birth of Tragedy* xvi, 102]) because, once destroyed, the creative forces of life are also reached, and it is now possible to create life anew. In other words, the "metaphysical solace" of the death-drive leads back to the contrary desire for individual existence because, out of the "rapturous superabundance" of "primal Being" (also referred to here as the "extravagant fecundity of the world will"), one can then, and only then, "take delight in" the concrete manifestations ("beings") of that same primal Being in the world.

Just as Nietzsche describes the process whereby the desire for Apol-

Ionian individuation and objectification is born from and returns to the "metaphysical delight" in undifferentiated primal Being, in this concluding section of *Beyond the Pleasure Principle* Freud too propounds a model leading *from* and *back to* the death-drive that circulates *to* and *from* the pleasure principle:

> We have found that one of the earliest and most important functions of the mental apparatus is to bind the instinctual impulses which impinge on it, to replace the primary process prevailing in them by the secondary process and convert their freely mobile cathectic energy into a mainly quiescent (tonic) cathexis. . . . the transformation occurs on behalf of the pleasure principle; the binding is a preparatory act which introduces and assures the dominance of the pleasure principle. . . .
>
> This raises the question of whether feelings of pleasure and unpleasure can be produced equally from bound and from unbound excitatory processes. *And there seems to be no doubt whatever that the unbound or primary processes give rise to far more intense feelings in both directions than the bound or secondary ones.* Moreover the primary processes are the earlier in time. . . . at the beginning of mental life the struggle for pleasure was far more intense than later but not so unrestricted: it had to submit to frequent interruptions. In later times the dominance of the pleasure principle is very much more secure, but it itself has no more escaped the process of taming than the other instincts in general.[35]

Freud speaks here of the "primary process" of "freely mobile," unbound cathexes from which the "later," "secondary" "mental" process of binding cathexes emerges and back to which these bound cathexes all desire to return: "It is clear that the function just described would be concerned with the most universal endeavour of all living substance—namely to return to the quiescence of the inorganic world."[36] This involuted model, whereby two opposing principles are actually one, is the same for both Freud and Nietzsche. For Freud, the binding of cathexes in the pleasure principle is actually preparatory to the ultimate goal of a return to the quiescence of death ("the greatest pleasure attainable by us, that of the sexual act, is associated with a momentary *extinction* of a highly intensified *excitation*"[37]). For Nietzsche, the Apollonian object of perception that is opposed to the "eternal Dionysian" is also a way of representing it: "Apollo overcomes individual suffering by the glorious apotheosis of what is eternal in appearance" (*Birth of Tragedy* xvi, 102).

Freud's description here of how the "primary" death-drive underlies the secondary "binding" of the pleasure principle thus parallels Nietzsche's description of how the primary Dionysian death-drive (where "the highest manifestation of the will, the tragic hero, is destroyed" [*Birth of*

Tragedy xvi, 102]) underlies the Apollonian creation of bound objects of pleasure with objective limitations.[38] The ultimate goal, in both cases, is the destruction of the very objects or cathexes that "hold down" or preserve the individual from destruction. In Nietzsche's case, as has been shown, the Apollonian object that, following the example from Schopenhauer, preserves the *principium individuationis* from metaphysical Oneness also mirrors the Dionysian death-drive in reducing—"petrifying," as it were—the world into its own kind of oneness, that afforded by the protection of the laws of identity. It is for this reason that, rather than opposing Apollo and Dionysus, Nietzsche refers to them as "fraternal twins," for the delightful illusions provided by Apollo in dreams, in art, and so forth are actually new objects that, as alternatives to the reality-principle of everyday life, mirror the "eternal" death-drive.

The Apollonian *principium individuationis* thus parallels the goal of the mental apparatus, which is "to bind the instinctual impulses which impinge on it, to replace the primary process prevailing in them by the secondary process and convert their freely mobile cathectic energy into a mainly quiescent (tonic) cathexis." Moreover, just as Nietzsche repeatedly insists on the association of this Apollonian principle with the visual, Freud too, as early as the unfinished *Project* of 1895, opposes the "primary" process of the unconscious to the field of perception and consciousness.[39]

Opposes, however, is clearly not the right word to use here. Following Freud's description, one begins with the notion of a primary, mobile field of energy fueled by instinctual drives but that is also "quiescent" and so closer to an original inanimate state because there are no perceptions, no cathexes, no consciousness of time, space, and so forth. This primary state, then, is at once more vital and yet also closer to death, thus resembling the Dionysian metaphysical Oneness described by Nietzsche in which the frenzied ("freely mobile") participant loses consciousness of self and merges with his or her surroundings.[40] The secondary state of consciousness described by Freud, which "holds down" ("cathects") and thus preserves particular objects of perception, serves, on the one hand, the erotic life-principle in establishing defined goals and objects of desire that, if they are safely achieved, satisfy the pleasure principle. On the other hand, the establishment of these objects and goals also serves the death-drive: first, because the very act of cathecting or preserving objects renders them immobile; and second, because the goal of all desire is to possess, consume, or otherwise destroy the very object of desire whose existence makes desire possible:

The pleasure principle, then, is a tendency operating in the service of a function whose business it is to free the mental apparatus entirely from excitation. . . . it is clear that the function just described would be concerned with the most universal endeavor of all living substance—namely to return to the quiescence of the inorganic world. We have all experienced how the greatest pleasure attainable by us, that of the sexual act, is associated with a momentary extinction of a highly intensified excitation. *The binding of an instinctual impulse would be a preliminary function designed to prepare the excitation for its elimination in the pleasure of discharge.*[41]

These descriptions of the erotic pleasure principle as at once separate from and the same as the death-drive are the very essence of tragedy. In Nietzschean terms, the problematic derivation of pleasure from the great havoc wreaked by tragic destruction is to be understood in terms of the primal, Dionysian desire to overcome all boundaries and other limits of perception. In Freudian terms, tragedy is to be understood as representing the ultimate goal of all desire, which is the desire for an end to all goals and other bound, perceptual objects that are both a function of and an obstacle to the fulfillment of the death-drive.[42] Freud was thus only partially correct when, in mentioning tragedy in *Beyond the Pleasure Principle,* he viewed its "motive for play" as "of no use for our purposes, since [it] presupposes the existence and dominance of the pleasure principle."[43] For, as he goes on to demonstrate in *Beyond the Pleasure Principle,* and as Nietzsche's *Birth of Tragedy* confirms, the pleasure principle and the death-drive are not mutually exclusive, and the tragic "game which the will, in its rapturous superabundance, plays with itself" (xxiv, 143) is the game of death.

5 The Life of Tragedy: Tragedy after Nietzsche

> One of the earliest and most enduring laments over the tragic condition of man is Cassandra's outcry in the courtyard of the house of Atreus. In the final, fragmentary scene of *Woyzeck* there are implications of grief no less universal.
>
> —Steiner, *The Death of Tragedy*

Contrary to Nietzsche's prediction—indeed, his "promise"— that tragedy would be the art of the future,[1] George Steiner has more recently declared the genre "dead on arrival" in the twentieth century, having long since been made obsolete by the evolution of human consciousness beyond its belief in a world of supernatural forces greater than itself: "In tragedy, lightning is a messenger. But it can no longer be so once Benjamin Franklin (the incarnation of the new rational man) has flown a kite to it. . . . at the touch of Hume and Voltaire the noble or hideous visitations which had haunted the mind since Agamemnon's blood cried out for vengeance disappeared altogether or took tawdry refuge among the gaslights of melodrama."[2]

Despite the influence of *The Death of Tragedy* it is unlikely that Steiner's work alone could be responsible for the popularity of this widespread but, as I shall argue, erroneous belief in the demise of the "greatest" literary genre.[3] Steiner's notion, as the passage just quoted confirms, is also informed by the commonly held (but seldom acknowledged as such[4]) Hegelian idea that modernism is defined by a process of increasing rationalism and individualization that would preclude the fundamental loss of objectivity, of grounding in reality, with which all tragedy is concerned. In other words, there can be no more tragedies because as "fallen," post-Copernican, decentered individuals, humans have nowhere left to fall—an argument that clearly ignores the fact that the original Fall of the Old Testament has hardly precluded further tragedies, such as that of the New Testament.

Steiner himself never attempted to place his argument in its Hegelian context because to do so would have meant acknowledging that his supposedly historical argument is ideologically suspect. Hegel's argument regarding the historical evolution of art from the symbolic materiality of Egyptian architecture through the mediated humanism of classical sculpture to modern "romantic" reality—in which the Spirit has finally freed itself from external forces greater than itself (leaving us, according to Hegel, with the very untragic art of Dutch still-life painting[5])—provides but one model for understanding the artistic predilections of any given period or for understanding the predilections for periods themselves. Having shown that *The Death of Tragedy* is, as its title suggests, a fictional drama[6] (in fact, a "period piece"), this chapter will then turn to essays by Albert Camus and Alain Robbe-Grillet that, although chronologically earlier than Steiner's work, explicitly address the "life of tragedy" in more modern works of art.

The scope, erudition, and artistry of Steiner's *Death of Tragedy* make it a work that, like Auerbach's *Mimesis,* will long be admired among comparatists for its intimate familiarity with the works of an impressive array of different languages, periods, and traditions. Unlike Auerbach's book, however, which sought only to compare the ways different literary traditions constructed their representations of reality, Steiner examines dramatic works from the Greeks to the twentieth century to prove his thesis that tragedy died sometime around the end of the seventeenth century, after Racine. It will be this chapter's contention that Steiner's impressive erudition serves to obscure rather than illuminate this thesis, which is never really proven. For all its influence Steiner's encyclopedic work, like the proverbial emperor's new clothes, is lacking in theoretical substance; for all his analyses of other works Steiner never analyzes, and scarcely even mentions, other theories of tragedy such as Hegel's, Nietzsche's, or the one closest to his own, Robbe-Grillet's.[7]

We can thus ignore, except where it is necessary to understand the substance of Steiner's argument, the elaborate wealth of allusive clothing, the countless textual references and digressions[8] in *The Death of*

Tragedy in order to focus on the author's statements regarding what tragedy is, and why it is no more. The problem of defining tragedy haunts Steiner's work like the ghost of Hamlet's father, and Steiner is no more diligent than Hamlet in attending to its behest. It is this lack of definition that gives *The Death of Tragedy* its fictional status: if one were to define tragedy in anything more than a specious or capricious way (for example, defining tragedy as requiring verse[9]), it would then no longer be possible to engage in the fantasy of declaring the genre dead.

Although Steiner states, at the conclusion of his introductory chapter, that "none of this, I know, is a definition of tragedy," he in fact comes closest here to saying what he thinks tragedy is: "Tragic drama arises out of precisely the contrary assertion: necessity is blind and man's encounter with it shall rob him of his eyes, whether it be in Thebes or in Gaza. The assertion is Greek, and the tragic sense of life built upon it is the foremost contribution of the Greek genius to our legacy."[10] Although the definition is inadequate, it is not inaccurate or unclear as far as it goes. Steiner is referring to the idea that tragedy hinges on a radical sense of dislocation or blindness that undermines humanity's fundamental sense of grounding or reality (not surprisingly, Steiner often refers to *King Lear* as a quintessential tragedy). If, Steiner goes on to argue, it is possible to redeem or otherwise recuperate from this fundamental loss—as supposedly happens when a Christian view of salvation or a modern, scientific view that purports to relegate or disown the irrational takes over—then tragedy is no longer possible.

Against and even reversing Steiner's notion that "the least touch of any theology which has a compensating Heaven to offer the tragic hero is fatal," this study has shown how Nietzsche maintains that chaotic, Dionysian suffering and destructiveness beget soothing objective realities such as the *principium individuationis* that save humanity from the turbulent, oceanic flux surrounding it.[11] Raphael's *Transfiguration* serves as a model for this in *The Birth of Tragedy* when the radiant figure of Christ "rises, like the fragrance of ambrosia," from the chaos of the lower half of the painting as a soothing illusion that saves us, redeems us, from the turbulence of the lower half of the painting:

> the original Oneness, the ground of Being, ever-suffering and contradictory, time and again has need of rapt vision and delightful illusion to redeem itself. . . . In the lower half of Raphael's "Transfiguration" . . . , through the figures of the possessed boy, the despairing bearers, the helpless, terrified disciples, we see a reflection of original pain, the sole ground of being: "illusion" here is a reflection of eternal contradiction, begetter

of all things. . . . Here we have, in a great symbol of art, both the fair world of Apollo and its substratum, the terrible wisdom of Silenus, and we can comprehend intuitively how they mutually require one another. But Apollo appears to us once again as the apotheosis of the principium individuationis, in whom the eternal goal of the original Oneness, namely its redemption through illusion, accomplishes itself. With august gesture the god shows us how there is need for a whole world of torment in order for the individual to produce the redemptive vision and to sit quietly in his rocking rowboat in mid-sea, absorbed in contemplation. (*Birth of Tragedy* iv, 33–34)

It is wrong to argue, then, that either redemption or the lack thereof is incompatible with tragedy, for it is their interplay that produces both nihilism and its denial in the work of art. In other words, tragic heroes like Oedipus, Christ, and Dionysus who are destroyed by the chaotic turbulence shown in the lower half of Raphael's painting ironically represent that reality for us and so inherently redeem us and themselves. It is no wonder that Nietzsche railed so violently against the tradition that sees such heroic figures as heavenly rather than earthly.[12] For, according to his interpretation, such tragic heroes are only martyred, heavenly figures because they "remained true to the earth" by embracing the inherent, abysmal contradictions (Oedipus's incest, Dionysus's frenzy, Christ's suicidal love for humanity) represented by the lower half of Raphael's *Transfiguration*.

All the tragedies this study has mentioned or will discuss, from the very first (Dionysian Greek drama) to the modern (*Hedda Gabler* and *The Cherry Orchard*), redeem the void by creating beautiful dramatic works and tragic heroes that represent it. Steiner himself suggests this when he describes how "man is ennobled by the vengeful spite or injustice of the gods,"[13] for how can one be "ennobled" but not redeemed? The passage cited from Nietzsche's *Birth of Tragedy*, however, explains the process that Steiner only mentions in passing. The confrontation with the abject suffering and pain of the "worst possible world" (the "terrible wisdom of Silenus") that always occurs in tragedy also produces the "fair Apollonian illusions" that save us from that suffering. This is Nietzsche's interpretation of the "serenity" of Greek culture, which he effectively turns on its head by comparing it to the emergence of a rose from a thicket of thorns (*Birth of Tragedy* iii, 30). The tragic hero is often ennobled or redeemed one way or the other (the masterful plot of *Oedipus Tyrannus;* its hero's martyrdom at Colonus; Lear's touching final scene with Cordelia, etc.), because his or her confrontation with catastrophe is alone capable of producing the "fair illusion" of heavenly, ambrosia- or rose-scented beauty that, like the Christ figure of Raphael's painting, emerges from life's richest frenzy of confusion.

I agree with Thomas Van Laan when he says that there is a "counter-argument" in Steiner's book that frequently contests the author's main argument about the supposed death of tragedy.[14] Steiner is right when he argues that tragedy—beginning with the *Iliad*—aesthetically represents the confrontation between the human and forces that exceed it. That is, tragedy necessarily involves a moment when human life, values, and expectations all come to grief—a time when one stares into the proverbial abyss, and the abyss does not stare back. But rather than examining this definition and exploring, as Nietzsche does, why this destructive confrontation should become the cause of aesthetic celebration,[15] Steiner shifts gears completely and invokes the notion that such a confrontation is historically determined, only occurring in what Hegel calls the middle, or mediated, period of Western art.[16] During that classical period, as described in the *Aesthetic Lectures*, humanism had emerged to challenge its subordination to "fate" or other cosmic forces but had not yet, as in the modern period, sufficiently extracted itself from this belief so as to make tragedy obsolete. There are thus two different arguments—one synchronic, the other diachronic—hiding behind each other in Steiner's work. The notion that tragedy involves an absurd confrontation with the meaninglessness of existence may indeed be related to the advent of humanism in the classical period, but one errs in maintaining that the syntactical requirements of periods mandate restricting the genre to this or that epoch.

The definition, then, of tragedy that informs Steiner's entire book—the idea that tragedy involves the separation of humans from their world—actually undermines the work's thesis concerning the death of tragedy. This is why Steiner denies that he has defined tragedy even though the same quasi-definition keeps cropping up throughout the book. By the work's end, the author has been forced to admit the "tragic grandeur" of so many works outside his periodic parameters that, in the words of Van Laan, "it is difficult to understand why anyone would write" such a patently self-undermining book.[17] It is for this reason that one needs to hear the title of Steiner's most famous book differently. One must hear *The Death of Tragedy* as bespeaking not the end of the genre but the catastrophic end (or death) of meaning that Steiner himself says all great tragedy entails.[18]

The "counter-argument" that "great tragedy is at all times timely" (289), which culminates in the work's final declaration that "the curve of tragedy is, perhaps, unbroken" (355), can be found throughout *The Death of Tragedy.*[19] Entire periods such as Romanticism that are viewed as in-compatible with tragedy nonetheless seem to contain more tragic works—by Hölderlin, Goethe, Kleist, Schiller, Keats, and others—than untragic. Verse, we are told, is synonymous with the extramundane greatness of tragedy, whereas "the association between comedy and prose is a very ancient and natural one." Yet Steiner admits, in the same paragraph, that "what has come down to us in Greek and Latin comedy is in verse. . . . But most probably there flourished below the level of literary drama traditions of folk comedy and farce presented in prose."[20] There are countless other examples (Hölderlin's *Empedokles*, for example, which "tells us how far it has been possible for a modern poet to adopt the tone and vision of the Greek tragic theatre," is not really tragic because it cannot be performed![21]) that challenge, like Oedipus's implication in the very crime he seeks to undo, the simultaneous attempt to do away with tragedy.

Plays like *Hedda Gabler*, which represent "the forces of disruption that have broken loose from the core of the spirit," prove more than they disprove the continued survival of tragedy:

> But the most dangerous assaults upon reason and life come not from without, as they do in Greek and Elizabethan tragedy. They arise in the unstable soul. Ibsen proceeds from the modern awareness that there is rivalry and unbalance in the individual psyche. The ghosts that haunt his characters are not the palpable heralds of damnation whom we find in *Hamlet* and *Macbeth*. They are forces of disruption that have broken loose from the core of the spirit. Or, more precisely, they are cancers growing in the soul. In Ibsen's vocabulary, the most deadly of these cancers is "idealism," the mask of hypocrisy and self-deception with which men seek to guard against the realities of social and personal life. When "ideals" seize upon an Ibsen character, they drive him to psychological and material ruin as the Weird Sisters drive Macbeth. Once the mask has grown close to the skin, it can be removed only at suicidal cost. When Rosmer and Rebecca West have attained the ability to confront life, they are on the verge of death. When the mask no longer shields her against the light, Hedda Gabler kills herself.[22]

What allows Steiner to maintain his thesis about *The Death of Trag-edy* despite the constant reminder of contrary evidence in passages such as this (note the allusion to Nietzsche's theory of the Apollonian mask and the Dionysian death-drive) is, again, the ideal inherited from Hegel that the gradual interiorization of truth in modern times precludes the fundamental loss of meaning that was possible in earlier, more outwardly centered (pre-Copernican) periods. But the proof that Hegel's thesis is misused when it is extended to mean the death of tragedy is readily evident here. For the conflict between "civilization and its discontents," the "unstable soul," and "'idealism,' the mask of hypocrisy and self-deception," has always been synonymous with tragedy. The numerous myths of Dionysus's conflicts with civilized rulers, such as the one depicted in Euripides' *Bacchae,* all retell the same story of the inherent conflict between society's "reality principle"[23] and the need for personal gratification. Seen in this light, the difference between Macbeth's seduction by the phantasmatic Weird Sisters, who tempt him with his own narcissistic omnipotence, and Hedda's refusal to obey society and relinquish her own destructive narcissism is less important than the similarity between the two works.

"When the mask [of idealism] no longer shields her against the light, Hedda Gabler kills herself." This statement is clearly as applicable to Phaedra and to Oedipus as it is to Hedda and, indeed, to all tragic heroes. Ibsen's play, in Steiner's own account of it, even gives us a hint of the Dionysian origins of all tragedy in its explicit reference to the "crown of vine leaves" with which Hedda hopes to crown a drunken, iconoclastic Loevborg: "Consider the stress of dramatic feeling and the complexity of meaning conveyed by the tarantella which Nora dances in *A Doll's House;* by Hedda Gabler's proposal to crown Lovborg with vine leaves. . . . Each is in itself a coherent episode in the play, yet it is at the same time a symbolic act which argues a specific vision of life. Ibsen arrived at this vision, and he devised the stylistic and theatrical means that give it dramatic life. This is his rare achievement."[24]

What Steiner is referring to here as Ibsen's "rare achievement" (through such symbols as Nora's tarantella and Hedda's crown of vine leaves) is his use of maenadic imagery to represent the fundamental conflict between society and chaos. It is "rare," according to Steiner, because tragic, Dionysian drama is not supposed to occur after the advent of such taming, modern influences as rationalism and Christianity. But such disruptive explosions of the unrepressed are not rare; they are even, as Yeats insisted,[25] synonymous with the inherent destructiveness of poetic rapture. If George Steiner recreates Pentheus's and other typologically similar figures' (Creon, Hippolytus, Tesman, Lopakhin in *The Cherry Orchard*) attempts to declare tragedy dead,[26] it is because tragedy's inherent threat to rationalism makes it both anathema and desirable to society. True, Steiner's work seems to elevate tragedy in its admiration for those supposedly rare periods of tragic accomplishment. But *The Death of Tragedy* is actually controlled by the rationalist's typical need to police society (in Steiner's case, Western society at large) and maintain order by refusing to grant works such as Ibsen's *Hedda Gabler* the full measure of their tragic greatness. It is important, in this regard, to note that there is no mention throughout Steiner's work of the aesthetic pleasure, or joy, that is obviously the raison d'être behind the creation, production, and enjoyment of tragic works of art. This, too, is the result of a Penthean, rationalistic approach whose seriousness is (quite literally in Steiner's book) the very death of tragedy. The notion that such seriousness is the appropriate response to tragedy is only one of the many pernicious notions inherited from the *Poetics,* which Plato/Socrates' famous equivocation at the end of the *Symposium,* and Longinus's more artistically uplifting but marginalized account of a "tragi-poetics," barely serves to correct.[27]

Steiner's rationalistic, Hegelian rejection of tragedy is even more obvious in his dismissal of Chekhov, who "knows grief and despair in the particular instance, but not tragedy."[28] Hegel, too, saw the particularization and "privatization" of modern art, its immersion in the details of everyday experience, as evidence of the falling away from the kind of classical idealism and universal conflicts that made tragedy possible. Music, which one might expect Hegel to oppose to such exteriorization, is in fact part of the same shift in periodicity, for, as the center of meaning shifts away from communal institutions such as religion, politics, and society, the privatization of experience elevates the inner thoughts of the individual as well as the everyday world of ordinary objects and places. Not surprisingly, then, Chekhov's mundane and therefore untragic concern with "the dry and private character of modern suffering" is, like the works of other dramatists of this period, coupled with "a special mood or atmosphere in which the shape of action becomes fluid and musical":

> The theatre of Chekhov always tends toward the condition of music. A Chekhov play is not directed primarily toward a representation of conflict or argument. It seeks to exteriorize, to make sensuously perceptible, certain crises of interior life. The characters move in an atmosphere receptive to the slightest shift in intonation. . . . This kind of drama is immensely difficult to produce because the means of realization are very close to music. A Chekhovian dialogue is a musical score set for speaking voice. . . . Pitch and timbre are often as meaningful as the explicit sense. . . . In the second Act of *The Cherry Orchard,* the voices of Madame Ranevsky, Lopakhin, Gayev, Trofimov, and Anya perform a quintet. The melodic lines move in isolation and seeming incongruence. Suddenly a mysterious sound is heard in the evening sky, "the sound of a snapped string." It changes the key of the entire play. The brittle weariness in the different voices now swells to a great sombre chord. "Well, good people, let us go," says Madame Ranevsky, "it's getting dark."
> But it is as difficult for the language of criticism to deal with the art of

Chekhov as it is for any language to deal with music. *All I would stress here is the fact that Chekhov lies outside a consideration of tragedy.*[29]

The notion that music and action are necessarily opposed ("a Chekhov play is not directed primarily toward a representation of conflict or argument") is much older than Hegel, extending as far back as the *Poetics'* well-known assertion that action is the most important part of the drama, whereas the musical component of Greek tragedy is relegated by Aristotle to the next-to-least important of tragedy's six elements (superior only to scenery). This is important because it shows that what is really at stake in this passage is the rationalist's necessary opposition between what is real and important because it can be objectively determined (for example, the plot that has a beginning, middle, and end) and between what is less important because it is only apprehended sensorily and cannot be understood by the intellect ("but it is as difficult for the language of criticism to deal with the art of Chekhov as it is for any language to deal with music"). But what if, as Nietzsche argued, music is not only not opposed to the action of the tragic drama but is its very essence?

Steiner rightly calls attention to the moment in *The Cherry Orchard* when "suddenly a mysterious sound is heard in the evening sky, 'the sound of a snapped string.' It changes the key of the entire play. The brittle weariness in the different voices now swells to a great sombre chord. 'Well, good people, let us go,' says Madame Ranevsky, 'it's getting dark.'" One does not oppose the rationalist tradition just discussed by accepting its oppositions and valorizing such previously devalorized elements as music but by rejecting the opposition altogether. This "mysterious," irrational sound cannot be opposed to the rational meaning of the play any more than the play's music can be opposed to its action. One may not know exactly what the "mournful sound" of a string snapping in Chekhov's play means, but the reader certainly knows that it accompanies the fall of aristocratic beauty as it is expelled from its edenic garden of overabundance by the encroaching forces of bourgeois realism. (It is astonishing that Steiner would say that a play like *The Cherry Orchard* "is not directed primarily toward a representation of conflict or argument.")

In *The Birth of Tragedy*, Nietzsche argued that the fall and its various versions, including, for example, that of the Prometheus myth, is the archetypal tragedy in depicting the self-destruction that ensues as a result of humanity's inevitable desire to challenge God, the gods, or its own "natural" limitations (ix). (Zarathustra "going down" among the people after filling his heart and mind with an overabundance of greatness is Nietzsche's own version of the myth.[30]) The sound that Chekhov keeps referring to in the play is not musical but unmusical: the mournful sound of a string snapping and dying away, of a bucket being cut loose, refers to the end of the musical, lyrical state of aristocratic beauty that is being displaced by Lopakhin, Trofimov, and the other modern, pragmatic forces of the play. (The last instance of this sound occurring is quickly followed by the sound of the cherry trees being chopped down.) Thus, what Steiner sees as a play about the irrational, musical condition of an interior, private space encroaching on the more classical space of objective action is actually about the opposite: the loss of the lyrical, rapturous overabundance equated with the aristocrats and their music in the face of more objective, rationalistic concerns.[31]

The Cherry Orchard, then, is not only a tragedy; it comes close to being *the* tragedy insofar as it is a tragedy about tragedy. The musical state of rapturous superabundance and excessive passion that leads Madame Ranevsky and her family to destruction is the same "siren song" that has been leading tragic heroes to their destruction since Achilles chose, despite the Lopakhinian warnings of his mother Thetis, a brief, incandescent life of fame and destruction over a less illustrious but longer life of more mundane accomplishments. The play's music, then, is not only not opposed to the tragedy's action; it is, as Nietzsche argued, its very essence. True, Chekhov designated *The Cherry Orchard* a comedy. But, discarding his own thesis regarding the "untragic" Chekhov, Steiner offers his own explanation of this apparent contradiction: "Or perhaps one should approach these elusive plays by discarding all traditions of dramatic genre. At the close of the *Symposium*, Socrates compelled his listeners to agree that the genius of comedy was the same as that of tragedy. Being drowsy with wine, they were unable to follow his argument. . . . Thus the Socratic demonstrating of the ultimate unity of tragic and comic drama is forever lost. *But the proof is in the art of Chekhov.*"[32]

I will now examine two works written before Steiner's that address, respectively, the life and the death of tragedy in the twentieth century. In choosing Sisyphus as his archetype of the "tragic" existential hero (*The Myth of Sisyphus*), Camus confirms Nietzsche's idea that tragedy is synonymous with the absurd loss of empirical/epistemological meaning that is inherent to all works of art, even to artworks of the modern period. Robbe-Grillet, on the other hand, argues for the "death of tragedy" in the modern era on the grounds that its aesthetic celebration of destruction is a ruse that confronts the void only to deny it.

The analysis of *The Myth of Sisyphus* will begin with an argument for the implicit importance of tragedy in Camus's initial arguments and end, as he does, with the explicit pronouncement that Sisyphus is himself a modern tragic hero. Camus rightly contends that all the major writers of the period that is now called "high modernism" are consumed by the philosophical problem of ascribing meaning to an inherently meaningless world. But this problem, as Camus also insists, is not limited to modern works like *The Trial, The Stranger, The Possessed*, and so forth. Other differences notwithstanding, classical works like *Oedipus* and *Medea* are no less concerned with the absurdity of existence than more modern works like *The Cherry Orchard* and *Waiting for Godot*. It is no more catastrophic for Meursault to confront the absurdity of his life than for Oedipus to realize his own ridiculous fate as the man who solved the riddle of the Sphinx only to ensure his own destruction. It is Camus's belief that the confrontation between absurdity and belief in some transcendental structure—be it that of the individual, society, religion, or philosophy—is as classical as it is modern. Camus's recognition of the broader application of this modern notion, his unwillingness to limit this problematic to one period or another, is our first indication of his disagreement with those who, like Steiner and Robbe-Grillet, rely on such period distinctions to declare the genre of tragedy dead.[33]

As evidence of the fact that one does not need a strong belief in God for the opposing force of tragic meaninglessness to occur, Camus speaks of the innately human "revolt of the flesh" that occurs when one confronts the absurdity of existence:

> Yet a day comes when one notices he or she is thirty. One asserts their youth. But simultaneously one situates oneself in relation to time, taking one's place in it. Tomorrow, one was longing for tomorrow, whereas everything ought to reject it. *That revolt of the flesh is the absurd.*
>
> A step lower and strangeness creeps in: perceiving that the world is "dense," sensing to what a degree a stone is foreign and irreducible to us, *with what intensity nature or a landscape can negate us.* . . . that denseness and that strangeness of the world is the absurd. People, too, secrete the inhuman. At certain moments of lucidity, the mechanical aspect of their gestures, their meaningless pantomime makes silly everything that surrounds them.[34]

Inherent to human existence, then, are such simple but profound transcendental structures as (in Kantian terms) our a priori consciousness of space and time, which deny the inherent "denseness and strangeness" of an absurd world. The "revolt of the flesh" is Camus's term for our inability to live with such transcendental structures and their denial of absurdity; as Nietzsche says in his essay "On Truth and Lies in an Extra-moral Sense," humans will always deny their decenteredness even if it means defining it as such. Steiner is correct in asserting that a world ruled by such absurdity, where (as in the case of *Waiting for Godot*) "the mechanical aspect of [one's] gestures, their meaningless pantomime makes silly everything that surrounds them," would be bereft of tragedy.[35] But *Waiting for Godot* and other examples of the theater of the absurd (where this mechanical pantomime predominates) *are* tragic because such absurdity always occurs as part of the conflict between such meaninglessness and the mind that rejects it. Robbe-Grillet is similarly correct when he says that Camus's notion of absurdity is always defined by the structures of meaning to which it is opposed, but he is wrong to condemn Camus—and tragedy—for this logical inconsistency. "To will," Camus writes, "is to stir up paradoxes."[36]

Just as consciousness is always consciousness of something, tragedy is always the tragedy of consciousness and its paradoxical knowledge of a lack of knowledge. Tragedy cannot exist without the consciousness, what Aristotle calls the "recognition" (*anagnorisis*), of its own failure.[37] Such a failure does not, however, preclude the consciousness of its recognition; indeed, Camus argues that consciousness begins with this fundamental recognition: "A stranger to myself and to the world, armed solely with a thought that negates itself as soon as it asserts, what is this condition in which I can have peace only by refusing to know and to live, in which the appetite for conquest bumps into walls that defy its assaults? To will is to stir up paradoxes. Everything is ordered in such a way as to bring into being that poisoned peace produced by thoughtlessness, lack of heart, or fatal renunciations."[38]

Thinking about the "meaning of meaninglessness" is not, as Robbe-Grillet argues, a useless self-contradiction; it is the essential stance of Camus's tragic hero of the absurd. Camus reverses our more customary notions by describing "peace" and "order" as a "poisoned" state of "thoughtlessness" that denies the essential "paradoxicality" of consciousness, of a "thought that negates itself as soon as it asserts." In other words, genuine thinking is not defined by the stability of its concepts but by the self-undermining[39] process of thought that depeoples the world of its self-enclosed concepts, beginning with the fundamental principle of consciousness, the principle of noncontradictory identity (one becomes "a stranger to myself and to the world"). It is in such a desert that thought becomes consciousness and, as this chapter will show, humanity becomes Sisyphean. As such, the desert is not really an unhappy place for Camus and his absurd, tragic heroes. If it is associated with death, that is because it is a place where humanity realizes itself by exceeding its limitations and definitions. The death of tragedy is thus as relevant a phrase for Camus as it is for Steiner and Robbe-Grillet, although it means something completely different for each.

In this early reference to the will's "bumping into walls that defy its assaults,"[40] Camus is preparing the reader for his later discussion of Sisyphus's eternal rock rolling as his emblem of the human condition. But Camus also prepares the reader for the final, climactic unveiling of Sisyphus as a modern, tragic hero in his analysis of Don Juan. Like Sisyphus, Camus's Don Juan also begins as a satyr-like figure who believes in nothing but erotic gratification; his conflict with society and the law is based squarely on his logical recourse to this principle of sensual gratification. Quite simply, Don Juan refuses to let anything interfere with his duty to live a life based on love, and so to love life: "This life gratifies his every wish, and nothing is worse than losing it."[41] Stated this way, it reminds one of what Nietzsche says about Achilles, that his intense love of life and preference for a short but illustrious career is the equivalent of Silenus's statement that "the best thing in life would be never to have been born" (*Birth of Tragedy* iii, 29), never to have to limit one's life in mortal terms but rather to live like a god (who is also never born). The satyric Don Juan, for whom "that laugh, the conquering insolence, that playfulness and love of the theater are all clear and joyous," is a tragic figure because a life that is based solely on the rapturous overabundance of sensual gratification must ultimately conclude in the soulless desert of an impoverished inhumanity that is the logical result of Don Juan's aesthetic indifference:

> But this symbolizes the grim ending of an existence turned toward short-lived joys. At this point sensual pleasure winds up in asceticism. It is essential to realize that they may be, as it were, the two aspects of the same destitution. . . . I see Don Juan in a cell of one of those Spanish monasteries lost on a hilltop. And if he contemplates anything at all, it is . . . a noble, soulless land in which he recognizes himself. Yet, it is on this melancholy and radiant image that the curtain must be rung down.[42]

The tragic lesson of Don Juan, according to Camus, is that having everything also means losing everything. The aesthetic life of boundless, satyric bliss leads logically and inevitably to the ascetic impoverishment of a life without meaning, for, in both cases, Don Juan's life is based on nothing. His life is truly tragic because, like Oedipus, he reveals how the plethora of excessiveness leads to the devastating loss of everything, even of one's own identity. Yet it is important to note that Don Juan's end, like

Oedipus's at Colonus, is not only melancholy but "radiant": if aesthetic excess leads to ascetic impoverishment for both, it is because they are "two aspects of the same destitution." Aesthetic, rapturous overabundance is inseparable from tragedy's requisite loss of meaning.

Sisyphus is not, on closer examination, unlike Don Juan and other figures who represent satyric, tragic transgression. For, as Camus retells the legend (of which there are many variants), Sisyphus was another of those Promethean trickster figures who could be "accused of a certain levity towards the gods." He bested Zeus himself in one of the god's many attempted seductions of a mortal woman, and he bested Hades by putting Death himself in chains. Perhaps most significantly, after having obtained a furlough from the underworld, Sisyphus so "enjoyed the water and the sun, warm stones and the sea, that he no longer wanted to go back to the infernal darkness."[43] It is by virtue of this passionate, limitless zeal for life—and not just his famous rock-rolling—that Camus labels Sisyphus an "absurd hero." For the actions just described all bespeak an insouciant disregard for seriousness and the authority figures who rely on it; these transgressive actions make it impossible, in turn, for society and its gods to tolerate Sisyphus's existence. Similarly, Don Juan, Oedipus, and Prometheus are also punished because they refused to take society seriously, because they were imbued with divine laughter, the levity of "perhaps" (*viel-leicht*) versus "it is" or "it ought to be." It is because all the tragic figures just mentioned are imbued with a comic spirit of excessive disregard for civilization that comedy, as Socrates realized, is inseparable from tragedy.

Turning to Sisyphus's later punishment, Camus does not, even here, single out the rock rolling itself as important. Rather, it is the "hour of consciousness" that occurs when Sisyphus knows the full, heart-rending truth about his inescapable predicament:

> It is during that return, that pause, that Sisyphus interests me. A face that toils so close to stones is already stone itself. I see that man going back down with a heavy yet measured step toward the torment of which he will never know the end. That hour like a breathing-space which returns as surely as his suffering, that is the hour of consciousness. At each of those moments when he leaves the heights and gradually sinks toward the lairs of the gods, he is superior to his fate. He is stronger than his rock.
>
> *If this myth is tragic, that is because its hero is conscious.* Where would the torture be, indeed, if at every step the hope of succeeding upheld him? The workman of today works every day in his life at the same tasks, and this fate is no less absurd. *But it is tragic* only at the rare moments when it becomes conscious. Sisyphus, proletarian of the gods, powerless and rebellious, knows the whole extent of this wretched con-

dition: it is what he thinks of during his descent. The lucidity that was to constitute his torture at the same time crowns his victory. There is no fate that cannot be surmounted by scorn. . . . One must imagine Sisyphus happy.[44]

If Steiner is right about the incompatibility of tragedy with a godless modern age, then why does Camus, who wore his atheism like a badge of honor, label his representative hero of the absurd "tragic" not once but twice? Clearly, one does not need a strong belief in the gods to experience the "bottom dropping out" of a life that has become absurd and meaningless. One does, however, need consciousness to fathom fully, as Sisyphus does here, the tragedy of a life that has been drained of all conscious meaning. And, if "one must imagine Sisyphus happy" in the consciousness of this absurdity, that is because his punishment is the "other side of the same destitution" that was his former career as a satyric trickster. The same exuberant vitality that had before caused Sisyphus to laugh at the gods now allows him to shoulder his rock with glee: once again, nothing exists, and so nothing truly matters. We are reminded of what Nietzsche says, in *Thus Spoke Zarathustra,* about the "greatest weight" (*Schwergewicht*) of the eternal return: we must "imagine ourselves happy" in shouldering the greatest burdens of life, replete with all its tragedies, if we are to remain true to the "rapturous overabundance" of which absurdity is only the rationalist equivalent.[45]

This analysis can now turn to a powerful advocate of the "death of tragedy" who, unlike Steiner, was fully aware of Camus's argument that modernist absurdity is synonymous with satyric exuberance and the tragedy of a life without meaning. Written shortly after Camus's work but before Steiner's *Death of Tragedy,* Robbe-Grillet argued in even more emphatic terms than Steiner against the practice of writing, or even continuing to read, tragedies. Robbe-Grillet's position grew out of the following passage by Roland Barthes, which Robbe-Grillet quotes at the beginning of his essay: "Tragedy is merely a means of 'recovering' human misery, of subsuming and thereby justifying it in the form of a necessity, a wisdom, or a purification. . . . nothing is more insidious than tragedy."[46]

Barthes's argument against tragedy's "recuperation" of meaning anticipates his later discussion in the masterful *S/Z* of the classic text's reliance on various strategies of Aristotelian unity. The passage also demonstrates typical Barthesian elegance in pointing out that tragedy actually has too much of the recuperation of meaning that it seems to be lacking. Against the notion that classical tragedies like Euripides' *Hippolytus* or Racine's *Phèdre* coyly flirt with disaster only to recuperate meaning later on, this chapter will now argue that such an argument is itself guilty of the coyness that it seeks to condemn.

The key to Robbe-Grillet's argument is in the title of the chapter from *For a New Novel* concerning tragedy. "Nature, Humanism, Tragedy" are all linked in his mind by their similar anthropomorphic projections of human consciousness onto an essentially foreign world. Robbe-Grillet argues that we have not progressed beyond the primitive assumption that the universe is governed by gods of our own making and that "nature" corresponds to the ideas that we project upon it. His attacks on "nature, humanism, and tragedy" are thus really attacks on projection, on the metaphorical, figurative displacements of improper meanings onto a world that should remain literal: "Metaphor, as a matter of fact, is never an innocent figure of speech. To say that the weather is 'capricious' or the mountain 'majestic,' to speak of the 'heart' of the forest, of a 'pitiless' sun . . . is to furnish clues to the things themselves. . . . In almost the whole of our contemporary literature, these anthropomorphic analogies are repeated too insistently, too coherently not to reveal an entire metaphysical system."[47]

Before leaping to metaphor's defense (not only is "leaping" a metaphor, but it is the metaphor of metaphorical expressions, which always leap, jump, or transgress from the literal), it should be noted that Robbe-Grillet's statements against metaphor derive from Kafka's own statements and his enormous influence on the French writer[48]—such national border crossings are, of course, their own form of metaphorical borrowings.[49] Like Robbe-Grillet, Kafka believes that metaphor impoverishes rather than enriches language by adulterating objectivity with a subjective impression "which does not properly belong."[50] Indeed, examples such as Kafka's "sad winter"[51] and Robbe-Grillet's "majestic mountain" would lead one to condemn the whole process as dull and uninteresting—certainly duller than Robbe-Grillet's novelistic world of untouched facticity or a world where a traveling salesman can be literally, not just figuratively, metamorphosed into a bug. Yet, if one were to choose "live metaphors" (as Paul Ricoeur would call them[52]) from actual, "living" poems, something that both Robbe-Grillet and Kafka avoid doing, then the criticism of metaphor as trivial and subjective would immediately vanish:

> Shall gods be said to thump the clouds
> When clouds are cursed by thunder,
> Be said to weep when weather howls?
> Shall rainbows be their tunics' colour? . . .

It shall be said that gods are stone.
Shall a dropped stone drum on the ground,
Flung gravel chime? Let the stones speak
With tongues that talk all tongues.[53]

Considering the myriad of living, poetical metaphors such as these, one quickly realizes that if metaphor "adulterates" language (Aristotle's word), its licentiousness adds to, rather than subtracts from, the objectivity and originality of a world that would otherwise be impoverished by the literal, which is synonymous with the proper, which is synonymous with the law. Kafka may have been true to his antimetaphorical position in studiously avoiding hackneyed expressions like "the sad winter" throughout his writings, but his literary world of human bugs, singing mice, and freak shows featuring starving artists is hardly unmetaphorical.

"The characteristic of humanism," Robbe-Grillet writes, "is to appropriate everything,"[54] and there is no doubt that the goal of Robbe-Grillet's essay is to rid us of this unfortunate tendency toward "appropriation" (the word, with its reference to the literal, or *propre*, warns us that the literal may be as much of an act of appropriation as the figurative). The reason, as this chapter has shown, that acts of appropriation, recuperation, and familiarization are condemned is that they all involve the illegitimate projection of the human onto a world to which one does not properly belong. It is for this reason that Robbe-Grillet is led to praise tools and condemn nature when one would have expected the opposite. For while tools are distinctly human, they reside securely within that realm and so do not encroach on the world outside humanity's ken. Nature, on the other hand, is that which by definition lies outside the sphere, and so Robbe-Grillet ridicules attempts such as those of the Romantics to experience the pantheistic world of "Nature" directly.

It is thus that Robbe-Grillet ridicules tragedy as a ruse, for however much tragedy might seem to concern estrangement, defamiliarization, and meaninglessness, it is in fact a surreptitious, Romantic attempt to experience the greater world of "Nature" (albeit negatively) and deny the phenomenological surface to which one is necessarily limited.[55] Even Camus errs, according to Robbe-Grillet, in fashioning a character whose very estrangement leads to a tragic confrontation with the meaninglessness of life that provides him with a new reason for living:

> The crucial scene of the novel affords the perfect image of a painful solidarity: the implacable sun is always "the same," its reflection on the blade of the knife the Arab is holding "strikes" the hero full in the face and "searches" his eyes. . . . *Absurdity, then, is really a form of tragic*

humanism. It is not an observation of the separation between man and things. . . . When Sartre writes that *The Stranger* "rejects anthropomorphism," he is giving us, as the quotations above show, an incomplete view of the work.[56]

The duplicitous, humanistic gestures of metaphor and tragedy are actually ways to give meaning to a world that is beyond us. This is true, but when one looks at "living" tragedies (as before we looked at "living metaphors") in their poetic contexts—tragedies like *Oedipus, Phèdre, Hamlet, A Streetcar Named Desire, Waiting for Godot*, and so forth— Robbe-Grillet's argument that the "divorce" becomes the new relationship between the human and its world dissolves in much the same way as we saw the condemnation of dead metaphors dissolve.[57] The destruction of meaning that occurs in particular metaphors and actual tragedies does indeed make the divorce of meaning into a "new relationship," but that is like saying that a new metaphor, or a new painting, is not really new because it must be part of our conceptual, visual framework to make sense. Tragedy and metaphor do exactly what Robbe-Grillet says they do not, and the literalness of the "new novel" is not doing what he claims it does. For metaphor and tragedy, in requiring the destruction of the literal and literal destruction respectively, violently overthrow the quotidian aspects of civilized meaning, whereas the pure descriptiveness of Robbe-Grillet's new novel risks cloyingly reiterating the most "human" of empirical objectifications.

Just as it is wrong to reject metaphysics as naive because it concerns itself with the end of knowledge (Kant was certainly not naive in arguing for the legitimacy of metaphysical speculation on the supersensible), it is wrong to condemn humanism for dealing with the end of human reality in its own distinctly human terms. Neither humanism nor metaphysics satisfies itself with merely restating the obvious in remaking the external world in its own image—something one could more easily say of the nouveau roman.[58] Like tragedy, both grapple with our problematic relationship with the inhuman world surrounding us; to dismiss that as Romantic and self-contradictory is partly true but totally naive. Tragedies like Hamlet's and Lear's, Phaedra's and Medea's, are about the fundamental loss of meaning that follows humanity around like a shadow; they are not just about the escape, or "recuperation," from that loss. That we take aesthetic delight in watching tragedies about our own destruction is no proof that tragedy is a sham but rather, as Nietzsche argued, proof that humans delight in metaphors and tragedies that represent things "greater than themselves" (Aristotle).

6 Nietzsche Sings the Blues: Tragedy and the Blues

> Music alone allows us to understand the delight felt at the annihilation of the individual.
>
> —Nietzsche, *The Birth of Tragedy*

> How is it that we gain definite pleasure by identifying with the singer's sadness? . . . A clarification of this problem is essential if we are to understand how and why we enjoy the blues.
>
> —Garon, *Blues and the Poetic Spirit*

In the first years of the twentieth century, when Nietzsche had completed his celebrated reversal (*Umkehrung*) of Western rationalism and Freud had just published his own monumental dismantling of rational consciousness in *The Interpretation of Dreams*, W. C. Handy penned the first description of a Delta blues singer:

> A lean, loose-jointed Negro had commenced plucking a guitar beside me while I slept. His clothes were rags; his feet peeped out of his shoes. His face had on it some of the sadness of the ages. As he played, he pressed a knife on the strings of the guitar in a manner popularized by Hawaiian guitarists who used steel bars. His song, too, struck me instantly:
>
> *Goin' where the Southern cross the Dog*
>
> The singer repeated the line three times, accompanying himself on the guitar with the weirdest music I had ever heard. The tune stayed in my mind.[1]

The general tendency among the writers and researchers who have attempted to understand the "weird music" that mysteriously emerged around the turn of the century from the Mississippi Delta is to stress the miserable sociopolitical conditions of the impoverished, segregated African Americans who created the genre.[2] These writers' strong (and, needless to say, legitimate) sense of social injustice has also led music writers and historians to refer the blues back to the African musical origins that newly freed slaves had heroically preserved from their cultural oppressors:

> From all this it may be seen that Negro traditions of music, song and dance had a long history extending far back in slavery and to an African heritage. Vestiges of Africa remained in their arts. . . . All this has relevance to the blues and has had, in some way, an influence on the shaping of the music, its content or its function.
> But the blues did not exist in slavery, at least in a form which can be identified with those which constitute "the blues."[3]

Notwithstanding the contradictory nature of an argument that derives the blues from Africa and from the suffering of blacks in America, from slavery and yet after slavery, the main objection to these sociopolitical theories is that their strong explanatory value has effaced other, more aesthetic ways of understanding the blues. Regarding the supposed African origins of the blues, Bruce Cook has written:

> Clearly, blues and jazz and the whole world of popular music that they have produced all find their source in the American Negro and his culture. Since he came from Africa and must have brought his music with him, reason seems to dictate that we have only to go back to Africa . . . to hear the roots of the music that came to bloom over here. As a result, nearly every book on blues and jazz . . . has had its obligatory first chapter on African origins. . . . *They are not the same music at all;* a much more profound and complete metamorphosis took place here in America during the nineteen century (perhaps starting even before then), producing a music that was more singular in nature than the historians of jazz and American popular music are willing to allow.[4]

Cook goes on to quote the eminent ethnomusicologist Richard A. Waterman, who emphatically states that "there are no African retentions, as such, in the blues."[5] And, even among those who, like the distinguished blues historian Paul Oliver, cling to the notion that the blues is of African origin, there is (as evident in the passage quoted above) considerable hesitancy and uncertainty.[6] The point here is not so much to enter into this debate as it is to move the discussion away from such widely accepted commonplaces and sociological explanations of the blues. As a musical art form the blues, this chapter will argue, is better understood in the aesthetic terms of Nietzsche's theory of tragic, Dionysian music: "Most critics regard the blues as a historically demarcated and easily classifiable trend. But the blues people themselves generally conceive their life's work to be 'timeless' and outside conventional critical frameworks. Thus Boogie Woogie Red tells us that 'blues have been goin' on for centuries and centuries, and the blues was written years and centuries ago—they was always here.'"[7]

Moreover, it is as much of a category mistake to define the blues as a direct expression of personal suffering as it is to define the blues as the direct expression of certain vaguely historical and not so vague social conditions.[8] Anyone who has listened closely to this music knows that such suffering is not the essential experience of the blues—indeed, the "specifically musical appeal of the blues" may even be described as antithetically related to what the lyrics as a rule describe.[9] Through the application of Nietzsche's theory of tragic suffering as an expression of aesthetic pleasure,[10] as well as through his related critique of so-called subjectivity in art ("Seine Subjektivität hat der Künstler bereits in dem dionysischen Prozess aufgegeben" [the artist has already relinquished his subjectivity in the Dionysian process]),[11] this chapter will provide a unique position through which to understand why the blues is not really about such suffering, even though its lyrics often say otherwise.[12]

For Nietzsche, all art is inherently an expression of overwhelming joy, or rapture (*Rausch*),[13] and it is from this premise that he seeks to explain, in *The Birth of Tragedy*, how the Athenian Greeks of the fifth century could have derived aesthetic pleasure from tragedy's spectacles of suffering. To explain this conundrum, Nietzsche refers tragedy back to its musical origins in the dithyrambic Dionysian chorus (the complete title of Nietzsche's first book is *The Birth of Tragedy out of the Spirit of Music* [Die Geburt der Tragödie aus dem Geiste der Musik]). Nietzsche's theory of the rapturous Dionysian spirit of music and its inherent relation to tragic nihilism will thus provide the key to solving what Paul Garon referred to as the "essential problem" of "how and why we enjoy the blues."[14]

The first part of this chapter will discuss how Nietzsche's theory of the musical origins of tragic art in original Dionysian pain and suffering relates to blues music in general. We will also consider Nietzsche's theory of the relation of Dionysian music to Apollonian objectivity insofar as it informs an understanding of the relation between rapturous blues music and its supposedly pessimistic lyrics. Then the second part of this chapter will move in the contrary direction and look more closely at the way certain defining characteristics of the blues, such as the dissonant "choking" of certain notes in the blues scale and the nihilistic tendencies of blues lyrics in general, also support a Nietzschean theory—or "singing"—of the blues.

Music and tragic myth are equally expressive of the Dionysiac talent of a nation and cannot be divorced from one another. Both have their origin in a realm of art which lies beyond the Apollonian; *both shed their transfiguring light on a region in whose rapt harmony dissonance and the horror of existence fade away in enchantment.* Confident of their supreme powers, *they both toy with the sting of displeasure, and by their toying they both justify the existence of even the "worst possible world."* Thus the Dionysiac element, as against the Apollonian, proves itself to be the eternal and original power of art, since it calls into being the entire world of phenomena. (*Birth of Tragedy* xxv, 145 [emphasis added])

There is a realm of art that causes the "horror of existence"—an ambiguous phrase by which Nietzsche means both the "worst possible world" depicted in tragedy as well as the horror of merely existing in the real world—to "fade away" (*verklingen*). The German term, unlike the English, is distinctly musical, although both provide alternatives to the idea of existence "disappearing," or "being destroyed," by art. Nietzsche uses *verklingen* to stress the musical dimension of the experience. Existence "fades away" because music does the opposite: it "drowns out" (*klingt*) reality by "fading in," by invading (or "in-fading") the "horrors" of our everyday lives.

This aural idea of "drowning out" is important in signaling Nietzsche's fundamental goal of dislodging Western metaphysics by challenging its key terms. Since Plato, Western thought has defined existence visually as definition and defined itself in opposition to the flux-based philosophies of pre-Socratic thinkers like Heracleitus and Protagoras. Nietzsche's goal of undermining this Platonic tradition is reflected in his preference here for "fading out" the foundational reality of existence: by using this musical term, Nietzsche avoids the logical trap of defining himself in opposition to definitions and thus creates a musical, Dionysian alternative to our largely visual Western metaphysics.

Music and tragedy, as explained in this passage, are part of a more original, artistic world ("Thus the Dionysiac element, as against the Apollonian, proves itself to be the eternal and original power of art, since it calls into being the entire world of phenomena") that is greater than ourselves and the entire objective world and, as such, is part of the dissonant, Dionysian world of suffering. But how can music overcome suffering and yet itself be suffering? *"In referring to primordial contradiction and pain* [music] symbolizes a sphere which is both earlier than appearance and beyond it" and so is different from the aforementioned "horror of *existence"* (*Birth of Tragedy* xxv, 145), the pain of quotidian reality. The former suffering, which occurs in a state of musical rapture,[15] occurs because of the ecstatic overabundance that destroys the *principium individuationis,* the everyday reality of the static individual as defined by the law of abiding identity, both personal and logical. And so Dionysian rapture is equated with suffering of a different nature,[16] the suffering of ecstasy that must simultaneously lament its destructiveness, including that of its own passing (for, to the extent to which it *is,* such joy is already extinct).

As aesthetic phenomena, music and tragedy paradoxically create "objects" that are closer to this destructive, Dionysian world than their Apollonian counterparts and thereby "shed their transfiguring light on a region in whose rapt harmony dissonance and the horror of existence fade away in enchantment." Such art is "supreme" and "supremely confident" because it has literally transcended any concern for this world, and so "toys with the sting of displeasure" and justifies even "the worst of all possible worlds." This is why the blues lyric, like the plot of tragedy, seems to return its audience to the very pain of existence and the anguish of alienation from which music sets us free:

> Standin' at the crossroad,
> tried to flag a ride.
> Oooo ooee eeeee
> tried to flag a ride.
> Didn't nobody seem to know me, babe
> everybody pass me by.
>> —Robert Johnson, "Cross Road Blues"
>> [my transcription]

> Well I got troubles, on my mind.
> Well I got troubles, on my mind.
> Well I just can't be satisfied.
> And I just can't keep from crying.
>> —Muddy Waters, "I Just Can't Be Satisfied"
>> [my transcription]

The blues song will often take the form of a plaintive cry of despair precisely when the music—"Orpheus ascending"—is in the process of liberating the musician from just those things that are the subject matter of the song: in the case of Robert Johnson's lyric quoted above, the loneliness of the world's contemptuous disregard; in Muddy Waters's words, the perennial discontent and frustration of living in the real world that is certainly felt more acutely, although not exclusively, by blacks. Like the surprising declaration of the archsatyr Silenus (Dionysus's mentor) that "the best thing in life would be never to have been born, the second best to die soon" (*Birth of Tragedy* iii, 29), the rapturous blues artist's objective lyrics of despair must be understood as the function of an overabundant will that can "toy with the sting of displeasure" and not as a function of any real unhappiness.

As *lyric* drama,[17] Greek tragedy's proximity to the musical, Dionysian origin of art in general (pace Aristotle[18]) explains the genre's well-known propensity for scenarios of nihilistic destruction, for the destruction of the tragic hero is actually, according to Nietzsche, a positive affirmation of "instinctive" Dionysian life. This is because, as a musical expression of "eternal," nonobjective superabundance, art finds its "symbolic expression" (*Birth of Tragedy* xvi, 101) in the Dionysian tragic hero who passionately exceeds her (Antigone, Clytemnestra, Medea, Phaedra) or his (Oedipus, Pentheus, Creon, Ajax) objective, individual limits. Although the tragic hero is always, either literally or figuratively, destroyed, this excessive overabundance paradoxically represents a greater, more vital force than that of the preservation of static, individual identity to which the tragic hero is almost always opposed.[19]

Tragedy is thus a "similitude," "parable," or "translation" (*Gleichnis, Übersetzung*) of "instinctive Dionysian wisdom into images" (xvi, 102). Nietzsche's emphasis on figurative language is important, because it explains why the blues lyric, like the plot of tragedy, cannot be taken literally, for the tragic heroes just described are all "parables" (*Gleichnisse*) of the "eternal, omnipotent will" that is more directly expressed not in images but in music. Metaphor, simile, parable, and such are thus inherently paradoxical entities that express an omnipotent, rapturous will, which always "remains invisible" behind the figures themselves.[20]

Tragedy is actually a joyous affirmation of the rapturous superabundance of the tragic hero who exceeds the limits of rational civilization and symbolizes the figurative essence of music. Like tragedy, the blues is also inherently nihilistic; the lyrics, like the tragic plot, express the singer's "loathing of existence," his or her loss of the very things whose possession would mean (supposedly) happiness and fulfillment. But if the blues resembles tragedy in this abiding sense of nihilistic despair, it also resembles tragedy in the "need to look and look beyond" (*Birth of Trag-*

edy xxiv, 123) such destructiveness as musically joyous and life-affirming. (This is even easier when listening to the blues, for the music that was such an integral part of Greek tragedy is for all intents and purposes lost.) Like tragedy the blues must, in the spirit of the Dionysian *sparagmos*,[21] tear apart all the individual objects and identities of ordinary, nonmusical experience. With Nietzsche's help one can now understand why the blues, while expressing this fundamental sense of loss, is nonetheless not about the pessimism of its lyrics but a musical expression of rapturous superabundance that, in the paradoxical words of the satyr Silenus, joyously affirms that the "next best thing in life would be to die soon" (*Birth of Tragedy* iii, 29).

Finally, Nietzsche's rejection of the traditional view of "subjectivity" in lyric poetry will help to understand the real nature of subjectivity in the modern blues lyric: "But to the extent that he interprets music through images he [the lyric poet] is dwelling on the still sea of Apollonian contemplation, no matter how turbulently all that he beholds through the musical medium may surge about him. *And when he looks at himself through that medium he will discover his own image in a state of turmoil: his own willing and desiring, his groans and jubilations, will all appear to him as a similitude [Gleichnis] by which music is interpreted*" (*Birth of Tragedy* vi, 45 [emphasis added]).

In yet another instance of Nietzsche's reversal (*Umkehrung*) of the foundations of Western metaphysics the philosopher states that the words of the poet are figuratively related to the literal significance of the music—and not the reverse. When the lyric poet or the blues artist laments his or her lost love, or the Chorus in *Oedipus Tyrannus* laments the loss of human values, one must understand those as figurative (and to that extent false) expressions of music's different expression of suffering and loss, the rapturous, "turbulent" state of excitement that likewise denies or destroys every object. And given the fact that music is the primary aesthetic representation, or *Abbild* (Aristotle's conception of *mimesis* as active re-presentation, versus copy, is directly relevant here), of an "original Oneness" that destroys individual boundaries, the lyric poet does not, contrary to the traditional misconception, represent his or her own "empirically real" (*empirisch, realen*) subjectivity in verse.

One might object that while tragedy's consistently destructive bent may be seen as representing Dionysian deindividuation, surely lyric poetry and the lyrics of blues songs represent subjective experience. If this is not the case, then how does one explain the omnipresent *wörtchen* (little word) "I" as the unmovable center, as it were, of the lyric experience? Surely, Archilochus, Sappho, and others are lyric *poets*, not *lyric* poets?

Archilochus, Sappho, Robert Johnson, and other lyric poets may appear to be singing primarily about their experience, but they do so, Nietzsche maintains, as sleepers whose imagistic poems/dreams represent not the empirical/real world of waking reality but the latent, unconscious forces[22] of desire that are reflected primarily in music. In other words, the poem's lyrics and its lyric "I" bear the same relationship to the poet's actual subjectivity as do the poet's dreams, which is to say that there is no relationship or, if Freud is right, only a marginal one based on "residues" of one's daily activities:

> The artist had abrogated his subjectivity earlier, during the Dionysiac phase: the image which now reveals to him his oneness with the heart of the world is a dream scene showing forth vividly, together with original pain, the original delight of illusion. The "I" thus sounds out of the depth of being; *what recent writers on esthetics speak of as "subjectivity" is a mere figment.* When Archilochus, the first lyric poet of the Greeks, hurls both his frantic love and his contempt at the daughters of Lycambes, *it is not his own passion that we see dancing before us in an orgiastic frenzy: we see Dionysos and the maenads,* we see the drunken reveler Archilochus, sunk down in sleep—as Euripides describes him for us in the *Bacchae,* asleep on a high mountain meadow, in the midday sun—and now Apollo approaches him and touches him with his laurel. The sleeper's enchantment through Dionysiac music now begins to emit sparks of imagery, poems which, at their point of highest evolution, will bear the name of tragedies and dramatic dithyrambs. (*Birth of Tragedy* v, 38)

What is expressed in Archilochus's lyrics, what is expressed in the lyrics of the blues poets and in "dramatic dithyrambs" and tragedies, is the verbal expression of orgiastic music (a redundancy for Nietzsche) that stands in the same relation to consciousness as does sleep. Nietzsche's reference to Euripides' *Bacchae*—the "tragedy of tragedy" that deals with the god of tragedy, Dionysus—is particularly apt at conveying this reversal of the traditional view of poetry's relationship to its musical origins: the poet, whether she or he be the lyric poet, the blues poet, or the tragic poet, is like a sleeping bacchante who finds momentary respite—"calm before the storm," if one recalls the scene from Euripides' play—in the poem/ dream whose fundamental reality is not the dreamer's waking life but the surrounding "tumult" of Dionysian frenzy.

The "I" of the lyric poet is thus not the "*empirisch/realen* I" but "his [or her] I-ness" (*Ichheit*), the subjective, musical will whose relation to images such as that of the "I" is that of the sleeper to the dream, not that of the poet to his or her waking reality. The lyric "I" is the "active center of the world," by which Nietzsche means that the lyric poet's world is a function of his or her subjective will; he does not mean that the poem is governed by the poet's waking reality: "Being the active center of that world the poet may boldly speak in the first person, only the 'I' is not that of the actual waking person, but the 'I' dwelling, truly and eternally, in the ground of being" [*Birth of Tragedy* v, 39].[23] And so one must not be misled into thinking that the personal goals, passions, and intentions of the *"wörtchen"* "I" are an issue in the lyric poem. Such intentions, Nietzsche insists, must not be confused with the lyrical essence of the poem ("Archilochus, the subjectively willing and desiring human being, can never be a poet" [*Birth of Tragedy* v, 40]), a lyrical essence whose "primordial suffering," in the case of the blues, is expressed poetically in the music and in the impersonal, nonsubjective "suffering" of the lyrics. Nietzsche's theory, which leads us to the conclusion that there can be little or nothing personal in the blues because what is really at stake is music's rapturous expression of "primordial contradiction and pain," is confirmed by a study of blues lyrics, wherein the most "intimate" artists tell listeners next to nothing of their own personal troubles or concerns:[24] "Music, in referring to primordial contradiction and pain, symbolizes a sphere which is both earlier than appearance and beyond it."

When the chorus of Sophocles' *Oedipus Tyrannus*, dismayed over the sorry revelations that have succeeded in undermining all its beliefs, utters its quintessential declaration of tragic nihilism—"Oh generations of mankind, how I reckon you as equal to those who live not at all!"[25]—it is expressing the same sentiment as countless blues artists:

> Can't tell my future, I can't tell my past,
> And it seems like every minute sure gonna be my last.
>> —Charles Patton, "Future Blues" [my transcription]

> Lord, I was troubled,
> I was all worried in mind.
> Well, honey, I couldn't never be satisfied,
> And I just couldn't keep from crying.
>> —Muddy Waters, "I Just Can't Be Satisfied"
>> [my transcription]

The traditional view is that such songs are derived from the blues musicians' personal frustrations in love and life—as well as their sufferings as an oppressed class in a racist locale and country. But, following Nietzsche, I have argued that these lyrics, like those of tragedy, must be understood as emerging from the impersonal qualities of the music, not the reverse. And so it is to the music itself, then, that one must first turn to understand the blues and its perennial "metaphysical complaint."

There are (at least) two consistently defining characteristics of almost every blues song:[26] first, the "twelve-bar" developmental ascent to the subdominant IV chord after the initial statement or presentation of the tonic I chord, which is followed by the verse's concluding fall or descent to the dominant V chord; and, second, the dissonant flattening (I prefer "choking") of the third, fifth, and seventh notes of the major scale.[27] Regarding the second characteristic, it is important to note that, while the result of this flattening is structurally similar to a minor scale, the effect of "choking" certain notes intermittently is different—a difference that is attested to by the noticeable paucity of blues songs in minor keys.[28]

Of the two characteristics just mentioned, the second—the flattening of certain key notes of the major scale—is fundamental and distinctive to the blues. The particular strophic form of I–IV–I–V–I, while of considerable importance, is more variable from song to song and is frequently present in other genres, such as gospel hymns and balladic folk music, from which the blues usage probably derives.[29] Although a blues song could dispense with the approximate twelve-bar, I–IV–I–V–I form, I shall argue later that this regular pattern is nonetheless part of the Apollonian form that, like the lyrics, is related but of secondary importance to the dissonant blues melody line. Finally, I would add that the primary emphasis on the flattened, or choked, blues melody also explains the crucial difference between the blues and jazz. For jazz, while developing from the blues in its evolution through ragtime and Dixieland, loses the blues when the proliferation of notes that is part of its inherent emphasis on improvisation and virtuosic technique is forced to obscure the blues melody's strong emphasis on the three flattened notes just mentioned.

These choked notes, then, are the essence of the blues.[30] As mentioned, no blues artist simply strikes these halftones as if they were part of a new, quasiminor scale. A successful blues style depends on the artist's ability to slide, bend, or waver between these halftones or even quarter tones. This technique creates a pleasing dissonance that excites the listener by suspending the ground of the major scale, neither abandoning it (as in a minor scale) nor quite returning to it, thereby ingeniously avoiding the reestablishment of a new ground.

It is significant that the dissonant blues melody bends and slides between precisely those dominant points on the scale (the first, third, and fifth) that are more rigidly imposed on the song by the rhythm and harmony of the standard chordal progression. This crucial dissonance is thus the equivalent of the "dissonant, primordial" Dionysian desire from which, according to Nietzsche, tragedy and music originate. As this study has already shown, such desire is inherently "dissonant" (Nietzsche's term) because it revels in the will's disattachment from the Apollonian world of stable objects controlled by the "law of identity," or *principium individuationis:*

> In order to understand the difficult phenomenon of Dionysiac art directly, we must now attend to the supreme significance of musical dissonance. The delight created by tragic myth has the same origin as the delight dissonance in music creates. That primal Dionysiac delight, experienced even in the presence of pain, is the source common to both music and tragic myth. . . . *musical dissonance, as used by a master, makes us need to hear and at the same time to go beyond that hearing.* This forward propulsion, notwithstanding our supreme delight in a reality perceived in all its features, *reminds us that both conditions are aspects of one and the same Dionysiac phenomenon, of that spirit which playfully shatters and rebuilds the teeming world of individuals*—much as, in Heracleitus, the plastic power of the universe is compared to a child tossing pebbles or building in a sand pile and then destroying what he has built. (*Birth of Tragedy* xxiv, 143–44 [emphasis added])

In this important passage Nietzsche describes how musical dissonance originates in a joyful exuberance that is "propelled beyond" the ordinary world of objects. We "delight in" dissonance and spectacles of tragic suffering, Nietzsche argues, because art must go beyond conventional wisdom to create anew, in the same way that a child "playfully shatters" to rebuild anew.[31] In its essential sliding and wavering, which earlier were compared to the melody's suspension between the static objects of the phenomenal world, the dissonant blues melody expresses a similar "primal Dionysian delight" in destroying and being destroyed by the "reality principles" of the world.[32] One can thus understand Nietzsche's crucial enjoinder that one "hear and go beyond hearing" tragedy's and the blues' lyrics of despair, which express the poet's "metaphysical complaints" of lost love, life, and happiness.

The standard form of the blues verse (I–IV–I–V–I) stands in relation to the Dionysian blues melody as its Apollonian counterpart. It is the latter that gives form to the relative formlessness of the melody (the chords, unlike the dissonance just described, can be repeated) by imposing rigid, logical (to use Nietzsche's term) patterns such as the oft-noted twelve-bar progression, where certain chordal changes can occur only at the beginning of certain measures. The Apollonian pattern of meter and chordal changes that accompanies the lyric is not allowed, except in the

rarest cases, to develop beyond this rigid structure, because the Dionysian essence of the blues, which is in the dissonant melody line, would
be lost as the music became more intricate and complicated. In most
blues, the same line can be repeated, without modification, over the I,
IV, or V chords. As mentioned before, the twelve-bar pattern, which resembles that of much folk music, was probably applied to the distinctive
melody line after the fact by the early composers of the blues and then
by the early blues musicians, such as Charley Patton and Son House, on
whom the influence of such chordal progressions in religious hymns is
well known.

In addition to these pleasing chordal changes, the dissonant blues
melody finds another Apollonian ally, that of the typical complaint of the
pessimistic blues lyric:

> Well I'm driftin' and driftin',
> Like a ship out on the sea.
> Well, I ain't got nobody
> In this world to care for me.
> —Johnny Moore, "Drifting Blues"
> [my transcription]

One recalls that Nietzsche warned against the notion that the lyric
poet—or, in this case, the blues musician—is speaking personally (*Birth
of Tragedy* vi), urging one instead to consider that the negative lyrics of
poetry, tragedy, and the blues are born out of the ecstatic "suffering" of
the melody itself. One could also point to common sense and the historical record to prove that the artists who achieved such great heights of
creation required considerable freedom from distraction to perfect their
craft.[33] It is only logical that the perfection of great works of art requires
a considerable degree of detachment from mainstream society; thus it is
a "category mistake" (if not racial slur) to emphasize socioeconomic
conditions more in discussing the blues than in discussing a painting by
Picasso or a symphony by Beethoven.

Following Nietzsche, it is possible to offer a more properly aesthetic
explanation of the birth of the blues lyric from its dissonant, Dionysian
melody: "In thus retracing the experiences of the truly responsive listener
we gain an understanding of the tragic artist, of how, like a prodigal deity of individuation, he creates his characters—a far cry from mere imitation of nature—and how his mighty Dionysiac desire then engulfs this
entire world of phenomena, in order to reveal behind it a sublime esthetic
joy in the heart of original Oneness" (*Birth of Tragedy* xxii, 133).

Here Nietzsche describes how the Dionysian artist creates Apollonian objects such as characters and plot not by observation ("a far cry from mere imitation of nature") but by rapturously overcoming the boundaries of individuation and then playfully recreating those objects in his or her own image. This, again, is what Nietzsche means when he elsewhere addresses the "need to look and go beyond the look" at such linguistic phenomena as words, characters, and plots to experience (not "see") the rapturous musical origin of such objects. Similarly, the tragic joy of blues music lies (or, better, moves) in its revelrous abandonment of the words, ideas, objects, and laws that are represented by the lyrics. One might even say that what the blues lament is precisely the lyrics themselves, the static, language-based quotidian world that the music overcomes.

But why do the "playful" lyrics of the blues express sorrow when the total aesthetic, musical effect of both the lyrics and the music is one of joy? First, one must correct the terms of the question, for the typical blues lyric is not really about sorrow but rather longing, frustration, disappointment, and loss—in other words, desire. And desire is not expressed logically in fulfillment but in the separation of the individual—including the individual note—from the desired loss of consciousness (which is always consciousness of separation) and individuation (which is the essence of our "primordial" desire).[34] The blues lyric is thus the limited linguistic/Apollonian expression of what the music accomplishes in its more fluid bendings and waverings: the end of separation, the loss of individuation, and the unity of metaphysical Oneness.

The words of the typical blues *lyric* ("I love my baby, but my baby don't love me") must not, then, keep one from recognizing that the *music* is accomplishing exactly what the words do not. The objective words must be "looked at and looked beyond" as affirmations of the music's rapturous overcoming of the separations inherent in everyday life, separations that are then expressed by lyrics that, as Apollonian products of the law of individuation, are actually the linguistic equivalent of the Dionysian music. When Buddy Guy angrily declares "Damn right I've got the blues!" in a song on his 1991 album of the same title, one can now understand this as the individual singer's veiled, verbal expression of the rapturous Dionysian music that resolves those very lyrics' complaint. For the "truly responsive listener" that Nietzsche describes, the blues has always been heard this way—despite the understandable tendency to respond primarily to the Apollonian/linguistic level of the song.[35]

7 On the Kindness of Strangers: Tragedy, Contingency, and the Holocaust

> Oh generations of mankind, how I reckon you as nothing at all!
> —Sophocles, *Oedipus Tyrannus*

Nothing unobjectionable has ever been—or will ever be—written or filmed about the Holocaust. The now massive number of essays, books, novels, documentaries, and films on the subject all attest to the fact that whatever it is that is essential about the Holocaust is inevitably missing from the most sensitive or ingenious book or film. In this respect, the Holocaust resembles a species of figurative language, such as metaphor or parable, that sits before us sphinx-like, throttling our attempts at answers or even, as in the case of Oedipus, at solutions. One could say, then, that the Holocaust is also about the extermination of the meaning of the Holocaust itself.

This is not to say, as some have argued, that one should be silent about the Holocaust;[1] such silence, to paraphrase Lacan, would be louder than words in essentializing the Holocaust, however negatively. But it is to say that one must, in any study of the subject, acknowledge the essential ineffability of the Holocaust—as if that "ineffable essence" were not as inadequate as the most searing photographic images of the event, telling us so much and yet so little.

Acknowledging the fundamental inadequacy of this and other attempts to understand the Holocaust is what leads one to ask whether the Holocaust is a tragedy. For tragedy—whether one thinks of the ancient Greek plays, more recent works, or even the most contemporary headlines—has always referred to an event of such overwhelming destructiveness as to defy our understanding. Even Nietzsche's Dionysian theory of tragic affirmation acknowledges the annihilation of meaning that our distinctly Western notion of tragedy everywhere entails: "It is as though the myth [of Oedipus] whispered to us that wisdom, and especially Dionysiac wisdom, is an unnatural crime, and that whoever hurls nature into the abyss of destruction must experience nature's disintegration. 'The edge of wisdom is turned against the wise; wisdom is a crime committed on nature'" (*Birth of Tragedy* ix, 61). While it remains to be seen whether the genre of tragedy or theories of tragedy such as Nietzsche's are legitimate ways to address the horror of the Holocaust, an investigation into this comparison seems justified in light of the same basic confrontation with the abyss of meaninglessness that defines both tragedy and the Holocaust:

> Alas poor men, their destiny.
> When all goes well
> A shadow will overthrow it—
> If it be unkind
> One stroke of a wet sponge wipes all the picture out,
> And that is far the unhappiest thing of all.[2]

Even more unfortunate than unhappiness, laments Cassandra, the Trojan princess, is happiness, for then we are deluded into thinking we are happy when another misfortune is bound to occur that will soon destroy us. Cassandra's trenchant, tragic irony—her devastating denial of even the possibility of happiness as a result of the recent annihilation of her people—merits consideration with the greatest unhappiness of our time.

———

In a section of his *Negative Dialectics* entitled "After Auschwitz," Theodor Adorno argues for a third new historical time period (to follow the periods "before" and "after" Christ) that would reflect the fundamental change brought about in the world after the Holocaust: "We cannot say any more that the immutable is truth, and that the mobile, transitory is appearance. . . . After Auschwitz, our feelings resist any claim of the positivity of existence as sanctimonious, as wronging the victims; they balk at squeezing any kind of sense, however bleached, out of the victims' fate."[3] Adorno's entire work exemplifies this new period, as it should if his theory is correct, by everywhere pointing to the negative underbelly of thought that undermines our sublime pretensions of recuperating meaning and happiness—both philosophically and morally:

> And in philosophy we experience a shock: the deeper, the more vigorous its penetration, the greater our suspicion that philosophy removes us from things as they are—that an unveiling of the essence might enable the most superficial and trivial views to prevail over the views that aim at the essence. . . . what must come to be known may resemble the down-to-earth more than it resembles the sublime; it might be that this premonition will be confirmed even beyond the pedestrian realm, although the happiness of thought, the promise of this truth, lies in sublimity alone.[4]

In addition to his own position as an "anti-philosopher" who systematically and paradoxically describes the inadequacies of philosophical reflection, Adorno cites the Holocaust survivor and characters in a Beckett drama as two other examples of those who live without the sublime "happiness of thought." But even more than the others, the Holocaust survivor is essentially a dead man or woman for whom every breath is a caustic reminder of the denial of negativity and suffering that characterized the executioners at Auschwitz and elsewhere.

Adorno is, of course, not alone in citing the materialistic rejection of idealism as characteristic of our postmodern, poststructuralist, post-Holocaust age.[5] For example, Alain Robbe-Grillet, too, declares an end to humanistic tendencies in favor of a new novelistic agenda of materialistic immanence: "the characteristic of humanism, whether Christian or not, is precisely to recover everything, including whatever attempts to trace its limits, even to impugn it as a whole. This is, in fact, one of the surest resources of its functioning. . . . On the pretext that man can achieve only a subjective knowledge of the world, humanism decides to elect man the justification of everything. A true bridge of souls thrown between man and things, the humanist outlook is preeminently a pledge of solidarity."[6] No longer, Robbe-Grillet argues, should we project onto the world more than is already there and so appropriate its indifference to our own distinctly human advantage.

This, one recalls, is the same argument that Robbe-Grillet uses to condemn tragedy as a surreptitious recuperation of meaning by means of its supposed rejection.[7] Although Robbe-Grillet does not, like Adorno, relate his argument for the postmodern contingency of human existence to the Holocaust, there is a work that allows one to understand the author's argument against tragedy in terms of the Nazis' attempted extermination of the Jews. Alain Resnais's 1955 film *Nuit et brouillard* (Night and fog), while not a product of the filmmaker's famous collaboration with Robbe-Grillet (*Last Year at Marienbad* was some five years later), nonetheless demonstrates how the Holocaust would be represented by someone who followed the latter's nouveau roman manifesto,[8] thus allowing one to consider why it would not be appropriate to view the Holocaust as a tragedy.

Many have interpreted the flat, dispassionate delivery of Resnais's short documentary as quietly reverential, as tenaciously retaining its objectivity to express more fully the horror of millions of innocent children, women, and men being calmly exterminated.[9] But this interpretation, which is suspect in itself as a strategy of moral reverence, is also contradicted when one understands the film in terms of the *nouveau roman*'s aesthetics in general—and of Robbe-Grillet's manifesto in particular. The lack of reference to the subjective suffering of the countless individuals and families who were forced to carry on with their solicitudinous pretenses in the face of imminent execution should also be seen as the logical result of the movement's celebrated insistence on total objectivity.

The fact that the most compelling scenes in Resnais's film, the ones used to demonstrate the director's humanity, are those showing piles of shoes, glasses, and human hair can also be explained in terms of Robbe-Grillet's rejection of the human in favor of the utensil as more important (because more objectively real) than the idealistically alienated human who creates it: "Man does not thereby refuse all contact with the world; he consents on the contrary to utilize it for material ends: a utensil as a utensil, never possesses 'depth'; a utensil is entirely form and matter—and purpose. . . . the hammer is no more than a thing among things; outside of his use, it has no signification."[10]

Contrast these scenes from Resnais's film with the famous and overtly emotional scene from Claude Lanzmann's 1985 film *Shoah*, where a barber is shown cutting hair in present-day Jerusalem while he retells the story of being forced to cut the hair of women on their way to the "showers" in the very next room. The climax of the scene (the very sort of climaxes eschewed by Robbe-Grillet and Resnais's film) occurs when the barber tells how the law of objectivity imposed by the Nazi overseers broke down one day when one of the other barbers suddenly recognized his "client":

> A friend of mine worked as a barber, when his wife and his sister came into the gas chamber. . . . I can't. It's too horrible. Please. [You have to do

it . . . .] They tried to talk to him. . . . [He] could not tell them this was the last time they stay alive, because behind them was the German Nazis, SS men, and they knew that if they said a word, not only the wife and the woman, who were dead already, also they would share the same thing with them. In a way, they tried to do the best for them, with a second longer, a minute longer, just to hug and kiss them, because they knew they would never see them again.[11]

It is doubtful, in light of these two examples, whether one could argue that Resnais's dispassionate exposition is necessary to do justice to the enormity of the subject. The calm and objectivity of Resnais's film is more understandable, one might suggest, in terms of its affinities with the explicit agenda spelled out in Robbe-Grillet's *For a New Novel* than it is as an attempt to do justice to the enormous human suffering of its content. Indeed, the latter explanation of Resnais's style in *Night and Fog* is more compelling, for it is doubtful whether the objectivity of Resnais's film can be said, following some sort of reverse logic, to represent the very thing—human cruelty and the suffering of the innocent—that it so studiously avoids.

Although Robbe-Grillet and Resnais would doubtless agree with Adorno in insisting on the end of human ideals "after Auschwitz," Adorno's "negative dialectics" would not necessarily embrace this reduction of the human to the inhuman,[12] of the ideal to the materially contingent. For to do so would imply a direct, empirical relation to the real world that Adorno's dialectic would deny. Thus, despite the fact that Robbe-Grillet (and, if I am right, Resnais) explicitly rejects tragedy as a surreptitious reintroduction of the truth, it does not necessarily follow that Adorno's negative dialectics would do the same. Indeed, neither Adorno, Beckett, nor Camus explicitly rejects the notion of tragedy to describe this fundamental loss of meaning; Beckett, one will recall, even describes the generic contents of *Waiting for Godot* as a "tragi-comedy." But, before attempting to decide whether this loss of idealism really allows for the continuation of tragedy, there is one other important voice on the subject of contingency and the Holocaust that needs to be heard.

In a 1989 collection of essays entitled *Contingency, Irony, and Solidarity*, Richard Rorty also insists on the postmodern notion, whether in the form of Adorno's negative dialectics or Derrida's *différance*, of liberating thought from the exigencies of traditional metaphysical thinking. In this respect, Nietzsche functions throughout Rorty's essays in much the same way as Camus does in Robbe-Grillet's manifesto, for Rorty criticizes Nietzsche for his too idealistic reversal of Plato (however else it may be described) and for his apocalyptic vision of a new world to be dominated by the *Übermensch*. This critique is key for analyzing Rorty's position, which is that all such speculative positions fall apart when confronted with the contingencies of our materialistic existence:

> Old metaphors are constantly dying off into literalness, and then serving as a platform and foil for new metaphors. This analogy lets us think of "our language"—that is, of the science and culture of twentieth-century Europe—as something that took shape as a result of a great number of sheer contingencies. Our language and our culture are as much a contingency, as much a result of thousands of small mutations finding niches (and millions of others finding no niches), as are the orchids and the anthropoids.[13]

Rorty's position seems closer to Robbe-Grillet than to Adorno, for his insistence on the contingency of human experience is embraced as liberating thought from its more conservative tendencies rather than lamented for drowning out the "music" of pre-Holocaust speculative thinking.[14] As one might expect, then, Rorty's position on the Holocaust, which he presents in one of the book's final essays, is closer to (but, as will be shown, not the same as) Robbe-Grillet's polite indifference than it is to Adorno's elegiac lament.

In an earlier chapter of *Contingency, Irony, and Solidarity* entitled "The Contingency of Selfhood," Rorty establishes the terms that will lead to his explicit views on the Holocaust and, for this study's purposes, tragedy. Taking his lead from Derrida, Rorty embraces the "playfulness" of a contingent selfhood that, he admits, cannot contest authority without risking the loss of its own peculiar "essence":

> This playfulness is the product of their [Freud and Henry James] shared ability to appreciate the power of redescribing . . . an appreciation which becomes possible only when one's aim becomes an expanding repertoire of alternative descriptions rather than The One Right Description. Such a shift in aim is possible only to the extent that both the world and the self have been de-divinized. . . . Both, however, have power over us—for example, the power to kill us. . . . Faced with the nonhuman, the nonlinguistic, we no longer have an ability to overcome contingency and pain by appropriation and transformation.[15]

Despite having the chimerical, protean power of its own insubstantiality, the contingent, metonymical self can do nothing—except, perhaps, write a great novel. Yet, even the category of the figurative/aesthetical is necessarily qualified by Rorty's emphasis on contingency, for in quoting Harold Bloom's notion that art has "no unity, form or meaning. . . . its unity is in the good will of the reader," Rorty implies that, except for the "good will" of its audience, the "kindness of strangers," the self and art are utterly contingent and so utterly meaningless in themselves.[16]

Rorty is nothing if not logically consistent, and the discussion of the Holocaust with which he concludes his book repeats this earlier essay almost to the letter. In "Solidarity," a discussion of socialized cruelty in general and the Holocaust in particular, Rorty contends that what saved more Jews in some countries, such as Italy, than in others, such as Belgium, was the utterly contingent "good will" of strangers that, as one might suspect, is sometimes found more in some places and less in others. Life, Rorty is urging us to admit, is really like that, and all of our attempts to believe otherwise are congruous (like Nietzsche's deifications) with the very structures of society that, because of their reliance on the "One Right Description," we ought to avoid. Furthermore, we ought to take comfort in the freedom of our contingent selfhoods despite the fact that, like the victims of the Holocaust, we are utterly helpless in the face of authoritative power. Hope is to be found, again, in the "kindness of strangers"; that is, in the fact that there are many like us, particularly in a liberal country like America, who believe more in their contingent selfhoods (Adorno's "human part, the very part resisted by its ideologists"[17]) than in the powerful structures of authority. Surprisingly, awareness of the irony that is inherent in this "comfort" is sometimes lacking in Rorty's defense of contingency—irony that is not at all lacking in the memorable lines of Blanche DuBois or in the grim scenario of Paul Schrader's 1990 film *The Comfort of Strangers:*

> *Faced with the nonhuman, the nonlinguistic, we no longer have an ability to overcome contingency and pain by appropriation and transformation. . . .* The final victory of poetry in its ancient quarrel with philosophy—the final victory of metaphors of self-creation over metaphors of discovery—would consist in our becoming reconciled to the thought that this is the only sort of power over the world which we can hope to have. For that would be the final abjuration of the notion that truth, and not just power and pain, is to be found "out there."[18]

Here Rorty is reminding us that the irony of the Nazis' "relocation" of the Jews, of *"Arbeit Macht Frei"* (work sets one free), and of the "delousing" procedures was no mere ironic reversal but the "nonhuman," "nonlinguistic" reference to nonexistent things. The contingency of the victims is defined by such nonrelational signs that have no relation, not even an ironic one, to the humans for whom they are intended. Language is not language, for the humans who read these signs are not considered human. The horror of this is compounded by the fact that the false signs are so much so that they are even, in a way, true: work does free one, and showers do rid one of lice.

The *trans-ports* that conveyed the victims of the Holocaust to the death camps and that, if Adorno is right, transported all of us into a different age, are literally, etymologically, and symbolically meta-phors. The victims—and we ourselves—are living with borrowed terms and on borrowed time; for in the same way that the victims thought they were being transported someplace else, we continue to think that our postmodern age can be defined, despite our gnawing uncertainty to the contrary. The utter contingency of our present condition, as defined by Robbe-Grillet, Adorno, and Rorty, is thus modeled on the contingency of the victims, the transportees of the Holocaust. Whatever it may be that we think about where we are or where we are going is so totally false, so utterly contingent in its nonrelation to the truth, that it may even be true.

Does this view of our contingent, ironic, metaphoric/metonymic selfhood preclude the possibility of viewing the Holocaust in the essentialist terms of tragedy? Or does Rorty's opposition to Robbe-Grillet's embrace of literalness and objectivity mean that he would also oppose Robbe-Grillet's condemnation of tragedy, despite their similar emphasis on contingency? And how does Rorty's contention that we can take comfort in our contingency and rely on the "kindness of strangers" fit with Adorno's more pessimistic, "negative" notion (which may or may not preclude tragedy) of an end to meaning "after Auschwitz"?

Rorty sees the potential for Derridean playfulness to take over once we have eliminated the traditional devalorization of nonserious structures of thought like metaphor and art in general. Rorty thus accepts what Adorno says about Auschwitz as the end of truth but allows for playfulness, metaphor, and art to survive as a result of our liberation from the exigencies of societal boundaries and definitions. In other words, Rorty takes to its logical conclusion a notion that is only implicit in Adorno: namely, that the "negative dialectics" of contingent truth—which are epitomized by Auschwitz—are conducive to the liberation of thought and the production of art in a postmodern, post-Auschwitz world. Thus, Rorty would not agree with Adorno that the Holocaust survivor must suffer from seeing him- or herself, by virtue of surviving, in the same terms as the Nazi guards who were indifferent to the cries of their victims.[19] Rather, Rorty might argue that the Holocaust survivor, while knowing better than most how contingent all our happiness is, experiences tragic joy—rapture—at being liberated from the nonsurvivor's (and the survivor's) world of meaning. Thus, a way has opened up that may allow us to reconcile Nietzsche's view of tragic rapture (*Rausch*) with the Holocaust.

Given the fact that tragedy from the time of the Greeks has always required, either literally or by implication, the nihilistic end of meaning and the destruction of the boundaries of moral, civilized society, the Holocaust should be not only *a* tragedy but *the* tragedy in the sense that it denies the most fundamental exigencies of civilized societies. And the postmodern age, which Adorno defines as the era "after Auschwitz," should also be designated as the age of tragedy. Robbe-Grillet, however, omits any mention of the Holocaust in his essay "Nature, Humanism, Tragedy" because he condemns the recognition of ironic and tragic structures of meaning that Adorno's and Rorty's essays, while also arguing for a new novelistic world of contingency, nonetheless clearly allow.[20]

By identifying Rorty's and Adorno's positions with the value of tragic destructiveness described by Nietzsche, this study is challenging the arguments of Robbe-Grillet and others who either explicitly or implicitly condemn tragedy's "insidious" recuperation of meaning ("Tragedy is merely a means of 'recovering' human misery, of subsuming and thereby justifying it in the form of a necessity, a wisdom, or a purification. . . . nothing is more insidious than tragedy"[21]). For, in a world of total contingency, the tragic recognition of absurd meaninglessness could not occur. In other words, contingent meaning—such as deferred, Derridean "meaning"—would make any form of tragic redemption (such as the *"Erlösung"* of Nietzsche's *Birth of Tragedy* or Sisyphus's happiness) seem excessively histrionic, insidious, and obsolete.

It is significant that the explicit declarations of the "death of tragedy"[22] by such writers as Robbe-Grillet and George Steiner are always coupled with denunciations of the heroic tradition that would limit tragedy to aristocratic protagonists such as Oedipus, Phaedra, Antigone, or Macbeth—tragic heroes who, according to Aristotle, must be "greater than us" for their tragic fall, or *peripeteia,* to shock or impress.[23] Yet there are other definitions of tragedy than Aristotle's, such as Nietzsche's, that do not require an aristocratic hero in the classical sense and thus do not vanish from the stage of Western art along with the end of aristocratic heroism that accompanies the advent of nineteenth-century realism and modernism.

For Nietzsche, tragedy is synonymous with the liberation of destructive Dionysian forces that are also creative in returning humanity to its musical, irrational (versus illogical), anti-Socratic origins. As an expression of the will's rapturous superabundance, tragedy is synonymous for Nietzsche with all great art (*Birth of Tragedy* xxi, 131) as a way of overcoming the laws and boundaries of rational, civilized behavior and consciousness. The identification of tragedy with aristocratic nobility is thus an effect, and not a cause, of the more important aesthetic notion of Dionysian excess that was first applied to those aristocratic individuals who—like Oedipus, Antigone, and Macbeth—could exceed the rational boundaries of more normative, civilized behavior. All that is left, then, that is needed to prove the viability of tragedy after Auschwitz is to show that the affirmative, redemptive recognition of such contingency through the fundamental loss of meaning in tragedy is neither contradictory nor immoral.

Robbe-Grillet's declaration of the death of tragedy may indeed apply to his own work, Resnais's *Nuit et brouillard,* and other works that proffer a world of total contingency wherein no special significance may be attached to anything in particular and then tragically lost. It would not apply, however, to Beckett's work, which, as I have suggested, is tragic (or at least, in Beckett's words, a "tragi-comedy") insofar as its contingent world is carefully placed alongside a more exigent, albeit missing, world—for example, the world of the idealized Godot. Note, too, the example of Camus's *Stranger,* which Robbe-Grillet condemns because, in the end, Meursault proves less than indifferent to his own indifference in defending his sense of absurdity. Contrariwise, it is doubtful whether Robbe-Grillet's purely contingent world—one that (unlike Rorty's) is bereft of all human hopes, fears, ideals, metaphors, personifications, projections, and expectations, a world where one does not stake claims and establish boundaries of even relative importance—has proven itself to be anything more than the aesthetic equivalent of a failed utopian experiment.

While it is certainly true that human contingency is an essential force in the modern, and especially the postmodern, world, the tragic drama that ensues as a result of this confrontation between contingency and the always already diminishing exigencies of civilized thought and values is and always has been, as Freud and Nietzsche argue, the very essence of art. We are thus in a position to understand why it is the case that the creation of great works of art has suffered not at all in the postmodern world, in the negative time of Adorno's "after Auschwitz." If, as was stated at the outset of this essay, the Holocaust is also about the extermination of the meaning of the Holocaust itself, then tragedy and art in general, which have always been unable to say what they mean (while always meaning what they say), are the only things left worth talking about, the only appropriate vehicles of meaning and representation in a post-Holocaust, postmodern world.

Unlike Steiner and Robbe-Grillet, neither Rorty nor Adorno explicitly declares the death of tragedy. This is because they realize that a world of pure contingency that is not opposed to the exigencies of human norms and values and where the human is no more important than its utensils is itself an all-too-human, all-too-unrealistic ideal. The Holocaust represents the triumph of contingency and, as Adorno maintains, denies forevermore the possibility of sustained belief in idealistic pronouncements and manifestos (such as Robbe-Grillet's) but not in the possibility of art, whose goal, as Rorty maintains, has always been to question such exigencies.

The postmodern reduction to contingency put forth by Rorty, Robbe-Grillet, and Adorno can take the horrifying form of the Holocaust, but it can also liberate us by its reduction of the human to the merely contingent. This is not, in any way, to mitigate the horror of the Holocaust. My point is that, as a tragedy, the Holocaust can and should redeem its survivors and observers—but not its executioners—by allowing them to embrace a contingent selfhood that is always the end result of tragedy's nihilistic destruction of meaning.

We can now return to the question with which we began: is the Holocaust a tragedy? It has been shown how opposition to such a notion is based on a number of more or less legitimate objections. The traditional notion that tragedy necessitates the heroic opposition to fate is obviously inappropriate to the Holocaust. However, this notion, derived from an Aristotelian understanding of tragedy that is as idiosyncratic as it is brilliant, was shown to be at most of secondary importance in tragedy and so not directly relevant to the definition in question here. More serious was the objection that tragedy insidiously recuperates the meaning of meaninglessness by projecting absurdity onto a world that is not even that (the gist of Robbe-Grillet's new novelistic objection to tragedy and to Camus). This would weigh heavily against any notion of the Holocaust as tragedy, because it would seem to appropriate and thus lessen the full extent of its horror.

The problem with this objection is that it assumes that any confrontation with or positing of meaninglessness, such as Camus's theory of the absurd, is a contradictory projection by humanity onto a world that is foreign to it. One cannot say, in other words, that life is meaningless, because that is to assume a meaning, albeit negatively, that the world lacks. This argument is valid, but only to a point. One need only recall Kant's arguments in defense of speculative, metaphysical thinking to realize that statements about a world that transcends human reality, such as statements about God, the sublime, or the supersensible, are a legitimate category of thought despite empiricists' claim of inconsistency. True, one is talking about something one does not ultimately know about, but that does not mean that speculative claims about such things (based on the different faculty of reason [*vernunft*]) are illegitimate.

To lament or to rejoice in the meaninglessness of life—as tragedy does—is thus neither irrational nor insidious because it projects human meaning onto a world that is supposedly meaningless. To paraphrase Camus, one might say that such a tragic confrontation with the meaninglessness of existence is in fact the only serious philosophical confrontation, one that, as we have seen, plays itself out in as many different ways—from Oedipus's sense of being fortune's fool to Hedda Gabler's sense of having stayed too long at the dance—as there are individual encounters with this abyss. The Holocaust, it was argued, is just such a tragic encounter with the void, both distinct from and the same as all other such encounters.

It is not, then, to contradict or cheapen the terrible experience of the Holocaust to define it as a tragic encounter with the meaninglessness of existence, despite the fact that such an ascription gives human meaning to something that it acknowledges is also beyond human meaning. The antitragic, empiricist, new novelist solution to this problem advocated by Robbe-Grillet and represented in Resnais's *Nuit et brouillard* (which steadfastly eschews the sort of emotional, human response to the Holocaust evident in films like *Shoah*) was viewed as an example of how the claim to deny the Holocaust its tragic depth is, at the least, morally as well as philosophically suspect. To dwell, as Resnais does, on such utensils as shoes (the famous footage of piles of shoes, eyeglasses, and other materials at Auschwitz) in order to avoid making speculative and emotional claims about the tragic horrors of the Holocaust is ultimately more idealistic than the histrionics such a gesture seeks to avoid.

One is left to consider the legitimacy of applying Nietzsche's definition of tragedy as a "game which the will, *in the eternal abundance of its pleasure,* plays with itself" (*Birth of Tragedy* xxiv, 143)[24] to the Holocaust. We should not, at the outset, reject such an application because of Nietzsche's use of the term "game" in his definition of tragedy. For we know that the term can mean, for Nietzsche as for countless other theoreticians after him (Freud, Gadamer, and others), something very serious: namely, an exercise of thought or of the will without regard for the real world's "reality principles."[25] This is not to say that the Holocaust should be considered a game even in this sense but only that the mere appearance of the term does not by itself disqualify the entire definition of tragedy as formulated by Nietzsche from consideration here.

Similarly, the reference to pleasure (*Lust*) needs to be qualified by its context: here, it is the "eternal fullness of [the will's] pleasure." As in our comparison of Freud's death-drive in *Beyond the Pleasure Principle* with Nietzsche's concept of the Dionysian in *The Birth of Tragedy* (chapter 4), such excessive, rapturous pleasure goes beyond its more conscious, Apollonian counterparts.

Nietzsche's complicated, pregnant definition (pregnant, in fact, with the "eternal fullness" of its own relevance to all of Nietzsche's key doctrines, both contemporary and future) refers tragedy to a state of rapturous overabundance in which embracing life to its fullest means experiencing the worst, as well as the best, that life has to offer. This is why Achilles' statement about the preciousness of life is actually synonymous, according to *The Birth of Tragedy*, with Silenus's statement about life as the "worst thing that could happen": Achilles' preference for a short, illustrious life over a long and less distinguished one actually illustrates the truth of both statements.

The Holocaust is unquestionably the "worst thing that could happen," an event that confirms more than any other the truth of Silenus's statement that "the best thing in life would be never to have been born" (*Birth of Tragedy* iii, 29). The real question, then, is whether such a tragedy conforms at all to Nietzsche's notion of an eternal overabundance of will. I would like to suggest that there is a way that it can—and, indeed, should. It is precisely because, to return to the notion with which this chapter began, one cannot ever understand the Holocaust, because it so totally overwhelms any attempt at understanding or representation, that it can only be understood in terms of a theory of tragic overabundance (such as Nietzsche's) that mocks the very category of understanding.[26] As such, the tragedy of the Holocaust can serve to liberate our consciousness from the constraints of the exigent reality principle and all nonaesthetic categories of thought that obey the laws of understanding. This is not to side with the executioners or to dishonor the memory of the victims. It is rather to bequeath a certain dignity on those who understand, or rather fail to understand, the tragic "game which the will, in the eternal abundance of its pleasure, plays with itself."

8 The Birth of Zarathustra from the Spirit of Tragedy

> Another ideal runs ahead of us, a strange, seductive,
> dangerous ideal . . . the ideal of a spirit who naively, that
> is to say impulsively and from overflowing plenitude
> [*überströmender Fülle*] plays with everything. . . . per-
> haps the *great seriousness* first arises, the real question
> mark is first set up, the destiny of the soul veers round,
> the clock hand moves on, the tragedy *begins.*
>
> —Nietzsche, *Ecce Homo*

The return to Nietzsche in the final chapter of this book is not due to any controversy regarding the continued importance of tragedy in the philosopher's later writings. Indeed, it is the general consensus among Nietzsche scholars (whenever they address the topic[1])—and the often re-peated declaration of Nietzsche himself—that *The Birth of Tragedy* pro-vides the cornerstone of the philosopher's entire oeuvre:

> The extent to which I therewith discovered the concept "tragic," the knowledge at last attained of what the psychology of tragedy is, I most recently expressed in the *Twilight of the Idols.* "Affirmation of life even in its strangest and sternest problems; the will to life rejoicing in its own inexhaustibility through the sacrifice of its highest types—that is what I called Dionysian that is what I recognized as the bridge to the psychol-ogy of the tragic poet.[2]

> When the thought of eternal return is thought, the tragic as such becomes the fundamental trait of beings. . . . Yet how does Nietzsche understand the essence of the tragic and of tragedy? We know that Nietzsche's first

treatise, published in 1872, was devoted to the question of "the birth of tragedy." *Experience of the tragic and meditation on its origin and essence pertain to the very basis of Nietzschean thought.*[3]

This chapter returns to Nietzsche to demonstrate that *Thus Spoke Zarathustra* contains the "eternal return of the same" theory of tragedy with which Nietzsche began his career. *"Incipit tragoedia":* tragedy begins. To understand the opening words—the beginning—of *Thus Spoke Zarathustra*, it is necessary to return to the theory of tragedy with which Nietzsche began his published writings.[4] And to understand the most important of Nietzsche's thoughts, the doctrine of the eternal return (as put forth in *Thus Spoke Zarathustra*), it is necessary to return to the same doctrine already present in Nietzsche's first book.

As in the opening chapter, Heidegger's *Nietzsche* will once again serve as our guide. Just as, before, this study followed and learned from Heidegger's insistence on rapture (*Rausch*) as the key to Nietzsche's concept of art, it will now follow Heidegger's study of *Thus Spoke Zarathustra*'s central doctrine of the eternal return of the same (*die ewige Widerkehr des Gleichen*) as centered on Nietzsche's theory of tragedy and tragic rapture: *"Incipit tragoedia.* The tragedy begins. Which tragedy? The tragedy of beings as such. But what does Nietzsche understand by 'tragedy'? Tragedy sings the tragic. We have to realize that Nietzsche defines the tragic purely in terms of the beginning of tragedy as he understands it. *When the thought of eternal return is thought, the tragic as such becomes the fundamental trait of beings.*"[5]

Heidegger is, of course, quoting the title of the Zarathustra aphorism (*Fröhliche Wissenschaft*) that later became the beginning of *Thus Spoke Zarathustra*. But what does Heidegger mean when he insists that "we have to realize that Nietzsche defines the tragic purely in terms of the beginning of tragedy as he understands it"? For Heidegger, "tragedy begins" means that tragedy, which always involves the abject, nihilistic end of things ("Oh generations of mankind, how I reckon you as equal to those who live not at all!"[6]) also always involves an aesthetic birth or beginning ("Trag-oedy sings the tragic"). *"Incipit tragoedia"* would then be a reiteration, a paraphrase even, of the title of Nietzsche's first book, *The Birth of Tragedy:* tragedy is the beginning of beings coming to be, the "metaphysical essence" and "fundamental trait of beings" that, as an end and a beginning, is synonymous with the much debated, much misunderstood doctrine of the eternal return of the same.[7] The goal of this chapter, then, is to clarify Heidegger's insight into the unity of Nietzsche's theory of tragedy and the eternal return of the same by reading *The Birth of Tragedy* back into *"Incipit tragoediac,"* tragedy begins. For despite Heidegger's insistence on the fundamental unity of Nietzsche's thought, he did not show that the key to many of his own insights concerning the eternal return of the same lies in a comparison with similar statements made in *The Birth of Tragedy.*

Nietzsche frequently refers to the eternal return of the same as "the heaviest," "the most burdensome" (*das grösste Schwergewicht*) of his many powerful thoughts.[8] And yet, Heidegger reminds us, the same doctrine is also referred to in *Ecce Homo* as "the highest formula of affirmation that can ever be achieved." Many interpreters, including Heidegger, have understood this burdensomeness to extend to the difficulty of understanding the doctrine itself, as well as to the oppressiveness of the thought once it is understood.[9] The former interpretation is less true, however, when one places the later communication of the doctrine back into the context of Nietzsche's other writings. For tragedy involves the same contradictory union of burdensomeness with joyous affirmation in its Dionysian denial of life and one's expectations of happiness as does the difficult later doctrine of the eternal return of the same.

The prologue of *Thus Spoke Zarathustra,* which includes the title *"Incipit tragoedia"* in *Fröhliche Wissenschaft,* offers up an example of burdensome affirmation under the explicit rubric of tragedy:

Incipit tragoedia. When Zarathustra was thirty years old he left Lake Urmi and his homeland and went into the mountains. There he communed with his spirit and his solitude and for ten years did not weary of them. But at last something in his heart turned—and one morning he rose with the dawn, confronted the sun, and addressed it in this way: You magnificent star! What would become of your happiness if you did not have those you illumine? For ten years you've been coming up here to my cave: you would have tired of your light and that path had it not been for me, my eagle, and my serpent. But every morning we waited for you, relieved you of your excess, and blessed you for it. Behold, I am overfilled with wisdom, like the bee that has gathered too much honey. I need hands that reach out, I want to give, to dispense, until the wise among men are happy again in their folly and the poor in their splendor. For that I must descend to the depths, as you do in the evening when you slip behind the sea and bring light to the very underworld you superabundant star! Like you, I must *go down,* as men call it, and it is men I want to go down to. So bless me then, tranquil eye that can look without envy upon a happiness that is all-too-great! Bless the cup that wants to overflow until the waters stream from it golden, bearing to all parts reflections of your delight! Behold, this cup wants to become empty again, and Zarathustra wants to become man again." Thus began Zarathustra's downgoing. (39)

We should not hurry past the initial fact that this is the only section of *Thus Spoke Zarathustra* to appear in its entirety twice, and is thus the eternal return of the same text that had ended the author's previous work and now begins the next. Moreover, the content of this prologue, which is a synecdoche for Zarathustra's repeated returns to isolation and "downgoing" throughout the work, is thus not only a foreshadowing of what is to come but also a "prepetition" of the doctrine of the eternal return of the same, the doctrine that, as Zarathustra himself states—and as Nietzsche and Heidegger both repeatedly maintain—is the central thought of *Thus Spoke Zarathustra*. How, then, can one read this prologue about the beginning of tragedy (*"Incipit tragoedia"*) as a synecdochal text about the "burdensome affirmation" of the eternal return that is to follow?

The ascent to and descent from his mountaintop with which Zarathustra's tragic "downgoing" (*Untergehen*) begins is not a unique event. For Zarathustra's retreat to his mountaintop at the age of thirty is repeated at the end of part 1, when Zarathustra again tires of mankind and returns to his mountain. Then, at the beginning of part 2, Zarathustra experiences the very same overabundant desire to revisit mankind that was experienced at the beginning of part 1:

> My wild Wisdom became pregnant upon lonely mountains; upon rough rocks she bore her young, her youngest.
>
> Now my wild Wisdom runs madly through the cruel desert and seeks and seeks for the soft grassland.
>
> Upon the soft grassland of your hearts, my friends, she would like to bed her dearest one! (pt. 2, 109)

Then, at the end of part 2, Zarathustra again returns to his mountaintop for the third and final time, where the original work (sans part 4) is concluded.

Critics have largely ignored this obvious manifestation of the eternal return,[10] but the value of this concrete instance of that idea in understanding the later communication of Zarathustra's doctrine is quickly apparent. For it is now clear why Zarathustra later rebukes the dwarf when he contemptuously interprets Zarathustra's most important truth about the repetition of discrete events within a framework of eternity to mean that "everything straight deceives, all truth is curved; time itself is a circle" (*Thus Spoke Zarathustra*, 178). For the small-minded dwarf's abstract formulation fails to account for the real relation between eternity and temporality, divinity and humanity, that the prologue describes. Zarathustra wills temporality and humanity ("Zarathustra wants to become man again") because the divine overabundance of eternity that he had earlier sought just as eagerly as overcoming all such empirical objects and realities now yearns to overcome itself and possess an object, a moment in time. *"Incipit tragoedia": the "birth of tragedy" is to be understood as the eternal repetition of the desire to become something that, because it is born from eternal overabundance, must later overcome itself, just as it overcame overcoming, in eternally returning to eternity.*

In contrast to the dwarf's reformulation, which says that every moment, in relation to eternity, has occurred before countless times and will recur again countless times, the prologue's tragic reformulation would be that the overabundance of eternity gives birth to each moment and to the human who lives in it; tragically, this moment does not exist in the eternity that gave birth to it. (This is the same tragic pathos expressed in Yeats's "Rose of the World."[11]) Zarathustra "wants to become man," wants to live in the moment; but the eternally recurring process of eternity that brought him to that point, or moment, is ironically indifferent to the creation of the meaning, moments, and humanity that it desires. This irony explains the contradiction of Zarathustra "wanting to become man again" so that he might begin preaching the doctrine of the Overman; it also explains one rendering of the phrase "the eternal return of the same": humanity (which is defined by the law of the same, the law of noncontradiction) is the sameness that is the eternal product of an eternity that is never the same: "Bless the cup that wants to overflow, that the waters may flow golden from him and bear the reflection of your joy all over the world!" (*Thus Spoke Zarathustra*, 39). The overabundance of joy and desire that wills to become human is an eternal, Dionysian desire that denies, with all the disdain of the other playful Olympians, the transitory objects of its own eternal desire (compare the frequent playful visitations to earth of the Greek gods).[12] As such, the beginning of tragedy is but another term for the eternal return of the same, the eternal return of a desire for the same (the human is the author of the doctrine of sameness, the "law of identity") that is denied the moment after it is born.

The prologue's emphasis on a rapturous overabundance ("like a bee that has gathered too much honey" [39]) that is form engendering[13] in its superfluity is related to the Dionysian/Apollonian relationship discussed in *The Birth of Tragedy* as well as to the doctrine of the eternal return of the same discussed later in *Thus Spoke Zarathustra*. In *The Birth of Tragedy*, the appearance (*Schein*) of visual arts (such as painting and sculpture) as well as the related linguistic arts (such as poetry and tragedy) is born from a nonobjective Dionysian state of rapturous Oneness that is closer to music:

> Music and tragic myth are equally expressive of the Dionysiac talent of a nation and cannot be divorced from one another. Both have their origin in a realm of art which lies beyond the Apollonian; *both shed their transfiguring light on a region in whose rapt harmony dissonance and the horror of existence fade away in enchantment.* Confident of their supreme powers, *they both toy with the sting of displeasure, and by their toying they both justify the existence of even the "worst possible world."* Thus the Dionysiac element, as against the Apollonian, proves itself to be the eternal and original power of art, since it calls into being the entire world of phenomena. (xxv, 145 [emphasis added])

The Dionysian realm is one of *"supreme* powers" "in whose *rapt* harmony dissonance and the horror of existence fade away in enchantment" because the empirical boundaries of everyday existence have ceased to exist in such a state of rapturous overcoming. Most important for our purposes is the reference to a turning back to the horror of existence that occurs as a result of this state of Dionysian rapture. If *rapture* is a *rupture* in its breaking the Apollonian boundaries of existence and overflowing with supreme power, then why return to the world of individuated forms, of empirical reality? The turn described here and throughout *The Birth of Tragedy* is exactly the same turn that returns Zarathustra to the real world so that he might preach his gospel of overcoming and eternal return. The "gospel of universal harmony" that is sounded in Dionysian ritual (*Birth of Tragedy* i, 23) rejoins the superhuman to the human because, ascending to its mountaintop and exceeding the world of men in the valleys below, the "transfiguring light" of amorphous Dionysian power reflects on, and thus recreates and gives birth to, a new world of objects that can hold and preserve it. When Nietzsche says that the Apollonian "at any moment makes life worth living and whets our appetite for the next moment" through such "illusions of fair semblance" (*Birth of Tragedy* xxv, 145), he is not contradicting his idea that the Dionysian is "the eternal and original power of art." The Apollonian makes life worth living because the overabundant power of Dionysian Oneness is reflected in an Apollonian object that is not really an object but rather the product of a transcendent power whose fulfillment is not to be found in an ideal, supersensible realm; rather, it appears in the fecund, orgiastic creation of objects in this world. Nietzsche's constant praise for the laughing Olympians (*Birth of Tragedy* iii, passim), the most human of all deities, is thus to be understood as part of his admonishment to "remain true to the earth" (*Thus Spoke Zarathustra*, 41–43), for in both cases the transcendent returns to earth from a state of rapturous overabundance.

It is likewise for Zarathustra, who in a state of rapturous overcoming—achieved through his own Olympian detachment—wishes to return to earth and "become man again." Zarathustra wants to resume his human form for no other reason than that described in *The Birth of Tragedy:* the Apollonian "twin brother" of the Dionysian is the product of an eternal, overabundant light or energy that returns to earth because it overflows—and such overabundant overflowing, given the "spirit of gravity," is always downwards. When Zarathustra goes down, he is in fact becoming the lame-footed dwarf (compare "Oedi-pous"—"swollen foot") who accompanies him, for the tragedy of the eternal return has always already begun: the gravity of the moment (which is described in *Thus Spoke Zarathustra*'s "On the Vision and the Riddle" as a stone archway) is desired by the overabundant energy that must also destroy it.

It has been the contention of this essay that one can understand *Thus Spoke Zarathustra*, especially the notoriously complex and controversial doctrine of the eternal return of the same, in terms of its relation to Nietzsche's foundational theory of tragedy as elaborated in the work of 1872 and before. Simply put, the eternal return of the same is the same theory of the Dionysian and the overabundant will as that which is expounded in *The Birth of Tragedy* (although there the idea is never designated as such). If all riddling involves placing a name with a missing definition, this may well be the ultimate riddle of the so-called "riddle" of the eternal return of the same.

The most explicit statement of the eternal return of the same occurs in the section of *Thus Spoke Zarathustra* entitled "On the Vision and the Riddle." As a confirmation of this identification of the doctrine with riddling, Zarathustra, whose fundamental thought is that of the eternal return, is himself referred to as the "Riddler" (pt. 3, 3). But the riddle in question is itself something of a riddle, for, to begin with, it is not altogether clear what the riddle in this section is, when it is being postulated as such, or how it differs from the "vision" of the eternal return of the same with which it is linked: "To you alone do I tell this riddle that I *saw*, the vision of the most solitary man" (176). What is referred to as a riddle (*Rätsel*) is thus also a parable (*Gleichnis*), an imagistic story that, like a riddle, must instead be interpreted or deciphered to reveal its hidden meaning.

In "On the Vision and the Riddle," Zarathustra begins by telling, à la Dante's allegorical riddles, of walking on a "wicked solitary mountain path" to overcome the dwarfish "spirit of gravity" (176–77) weighing him down; then he speaks to the dwarf of the gateway with the word "moment" (*Augenblick*) written above it that interrupts the infinite progression of time backward and forward. Finally, Zarathustra concludes this parable of the eternal return by telling of a shepherd choking on a snake who proceeds, following Zarathustra's urging, to bite off its head, whereupon the shepherd becomes a "transformed being, no longer a man, surrounded with light, laughing . . . a laughter that was no human laughter" (180).

One should not fault Nietzsche if he loosely uses the term riddle to describe what is more correctly described as an imagistic parable, for such terms for tropes and figures are often themselves tropes and figures of each other (compare metaphor, which is often used as a generic term for the way many tropes and figures use an inappropriate term to convey some new meaning[14]). Nietzsche's classical training and lecture courses on ancient rhetoric[15] made him more familiar than most with the precise definitions of such terms, and so if he uses the figurative term here figuratively it is because this parable, like most parables, needs to be solved like a riddle needs to be solved.

To answer the riddles of the three parts of "On the Vision and the Riddle," one needs to place them back into the context of Nietzsche's earlier writings on tragedy, where similar riddles are enunciated that will help to understand "On the Vision and the Riddle." Nor should it surprise one if the way to understand the later riddle is not to try and fathom some abstract solution but rather to place the riddle alongside itself in the larger context of the section and also alongside earlier formulations by Nietzsche of the same puzzle. For this would simply mean that the way to understand Nietzsche's most fundamental idea is not to place one's own meaning on it but rather to place it back into the context of Nietzsche's own thought—which is, in fact, precisely what one is supposed to do when solving riddles.

The section begins with Zarathustra telling his parable to an audience of "bold adventurers" who have left the land behind to set sail on perilous seas: "To you, the bold adventurers . . . who are intoxicated by riddles, who take pleasure in twilight, whose soul is lured with flutes to every treacherous abyss—for you do not desire to feel for a rope with cowardly hand; and where you can guess you hate to calculate" (*Thus Spoke Zarathustra*, 176).

The sea as an image of groundless Dionysian excess that represents humanity's "going-beyond-itself" (*hinübergehen*) is a consistent figure in

Nietzsche's writings that, like the sea itself, stretches from his earliest writings to his last.[16] This prelude to the telling of the parable of the eternal return of the same is thus itself a parable, and it is just as essential for understanding the doctrine as the aforementioned three parts in "Of the Vision and the Riddle" that follow. What does this beginning tell us? First, that "those who are *intoxicated* by riddles" (*den Rätsel-Trunkenen*) are not to be confused with those who patiently calculate (*erschliessen*) the solutions of problems. Rather, they are those who navigate their way while venturing beyond themselves and their knowledge ("whoever has embarked with cunning sails upon dreadful seas" [*Thus Spoke Zarathustra*, 176]). One must not confuse these two different forms of riddle solving and knowledge, for the latter *Fröhliche Wissenschaft* uses intuition rather than calculation ("where you can guess you hate to calculate"), which leaps over itself by plunging into the abyss rather than preserving itself: "you do not desire to feel for a rope with cowardly hand."

This beginning is not unrelated, or even merely ancillary, to the parable of the eternal return of the same that follows. Indeed, the adventurers' "intoxicated" Dionysian relation to eternity *is* the eternal return of the same. The rope that they do not need to feel beneath them (compare the *Seiltänzer* [tightrope walker] of the prologue), protecting them from the abyss, will soon become the stone passageway that blocks the flow of eternity through a contrary moment that is the eternal repetition of sameness inherent in empirical thought ("reality") and in the Platonic/Aristotelian *eidos* as *hauto kath auton* ("itself according to itself"). Likewise, the shepherd whose tongue is being bitten off by a snake, and who must reverse the process to emerge "no longer a man, . . . laughing," is the same as the adventurers who must bite off their own tongues in going beyond themselves by sailing into the horrors of a "treacherous abyss."

These "bold adventurers" are preceded in Nietzsche's "earlier" writings by other examples of tragic heroes "intoxicated by riddles" of the eternal return of the same:

> the poet's [Sophocles'] entire conception was nothing more nor less than the luminous afterimage which kind nature provides our eyes after a look into the abyss. Oedipus, his father's murderer, his mother's lover, solver of the Sphinx's riddle! What is the meaning of this triple fate? An ancient popular belief, *especially strong in Persia*, holds that a wise magus must be incestuously begotten. If we examine Oedipus, the solver of riddles and the liberator of his mother, in the light of this Parsee belief, we may conclude that *wherever soothsaying and magical powers have broken the spell of present and future, the rigid law of individuation, the magic circle of nature*, extreme unnaturalness—in this case incest—is the

necessary antecedent; for how should man force nature to yield up her secrets but by successfully resisting her, that is to say, by unnatural acts? . . . the same man who solved the riddle of nature (the ambiguous Sphinx) must also, as murderer of his father and husband of his mother, break the consecrated tables of the natural order. . . . wisdom, Dionysiac wisdom, is an unnatural crime, and whoever, in pride of knowledge, hurls nature into the abyss of destruction, must experience nature's disintegration. (*Birth of Tragedy* ix, 61)

Nietzsche probably did not have Zarathustra in mind when he referred in *The Birth of Tragedy* to Persian myth as the hidden truth of Oedipus's fate, but there is much to connect the latter with the former and its doctrine of the eternal return of the same. As earlier noted, riddle solving in *Thus Spoke Zarathustra* is not mere cogitation but willingness to immerse oneself in the mystery of overwhelming nature; the solution is neither in resolving this mystery nor in leaving it unresolved (which is also a form of solution) but in going beyond the boundaries of the known. Similarly, Oedipus's riddle solving as described here has little to do with the specific answer to the famous question posed by the Sphinx (which Nietzsche ignores) but with Oedipus's repeated attempts, his "triple fate," to overstep the limits of the known, the boundaries of nature, the laws of individuation. In referring to Oedipus as a "solver of riddles" Nietzsche is referring to Oedipus's intrication into the enigma of nature, his dissolution into a Oneness that denies all boundaries, that "hurls nature into the abyss of destruction." According to Nietzsche, Oedipus's riddle solving is synonymous with his incestuousness, for both involve the same immersion into the deindividuated forms of nature, such as reflected here in the deindividuated form of the Sphinx her/itself.

Tragedy begins with the eternal return of the same because those who, like Oedipus, deny the Apollonian law of individuation and the law of identity on which it is based by embracing the intoxicated bliss of nature's riddling disintegration "must experience nature's disintegration." One can thus understand the shepherd of *Thus Spoke Zarathustra* and his triumph as a version of Oedipus's fate, for biting off the head of the snake that is itself biting off the shepherd's head is a variant on Oedipus's confrontation with the riddling Sphinx; each triumphs by biting into the "extreme unnaturalness" that is biting into them. That is, each eschews sameness and enters into the horrifying flow of deindividuated nature (the chimerical Sphinx, the "eternal" snake) and, as such, reemerges "no longer a man."

The "luminous afterimage" of Sophocles' conception of this myth is the bright image that is left after Oedipus has experienced the disinte-

gration of nature in the form of the Sphinx, the incest, and the parricide
(Oedipus's "triple fate"). Nietzsche's repeated references in *The Birth of
Tragedy* to the emergence of luminous, Apollonian reality from the matrix of Dionysian dissolution are key to understanding the relation of the
luminous gateway moment to the eternal flow of time that surrounds it.
In the images of the negative sunspots with which Nietzsche begins the
ninth section of *The Birth of Tragedy*, of the "gently rocking rowboat"
that Nietzsche borrows from Schopenhauer (i, 22), and of the transfigured
Christ that Nietzsche borrows from Raphael (iv, 33), such soothing Apollonian objects are always to be understood in relation to the turbulence
of excessive Dionysian Oneness that surrounds them and to which they
provide welcome, luminous relief. From this, one understands the prologue in which Zarathustra compares himself to the overabundant sun
needing to "go down," to rid himself of the embarrassment of his rich-
es" in becoming man again, not as a moral imperative but rather as the
physiological desire for an object whose beauty is a direct result of the
excessiveness—the excessiveness of excessiveness—that preceded it.
Likewise, the gateway moment of the eternal return of the same is to be
understood as the same need of superabundant eternity to discharge itself in the form of something that, as something, is always the same.
The relation of eternity to luminous temporality in the eternal return
of the same is nothing more nor less than the relation of the Dionysian
to the Apollonian in *The Birth of Tragedy*; as such, one must understand
the tragedy of the eternal return as the tragic desire "to become man
again" of the god that exceeds him.

"If we examine Oedipus, the solver of riddles and the liberator of this
mother, in the light of this Parsee belief, we may conclude that wherev-
er soothsaying and magical powers have broken the spell of present and
future, the rigid law of individuation, the magic circle of nature, extreme
unnaturalness—in this case incest—is the necessary antecedent." We can
now read this passage as an interpretation of the eternal return of the
same—here, "the spell of present and future." The "solver of riddles," as
has been shown, means one who sets out to sea, an adventurer who
embarks on a voyage where questions, doubts, and uncertainties replace
the solid ground of meaning. To solve this means to perish; but, in so
doing, the hero becomes one with something greater and thereby triumphs. Oedipus's encounter with the Sphinx must, then, be reconsidered
in this light. His triumph is not in finding the correct answer to the
Sphinx's question (it certainly cannot be said that Oedipus wins the contest with the riddling Sphinx) but rather in desiring the uncertainty that
the monstrous Sphinx and its chimerical language equally represent. This

is why Nietzsche insists on joining together the encounter with the Sphinx with the incestuous encounter with Jocasta: the "extreme unnaturalness" of both belong together if one is to break the laws of nature and expose oneself to the metaphorical impurity of language. To say, as Hegel and others do, that Oedipus triumphs over the Sphinx by finding a human solution to its metaphorical expression ("the answer is man")[17] is to ignore that it is precisely such human answers that the entire myth puts into question.

In likening Oedipus to the Persian magus who has "broken the spell of present and future, the rigid law [*das starre Gesetz*] of individuation," Nietzsche is referring to the fact that Oedipus has overstepped the boundary of boundaries in general, of rigidity and of the lawfulness that requires it, of "the consecrated tables of the natural order." Oedipus is thus not only a tragic hero, he is a hero of the eternal return of the same. The stone doorway moment that blocks the flow of eternity with a present that separates and thus delineates a separate future and past must be overcome, its head must be bitten off, and this can only be done by the "extreme unnaturalness" of "incest" (understood in the largest sense of impurity). That is, the eternal return of the same, the doorway of separation that requires the law of identity, of sameness, to establish such purity, can only be overcome by such unnatural, incestuous acts as encountering the Sphinx (whose name refers to choking or throttling) and biting the head off of a snake that, like a riddle and/or metaphor,[18] has crawled into one's mouth and is biting off one's tongue. Oedipus's apotheosis at Colonus and the shepherd's final apotheosis are thus one and the same: each has become eternal by committing an impure, incestuous act that is the only way to overcome the *principium individuationis*, the law of sameness.

Commenting on the moment in *Thus Spoke Zarathustra* when the snake crawls into the shepherd's mouth, Heidegger writes: "Pity has not an inkling of the extent to which suffering and outrage crawl down the throat and choke a man until he has to cry out, nor does it know the extent to which this is 'necessary to attain the best' in man. *Precisely the knowledge that chokes us is what must be known if being as a whole is to be thought.*"[19] It is a pity that this explicit disavowal of pity as irrelevant to the greatness of tragic suffering—the suffering of the human who aspires to be more—has not been used to reject or at least qualify Aristotle's celebrated but misunderstood formula.[20] Throughout *Thus Spoke Zarathustra* one encounters the notion, which Heidegger in turn rightly stresses here, that "from unfathomable depths come the highest heights" (175). The return of this notion in the sections of *Thus Spoke Zarathus-*

tra concerning the eternal return of the same signals the connection between these two fundamental ideas and their relation to Nietzsche's equally fundamental notion of tragedy.

"From unfathomable depths come the highest heights": by immersing himself in the depths of being, the shepherd emerges as "a transformed being, surrounded with light, *laughing*! Never yet on earth had any man laughed as he laughed!" (*Thus Spoke Zarathustra*, 180). One recalls Nietzsche's numerous remarks censoring gods and humans who, unlike the Greeks and their deities, do not laugh; the shepherd is transformed into an illuminated, divine, laughing god because by biting off the head of the snake that has crawled into his mouth he has ingested the chaotic turbulence of the eternal Dionysian. This passage from *Thus Spoke Zarathustra* recalls the description in *The Birth of Tragedy* (iv, 33) of Raphael's *Transfiguration*, where the radiant, Apollonian Christ arises from the human madness and chaos below. Understood thus, Christ also represents the eternal return (parallels between *Thus Spoke Zarathustra* and the New Testament are numerous): his divinity, like the shepherd's, is based on the affirmation, the *Ja-sagen*, the love of life in its eternal entirety, beyond good and evil. (This is not contradicted by Nietzsche's famous battle with Christianity; rather, it illuminates the source of Nietzsche's anger.)

The shepherd scene and Heidegger's comment on it recall the riddle of the pastoral figure Silenus who, as Dionysus's tutor and as a satyr, is also one of the early versions of the *Übermensch:*

> An old legend has it that King Midas hunted a long time in the woods for the wise Silenus, companion of Dionysos, without being able to catch him. When he had finally caught him the king asked him what he considered man's greatest good. The daemon remained sullen and uncommunicative until finally, forced by the king, he broke into a shrill laugh and spoke: "Ephemeral wretch, begotten by accident and toil, why do you force me to tell you what it would be your greatest boon not to hear? What would be best for you is quite beyond your reach: not to have been born, not to be, to be nothing. But the second best is to die soon." (*Birth of Tragedy* iii, 29)

That this riddle comes in the form of an answer, not a question, should not surprise us, given the numerous warnings about Nietzschean riddles as parabolic, paradoxical statements that go beyond the simple question/answer format. The satyr's notion that "the best thing in life is never to have been born" is the same knowledge that Heidegger refers to as "knowledge that chokes us as what must be known if being as a whole is to be thought" and that is "necessary to attain the best." For mortality is that which is, by definition, defined by limits, beginning with the limit imposed by death, whereas to "attain the best" and become godlike ("immortal," literally "undying") it is necessary to exceed human limits. To choke on the wisdom of Silenus is thus to understand the inherent nature of human suffering by mere virtue of becoming human and thereby limiting its transcendent, transformative potential.

This most tragic, most abysmal of statements is key, Nietzsche insists,[21] to understanding the birth of the laughing Olympians, for it is only by acknowledging life as a whole world of torment wherein nothing ("no thing") is preserved that eternity is born. If Zarathustra chooses to "become man again," to return to this mortal world of torment and destruction, it is not because he has forgotten the miserable reality of the world after all his years of isolation but because his eternal, rapturous overabundance wills the recreation of the same forms that his overabundant spirit also denies.[22] The Dionysian wills the Apollonian, it desires to become human again, because the overabundant spirit, out of its overabundance, is now ready to begin again. "Tragedy begins" can now be understood as this birthing, or beginning, of forms that emerge from an excessiveness that must always return, in the end, to destroy them.

Notes

Introduction

1. In *Origin and Early Form of Greek Tragedy* (New York: Norton, 1965), Gerald Else discusses this phrase reported in the Suda and elsewhere, which he analyzes as the complaint about the movement away from Dionysian revelry and toward seriousness.

2. Jacques Derrida, "The Law of Genre," *Glyph* 7 (1980): 176–201.

3. Each of the six constituent elements of tragedy is superior or inferior to another, the choral ode is excluded from the discussion, tragedy is superior to epic, and so forth. See Paul Gordon, "Enigma of Aristotelian Metaphor," *Metaphor and Symbolic Activity* 5.2 (1990): 83–90.

4. "To resist Dionysus is to repress the elemental in one's own nature; the punishment is the sudden complete collapse of the inward dikes when the elemental breaks through perforce and civilization vanishes" (E. R. Dodds, "Introduction," in *The Bacchae*, ed. E. R. Dodds [New York: Oxford University Press, 1944], xvi).

5. Aristotle, *Poetics* (Ann Arbor: University of Michigan Press, 1970), 29.

6. "It is important to make fitting use of all the devices we have mentioned, including compounds and foreign words, *but by far the most important thing is to be good at metaphor.* This is the only part of the job that cannot be learned from others; on the contrary it is a token of high native gifts" (ibid., xxii, 60 [emphasis added]).

7. Parallels to the story of Pentheus's resistance are numerous; for example, the myth of Lycurgus (Homer, *Iliad* [New York: Penguin, 1990], 199).

8. Nietzsche emphasizes the "fraternal union" between the Apollonian and Dionysian throughout *The Birth of Tragedy* (Garden City, N.Y.: Doubleday, 1956), xxi, 131. Subsequent references to this work appear parenthetically in the text (section numbers are in roman, page numbers in arabic).

9. Dodds, "Introduction," xi–xii.

10. In *The Birth of Tragedy*, Nietzsche writes: "Dionysus remains the sole dramatic protagonist and all the famous characters of the Greek stage, Prometheus, Oedipus, etc. are only masks of that original hero" (x, 66).

11. See my essay "Misogyny, Dionysianism, and a New Model of Greek Tragedy," *Women's Studies* 17.3 (1989): 211–18.

12. Martha Nussbaum, *The Fragility of Goodness* (Cambridge: Cambridge University Press, 1986), 25 (emphasis added). I should state that I am not opposed to a moralistic reading of tragedy such as Nussbaum's, except where it leaves out the Dionysian element against which such Penthean seriousness is displayed. As I have argued elsewhere (see *"Lord Jim*, Paul de Man, and the Debate between Deconstructive and Humanistic Criticism," *Literature/Interpretation/Theory* 9 [1998]: 65–84), morality is not anathema to art—or to Nietzsche studies, for that matter—except when it is used to stop the work from saying more than what is moralistically defined as such.

13. In *Tragic Themes in Western Literature* (New Haven, Conn.: Yale University Press, 1955), Cleanth Brooks writes: "Under the circumstances, it is a temptation to say that all these 'tragedies' treat *seriously* a life-and-death problem. . . . On the tragic hero, suffering is never merely imposed: he incurs it by his own decision" (4 [emphasis added]). For writers such as Richard Sewall, in *The Vision of Tragedy* (New Haven, Conn.: Yale University Press, 1980), the sense of a confrontation in tragedy with the ultimate meaning, or meaninglessness, of existence is compatible with (but essentially different from) the view of tragic rapture being proffered here.

14. Sigmund Freud, *Introductory Lectures on Psychoanalysis* (New York: Norton, 1966), 231.

15. Among other places that Freud posits his interpretation of Sophocles' play, see ibid., 330–31. In *Mythe et tragédie en Grèce ancienne* (Paris: Maspero, 1981), 75–94, Jean Pierre Vernant argues, somewhat surprisingly, that Oedipus's conscious ignorance of his transgression refutes Freud's reading.

16. For example: "Many things the gods / Achieve beyond our judgment. What we thought / Is not confirmed and what we thought not god / Contrives. And so it happens in this story" (*Euripides I* [Chicago: University of Chicago Press, 1955], 108).

17. Although Nietzsche does not always use the term "rapture" (*Rausch*) in *The Birth of Tragedy* to describe what is here referred to as the *Urlust* of "primal Dionysiac delight," his reliance on the notion of rapture throughout his writings as an "overfull, teeming will that comes as a consequence of all great desires, all strong affects" (*Twilight of the Idols*, qtd. in Martin Heidegger, *Nietzsche*, trans. David Krell, 2 vols. [San Francisco: HarperCollins, 1991], 1:96–97) is clear and consistent.

18. I support this bold claim in the final chapter, which interprets *Thus Spoke Zarathustra* and its doctrine of "the eternal return of the same" through similar terms established in *The Birth of Tragedy*.

19. Nietzsche discusses the wisdom of Silenus in chapter 3 of *The Birth of Tragedy*. This concept will be referred to numerous times in this book.

20. Heidegger, *Nietzsche*, 1:97.

21. Michel Deguy, "The Discourse of Exaltation: Contribution to a Rereading

of Pseudo-Longinus," in *Of the Sublime: Presence in Question*, ed. Jeffrey S. Librett (Albany: State University of New York Press, 1993), 5–6.

22. Longinus, *On the Sublime* (Cambridge, Mass.: Harvard University Press, 1960), 227.

23. W. B. Yeats, *Ideas of Good and Evil* (London: Bullen, 1903), 279–80.

24. Freud, *Introductory Lectures on Psychoanalysis*, 50 (emphasis added).

25. Paul Garon, *Blues and the Poetic Spirit* (London: Eddison Press, 1975), 37.

26. Theodor Adorno, *Negative Dialectics* (New York: Seabury Press, 1973), 361.

27. Cf. "Indeed, my friends, believe with me in this Dionysiac life and in the rebirth of tragedy!" (Nietzsche, *Birth of Tragedy* xx, 124).

28. George Steiner, *The Death of Tragedy* (New York: Knopf, 1961), 194.

29. Alain Robbe-Grillet, "Nature, Humanism, Tragedy," in *For a New Novel*, trans. Richard Howard (New York: Grove Press, 1965), 49–75.

30. In *The Tragic Sense of Life* (Philadelphia: University of Pennsylvania Press, 1921), Miguel de Unamuno argues that the tragic conflict between humanity's mortal limits and immortal aspirations is timeless. However, he insists on defining this conflict in pessimistic terms (e.g., "he sinks into the despair of the critical century whose two greatest victims were Nietzsche and Tolstoy" [328]). Unamuno thereby differs with the present work's view of Nietzsche's tragic rapture as life-affirming.

Chapter 1: Nietzsche's Double Vision of Tragedy

1. In *Nietzsche's Voice* (Ithaca, N.Y.: Cornell University Press, 1990), Henry Staten speaks of "the notorious complexity of *The Birth of Tragedy* itself, even apart from any critical methodology one might bring to it, the labyrinthine crossings and returns of its argument that baffle any summary that tries to be faithful to the nuance and apparent contradiction on major points that we find there" (188). Without explicit reference to Staten's work, John Sallis refers to the same intricate pattern of overlapping and intersecting ideas in *Crossings: Nietzsche and the Space of Tragedy* (Chicago: University of Chicago Press, 1991).

2. In *Versuch über das Tragische* (Frankfurt: Insel, 1961), Peter Szondi writes: "Die Geburt der Tragödie hat ihr Pathos zwar in der Abwehr der Resignationslehre Schopenhauers, ist aber bis ins einzelne von dessen System geprägt" (45; The *Birth of Tragedy* certainly rejects Schopenhauer's notion of resignation but is nonetheless influenced in its details by the Schopenhauerian system). Ivan Soll's "Pessimism and the Tragic View of Life: Reconsiderations of Nietzsche's *Birth of Tragedy*" (in *Reading Nietzsche*, ed. Robert Solomon and Kathleen Higgins [New York: Oxford University Press, 1988], 104–31) provides an excellent analysis of the Schopenhauerian and Kantian concepts behind many of the key formulations in Nietzsche's work. I would disagree, however, with the author's contention that Nietzsche was not aware, in *The Birth of Tragedy*, of the weaknesses in Schopenhauer's position. For example, Nietzsche writes: "being in danger of longing for a Buddhistic negation of the will . . . art saves him [the profound Hellene], and through art, life" (*Birth of Tragedy* vii, 51).

3. For example, see Nietzsche's claim that "myth was now seized by the newborn genius of Dionysiac music, in whose hands it flowered once more" (*Birth of*

Tragedy x, 68). The most vicious attack on Nietzsche's questionable (and, at times, anachronistic) assumptions about the origin of Greek tragedy is still the very first: Wilamowitz-Moellendorff's famous refutation, "Zukunftsphilologie," which was published the same year as the *Geburt.* See Ulrich von Wilamowitz-Moellendorff, "Zukunftsphilologie" (in *Der Streit um Nietzsches "Geburt der Tragödie,"* ed. Karlfried Gründer [Hildesheim: Olms, 1969], 27–55) regarding Nietzsche's Schopenhauerian assumptions.

4. In *The Birth of Tragedy,* Nietzsche writes: "The metaphysical solace with which, I wish to say at once, all true tragedy sends us away" (vii, 50). He clearly identifies the goal of tragedy with that of art in general when he refers, for example, to "the highest goal of tragedy and art in general" as synonymous (xxi, 131).

5. "Spiel . . . welches der Wille, *in der ewigen Fülle seiner Lust,* mit sich selbst spielt" (Friedrich Nietzsche, *Werke,* ed. Karl Schlechta, vol. 1 [Frankfurt: Ulstein, 1969], 131). This crucial statement needs to be read alongside Nietzsche's description of the world, in *Philosophy in the Age of Tragedy,* as a "spiel der Zeus oder physikalischer ausgedruckt des Feuers mit sich selbst" (qtd. in Thomas Böning, *Metaphysik, Kunst und Sprache beim frühen Nietzsche* [Berlin: de Gruyter, 1988], 245; Zeus's game or, expressed physically, of fire with itself). Although I disagree with a number of the main assertions of "Genesis and Genealogy," Paul de Man's important essay on *The Birth of Tragedy* in his *Allegories of Reading* (New Haven, Conn.: Yale University Press, 1979)—e.g., his mockery of the "deadly power of [Dionysian] music" as a "myth that can not stand the ridicule of literal description" (97–98)—his gloss on the phrase that I have singled out for analysis here occurs at the point in the essay where de Man decides to honor Nietzsche, "not to bury him": "This process is itself called 'an artistic game that the will, in the eternal plenitude of its pleasure, plays with itself,' a formulation in which every word is ambivalent and enigmatic, since the will has been discredited as a self, the pleasure shown to be a lie, the fullness to be absence of meaning, and the play the endless tension of a nonidentity, a pattern of dissonance that contaminates the very source of the will, the will as a source" (99). For more on the disagreement with de Man's treatment of *The Birth of Tragedy,* see Henry Staten's fairminded "Appendix: *The Birth of Tragedy* Reconstructed" in *Nietzsche's Voice* (187–216).

6. Arthur Schopenhauer, *The World as Will and Representation* (Indian Hills, Colo.: Falcon's Wing Press, 1958).

7. In *Nietzsche,* Heidegger writes: "When the thought of the eternal return is thought, the tragic becomes the fundamental trait of beings" (2:28). Occasional references to volume 1 of the Neske edition of Heidegger's German text (*Nietzsche* [Pfullingen: Neske, 1961] give the letter "G" before the page number.

8. Nietzsche's *Thus Spoke Zarathustra,* trans. R. J. Hollingdale (New York: Penguin, 1961) begins with such superabundant overflowing, which then extends to such notions as that of the "Over-man" (39).

9. Heidegger, *Nietzsche,* 2:28–29.

10. As Staten makes clear in *Nietzsche's Voice* (187–216), even so rigorous a critic as de Man is not immune to this tendency to read *The Birth of Tragedy* "too quickly" (to quote Pascal). M. S. Silk and J. P. Stern's *Nietzsche on Tragedy* (London: Cambridge University Press, 1981) was the only work, until quite recently, to focus solely on *The Birth of Tragedy.* Unfortunately, given their lengthy inclu-

sion of biographical information, chapter summaries, and so forth, their unphilo-sophical book does not really fill the gap that they deplore.

11. References to other theories of Nietzsche's theory of tragedy are found throughout this chapter and this book. I would mention, though, as an example of the tendency to avoid the issue of "rapturously engendered form," Tracy Strong's writings on Nietzsche, specifically his essay on *The Birth of Tragedy*, "Aesthetic Authority and Tradition: Nietzsche and the Greeks," *History of European Ideas* 11 (1989): 989–1007. Strong argues for a theory of tragedy as "metaphoricity" that is never clearly defined but seems related to a sense of the genre's openness to different meanings (à la New Criticism or reader response criticism). Strong wrongly rejects, I think, the notion that Nietzsche places tragedy in the context of a specific philosophy of *nature* as rapturous, Dionysian excess (998, 1001).

12. While not all critical attention to Heidegger's two volumes on *Nietzsche* has been as hostile as Walter Kaufmann's foreword in *Philosophy and Truth*, ed. D. Breazele (Atlantic Highlands, N.J.: Humanities Press, 1979), the "benign neglect" of most writers is, perhaps, just as damning. Anglo-American studies have largely neglected the work: for example, *Nietzsche as Affirmative Thinker: Papers Presented at the Fifth Jerusalem Philosophical Encounter, April 1983*, ed. Yirmiahu Yovel (Boston: Nijhof, 1986); and *Reading Nietzsche*, ed. Robert C. Solomon and Kathleen M. Higgins (Oxford: Oxford University Press, 1988). Alexander Nehamas's *Nietzsche: Life as Literature* (Cambridge, Mass.: Harvard University Press, 1985), which resembles Heidegger's work in emphasizing the fragmentary will-to-power, nonetheless avoids any confrontation with Heidegger's *Nietzsche*. A notable exception to this neglect is Gianni Vattimo's discussion of Heidegger's *Nietzsche* in *The Adventure of Difference* (Baltimore: Johns Hopkins University Press, 1993). Vattimo notes at the outset that "[Heidegger's] book on Nietzsche has answered a real need in Nietzsche criticism" (85), although I would disagree with his assertion that Heidegger does not pay "sufficient attention to the aesthetic model which in reality underlies the will to power" (88).

13. In *Metaphysik, Kunst und Sprache beim frühen Nietzsche*, Böning writes concerning Nietzsche's identification of all the arts with tragedy: "Sie all erwachsen aus jener tragische Erkenntnis—schöpferisch macht für Nietzsche allein das Leiden" (235; All [the arts] are derived from tragic knowledge; for Nietzsche only suffering leads to creatvity).

14. In *Nietzsche*, Heidegger writes: "in willing we know ourselves as out beyond ourselves; we sense a mastery over . . . a thrill of pleasure announces to us the power attained, a power that enhances itself" (1:52; "wissen wir uns als über uns hinaus; ein irgendwie errichtes Herrsein über . . . wird fühlbar; eine Lust gibt die erreichte und sich steigende Macht zu wissen" [G.64]).

15. From Nietzsche's *Twilight of the Idols*, qtd. in Heidegger, *Nietzsche*, 1:96–97 (G.115).

16. Ibid., 1:97.

17. In *Nietzsche and Greek Thought* (Dordrecht: Nijhoff, 1987), Victorino Tejera is acutely sensitive to the similarity and opposition of the Dionysian and Apollonian: "both of them are instinct-driven social formations . . . [but] the two art-impulses out of whose mixing tragedy was born are not reducible to each other" (59–60). It is not possible, in other words, to oppose the Apollonian and Di-

onysian in terms of intellect versus passion, as often occurs. Heidegger's statement that "the formula of Apollonian and Dionysian opposition has long been the refuge of all confused and confusing talk and writing about art and about Nietzsche" (*Nietzsche*, 1:103) reflects the feelings of many Nietzsche scholars.

18. Heidegger, *Nietzsche*, 1:97, 98.

19. Like Heidegger, Sallis argues in *Crossings* for the continued importance of *The Birth of Tragedy* to Nietzsche's later work.

20. Heidegger, *Nietzsche*, 1:120 (G.141).

21. Ibid., 1:116 (G.137).

22. Ibid., 1:117. "Schaffen ist das einfacher und stärker sehende Heraustreiben der Hauptzüge" (G.137).

23. From Nietzsche's *Will to Power*, qtd. in ibid., 1:116 (emphasis added) (G.136).

24. Ibid., 1:137. "Des Schrecklichen Anfang, den wir noch gerade ertragen"; "wovor wir noch gerade bestehen könnten" (G.116).

25. Ibid., 1:122 (G.144).

26. Ibid., 1:144, 145.

27. From Nietzsche's *Will to Power*, qtd. in ibid., 1:73, 75.

28. See chapter 3, in which the very similar view of creative destruction in Yeats's "Lapis Lazuli" and other poems is discussed.

29. From Nietzsche's *Twilight of the Idols* and *The Will to Power*, respectively, qtd. in Heidegger, *Nietzsche*, 1:96, 71.

30. Ibid., 1:72–73.

31. Ibid., 1:98, 100 (emphasis added).

32. In *Claim of Reason* (Oxford: Oxford University Press, 1979), Stanley Cavell suggests that the tragic moment is the moment of recognition (*anagnorisis*) when the hero realizes (as Oedipus, Lear, Phaedra, and so many others do) who he or she is: "Here the tragedy is that the cost of claiming one's identity may claim one's life" (389). This might seem opposed to a view of tragedy as "rapturous overabundance" but actually complements it, for the anagnoristic moment of recognition, of naming comes after, as a moment of re-cognition, when the tragic hero has in some way already denied his or her "good name."

33. From Nietzsche's *Will to Power*, qtd. in Heidegger, *Nietzsche*, 1:101.

34. Sophocles' Antigone, for example, is often misread as a virtuous character rather than as the headstrong, noble-minded daughter of Oedipus that the play clearly presents (pace Hegel).

35. Cavell, *Claim of Reason*, 389.

36. Qtd. in Heidegger, *Nietzsche*, 1:116.

37. For example, see Else, *Origin and Early Form of Greek Tragedy*.

38. Nietzsche identifies the supreme accomplishment of tragedy with "art in general" (*Birth of Tragedy* xxi, 131). See also Böning, *Metaphysik, Kunst und Sprache beim frühen Nietzsche*, 235.

39. See the introduction.

40. Freud discusses Sophocles' play in *Introductory Lectures on Psychoanalysis*, 330–32.

41. "It was Apollo that brought this bitterness, / But the hand that struck me was none but my own" (Sophocles, *Oedipus the King*, trans. David Grene, in *Sophocles*, vol. 1 [Chicago: University of Chicago Press, 1954], 38–39).

42. In *Mythe et tragédie en Grèce ancienne*, Vernant explicitly rejects Freud's

ascription of an "Oedipus complex" to the Oedipus of Sophocles' play, while Bernard Knox, in *Oedipus at Thebes* (New Haven, Conn.: Yale University Press, 1957), emphasizes the contemporary political relevance of Sophocles' play.

43. In "Pessimism and the Tragic View of Life," Soll analyzes ways that this concept of original Being as suffering derives from Schopenhauer's reading of Kant: "Nietzsche refers to 'the truly existent primal unity, eternally suffering and contradictory.' The emphasis upon the world of things as they really are in themselves as being a 'primal unity' is almost a sure sign that Nietzsche had accepted and was working with Schopenhauer's revision of Kant's theory" (109).

44. Sui generis, but not idiosyncratic. Dodds's studies of Dionysianism among the Greeks support Nietzsche's notion of an ecstatic celebration of destruction, although Dodds does not have Nietzsche's philosophical sense of the origin of Dionysianism itself.

45. In *Nietzsche's Voice*, Staten notes a profound "ambivalence" toward this "joyful suffering" due to Nietzsche's supposed unwillingness to accept the dismemberment (*sparagmos*) of Dionysus and the individual in general. The author also relates this ambivalence to Nietzsche's elevation of the individual over the state at the same time that he insists on subordinating the meaningless individual to some higher purpose (110–11). The only qualification I would add to Staten's brilliant interpretation is that what he notes as Nietzsche's "ambiguity" is already referred to by Nietzsche himself as the Dionysian worshiper's *"Doppelheit"* in the passage just quoted. That is to say, the ambivalence toward Dionysianism (most evident in its relation to the Apollonian) is inscribed within Nietzsche's text.

46. Qtd. in Böning, *Metaphysik, Kunst und Sprache beim frühen Nietzsche*, 11.

47. Nietzsche's version of the story of Silenus and Midas is a variant on the better-known version that has Silenus granting Midas the "golden touch." See Ovid, *Metamorphoses* (New York: Viking, 1958), bk. 11, 301–2.

48. This comes, of course, from Homer's *Odyssey*, bk. 11, when Odysseus confronts the shade of the fallen hero in Hades.

49. Nehamas is a little careless when, in discussing Nietzsche's Hamlet reference, he says: "Too much [Dionysian] insight into the reality of life leads to despair and inaction: 'Knowledge kills action; action requires the veils of illusion': that is the doctrine of Hamlet" (*Nietzsche*, 119). Hamlet's inaction, it was just argued, is midway between Apollonian and Dionysian insight.

50. Sigmund Freud, "Mourning and Melancholia," in *Standard Edition*, 24 vols. (London: Hogarth, 1953–74), 14:243–58.

51. Aristotle, *Poetics* (1970), sec. viii.

52. Nietzsche uses Raphael's *Transfiguration* to illustrate the Apollonian/Dionysian forces (*Birth of Tragedy* iv, 33).

53. Nietzsche writes: "Poetry does not lie outside the world as a fantastic impossibility begotten of the poet's brain; it seeks to be the exact opposite, an unvarnished expression, and for this reason must cast away the trumpery garments worn by the supposed reality of civilized man" (*Birth of Tragedy* viii, 53). James Joyce's version of this "duperie" is evident in *Ulysses* (New York: Modern Library, 1946), where the "moody brooding" of the artist Stephan Dedalus is overshadowed by the more sensual intellect of Leopold Bloom (11).

54. The inherent tragedy of civilization from a psychoanalytic viewpoint is

discussed in chapter 4 of Sigmund Freud's *Tragedy and Psychoanalysis: Beyond the Pleasure Principle* (New York: Liveright, 1970).

55. In *Thus Spoke Zarathustra*, Nietzsche writes: "Whenever your spirit wants to speak in images, pay heed; for that is when your virtue has its origin and beginning" (101).

56. I discuss the "pyramid" of tragedy's six constitutive elements (according to Aristotle) in "The Enigma of Aristotelian Metaphor."

57. Paul de Man and others have rightly pointed to the importance of metonymy among Nietzsche's catalog of tropes (see de Man, *Allegories of Reading*, 103–18). In his course on rhetoric delivered in 1870, Nietzsche singled out metonymy as "very powerful in speech" (*Friedrich Nietzsche on Rhetoric and Language*, ed. Sander L. Gilman, Carole Blair, and David J. Parent [New York: Oxford University Press, 1989], 58–59).

58. Sophocles, *Oedipus the King*, 27.

59. This is not meant to contradict the excellent point made by Tejera in *Nietzsche and Greek Thought*, and by others, that the Apollonian beauty of the play—as evident in its masterful manipulation of irony and plot—is directly related to its horrible, repressed subject matter: "Thus, if the dialogue of tragedy is 'lucid and precise' (Apollonian), it is so in compensation for the fact that its subject-matter consists of the worse and most horrible things that can happen to a human, as in the Oedipus plays" (63–64).

60. Tracy Strong's "Oedipus as Hero: Family and Family Metaphors in Nietzsche" (in *Why Nietzsche Now?* ed. Daniel O'Hara [Bloomington: Indiana University Press, 1985], 311–36) attempts a brilliant, if inconclusive, reading of this passage (and others) in an attempt to show that, both personally and intellectually, Nietzsche's "wager is that one can go through the abyss of selflessness in order to build a transfigured world from the destruction of the old" (332). Strong offers some delectable items about Nietzsche's family relations to support his impressive "psychopathological" reading of Nietzsche's work.

61. For example, see Sophocles, *Antigone*, trans. E. Wyckoff, in *Sophocles*, vol. 1 (Chicago: University of Chicago Press, 1954), 160, and passim.

62. Sophocles, *Oedipus the King*, 64.

63. This same "invitation" is later repeated in Yeats's Fergus poems and throughout his celebration of tragic destructiveness. See chapter 3.

64. W. B. Yeats, "Lapis Lazuli," in *Collected Poems* (New York: Macmillan, 1964), 291. There is of course much yet to be said about the influence of Nietzsche on Yeats. The poem quoted, with its numerous references to Nietzschean "gaiety," recalls such lines from Nietzsche's *Also Sprach Zarathustra* (Munich: Goldmann, n.d.) as "Wer auf den höchsten Berg steigt, der lacht über alle Trauer-Spiele" (34; Whoever wishes to climb the highest mountain will laugh at all tragedies). See also chapter 3 in this book.

Chapter 2: Fulgurations

1. Phillipe Lacoue-Labarthe, "Sublime Truth," in *Of the Sublime: Presence in Question*, ed. Librett, 77.

2. Actually, the inscription is not "on the veil" (as Lacoue-Labarthe but not his translator doubtless realizes) but "on the temple of Isis." In Schiller's poem "The

Veiled Statue at Saïs," the inscription Kant refers to is repeated with significant changes in the form of indirect address spoken by the priest initiating Schiller's romantic hero.

3. Lacoue-Labarthe, "Sublime Truth," 74.

4. Ibid., 96.

5. Longinus, *On the Sublime*, xvii, 1

6. Lacoue-Labarthe, "Sublime Truth," 100.

7. In *The Birth of Tragedy*, Nietzsche speaks of painting, lyric poetry, music, and so forth, as functions of his essential aesthetic opposition between the Apollonian and the Dionysian.

8. Lacoue-Labarthe, "Sublime Truth," 103.

9. In "Tragedy and Sublimity" (in *Of the Sublime*, ed. Librett, 157–76), Jean-Francois Courtine also discusses the sublime: "Finally I will ask whether one can view tragedy, in accordance with the triple function Schelling assigns to art at the end of the *System of Transcendental Idealism*, as the supreme accomplishment of art, as the work *par excellence*, that work which more than any other illuminates the essence of art and its properly philosophical or speculative import" (158).

10. Longinus, *On the Sublime*, i, 227, xvi, 215, 235, ixx, 191.

11. Ibid., xxxv, 181, 139, i, 225–27.

12. In "Sublime Truth," Lacoue-Labarthe writes: "what is at stake in the sublime, since Longinus, will always have been the presentation of the meta-physical as such" (72).

13. Longinus, *On the Sublime*, xxxiv, 225.

14. Ibid., 225.

15. The "tenor" of metaphor, as described by Richards, Black, and other "interactionists" is not to be construed as the "meaning" of the metaphor. For a discussion of these theories see my book *The Critical Double: Figurative Meaning in Aesthetic Discourse* (Tuscaloosa: University of Alabama Press, 1995), 19–37.

16. In *The Birth of Tragedy*, Nietzsche writes that tragedy is a "game which the will, in the eternal superabundance of its pleasure, plays with itself" (xxiv, 143).

17. Immanuel Kant, *The Critique of Judgement*, trans. James Creed Meredith (Oxford: Clarendon Press, 1952), 179 (emphasis added).

18. Ibid., 107. The bracketed German phrases are from Immanuel Kant, *Kritik der Urteilskraft* (Frankfurt: Suhrkamp, 1979), 181.

19. For example, Nietzsche speaks of the "überschwänglichen Fruchtbarkeit des Weltwillens" (the overflowing fecundity of the primordial will) that is expressed in the destructiveness of "die dionysische Kunst [Dionysian art]" (*Werke*, 1:93).

20. Kant, *Critique of Judgement*, 94.

21. Ibid., 90.

22. Ibid., 110; Aristotle, *Poetics* (Cambridge, Mass.: Harvard University Press, 1973), 45.

23. Kant, *Critique of Judgement*, 111.

24. This, as well as the Christian appropriation of the term, is the essence of Nietzsche's rejection of the idea of *hamartia*. See chapter 1 for a discussion of Nietzsche's statement that "a truly noble soul [Oedipus] is incapable of sin" (*Birth of Tragedy* ix, 60).

25. Aristotle, *Poetics* (1973), 9.

26. "The human intelligence which Oedipus represents" (125) is the subject of

Bernard Knox's careful examination of the language of logic, science, and evidentiary reasoning in Sophocles' play. See Bernard Knox, *Oedipus at Thebes* (New Haven, Conn.: Yale University Press, 1957), esp. chap. 3.

27. Kant, *Critique of Judgement*, 91.

28. Ibid., 90.

29. Although Kant discusses music briefly in the "Analytic of the Sublime," he does not consider it sublime (to say the least) but rather discusses only its "comparative estimate of aesthetic worth among the fine arts" (ibid., 191).

30. Ibid., 120.

31. Although his "estimation" of music's worth is generally lacking, even Kant acknowledges that "mathematics, certainly, does not play the smallest part in the charm and movement of the mind produced by music" (ibid., 195).

32. In *Aesthetics* (trans. F. B. Osmaston, 2 vols. [London: Bell and Sons, 1920]), G. W. F. Hegel writes: "We find as nowhere else this art of the Sublime, as a mode of its original appearance, in the religious conceptions of the Hebrew race and their sacred poetry . . . what we are most amazed at here is the power of spiritual exaltation which suffers everything else to fall way that it may declare the unique Almightiness of God" (2:99, 103).

33. The veil is a popular figure among most theoreticians/philosophers concerned with knowledge and its limits, and Nietzsche is no exception. In *The Birth of Tragedy*, the image is frequently used (and even more often implied—e.g., "the true goal is covered over by a phantasm" [iii, 31]) to represent the Apollonian appearance of the Dionysian "in-itself": "In the Dionysiac dithyramb man is incited to strain his symbolic faculties to the utmost; something quite unheard of is now clamoring to be heard: the desire to tear asunder the veil of Maya, to sink back into the original oneness of nature" (ii, 27).

Chapter 3: "Troubled Ecstasy"

1. Frances Oppel, "Thinking about Tragedy: Yeats's *Purgatory* and Modern Tragic Theory," *Genre* 23 (Spring 1990): 33–46.

2. Timothy Reiss's *Tragedy and Truth* (New Haven, Conn.: Yale University Press, 1980) makes a very useful distinction between *tragedy* and the *tragic*, the latter being the real situation of meaninglessness that "has no possible resolution," the former being the artistic system of discourse that orders, and defines, that lack (17). My main problem with Reiss's distinction is that it "excludes the middle" possibility that is common to each.

3. Richard Ellmann's *Yeats: The Man and the Masks* (New York: Macmillan, 1948) sees Yeats's growth as a poet in symbolic terms as a movement away from the more romantic rose to the more subjective and (somewhat paradoxically) systematic mask.

4. The reference is of course to Steiner's *Death of Tragedy*. I disagree strongly with Steiner's notion that modern tragedy, with its lack of any transcendental framework such as that against which Greek and Elizabethan drama stood, is inherently impossible. One need only look to Nietzsche for confirmation that the "death of God" can (and for Nietzsche certainly does) coexist with a tragic view of life.

5. See Eitel Timm, *William Butler Yeats und Friedrich Nietzsche* (Würzburg:

Königshausen and Neumann, 1980), 312. The other main works on Yeats and Nietzsche are Frances Oppel's *Mask and Tragedy: Yeats and Nietzsche, 1902–10* (Charlottesville: University Press of Virginia, 1987) and Otto Bohlmann's *Yeats and Nietzsche* (Totowa, N.J.: Barnes and Noble, 1982). The consensus of these works is that the precise nature of the Yeats-Nietzsche relationship is left ambiguous. We know that Yeats mentions Nietzsche as early as his collection of essays *Ideas of Good and Evil* (1903), that he probably was aware of Nietzsche's ideas from an article by Ellis in 1896, and that as early as 1902 he owned a copy of Common's edition of *Nietzsche,* in which he added many notes of his own. I agree wholeheartedly with the middle position held by Alex Zwerdling in *Yeats and the Heroic Ideal* (New York: New York University Press, 1965), which urges us to "remember that the ideas which we might think were actually derived from the philosopher can in fact be seen in Yeats' own work before 1902" (21).

6. In *Tragic Victory: The Doctrine of Subjective Salvation in the Poetry of W. B. Yeats* (Troy, N.Y.: Whitston Press, 1987), Larry Brunner writes of Yeats: "As he progressed as a poet . . . art revealed more and more to Yeats that the essence of human experience is tragic" (2). Although he lends support to the widespread but pernicious notion of Yeats's supposedly inferior early work, Brunner does include a number of early poems in his study.

7. Yeats, *Collected Poems,* 36.

8. "Man can embody truth but he cannot know it. I must embody it in the completion of my life" (*Letters of W. B. Yeats,* ed. Allan Wade [London: Rupert Hart-Davis, 1954], 922).

9. Yeats's borrowings from Plato and the Neoplatonists are well known. See, for example, Robert Snukal, *High Talk: The Philosophical Poetry of W. B. Yeats* (Cambridge: Cambridge University Press, 1973), 23, for Yeats's philosophical idealism.

10. Yeats constantly plays on the homonyms of "rose" throughout his *Rose* collection. For example, see "Sorrow of Love": "A girl arose that had red mournful lips" (*Collected Poems,* 40).

11. Ibid., 40.

12. See Paul de Man's chapter "Image and Emblem in Yeats" in his *Rhetoric of Romanticism* (New York: Columbia University Press, 1984), 145–238.

13. See Harold Bloom, *Yeats* (New York: Oxford University Press, 1970), 108; William Empson, *Seven Types of Ambiguity* (New York: New Directions, 1966), 187–91.

14. In *Yeats and the Poetry of Death* (New Haven, Conn.: Yale University Press, 1990), Jahan Ramazani discusses Yeats's controversial flirtation with fascism in the 1930s. One should also consult Elizabeth Butler Cullingford's fair-minded analysis *Yeats, Ireland, and Fascism* (New York: New York University Press, 1981) for further discussion of this matter.

15. Yeats, *Collected Poems,* 32.

16. In *Yeats,* Bloom writes: "This ['Who Goes with Fergus?'] is not the defeated Fergus of 'Fergus and the Druid'" (112).

17. Yeats, *Ideas of Good and Evil,* 286.

18. This felicitous phrase comes from Brunner's *Tragic Victory.* He sees, as I do, that "to Yeats the essence of human experience is tragic" (2), but he does not stress the positive value of this experience for the poet's sense of beauty.

19. Compare another of Yeats's remarkable early poems, "The Stolen Child":

Where dips the rocky highland
Of Sleuth Wood in the lake,
There lies a leafy island
Where flapping herons wake
The drowsy water-rats;
There we've hid our faery vats,
Full of berries
And of reddest stolen cherries.
Come away, O human child!
To the waters and the wild
With a faery, hand in hand,
For the world's more full of weeping than
    you can understand. (Collected Poems, 18)

20. In *The Birth of Tragedy*, Nietzsche asks: "How can ugliness and disharmony, which are the content of tragic myth, inspire an esthetic delight?" (xxiv, 143).

21. Sophocles, *Oedipus the King*, 64.

22. In *Gaiety of Language* (Berkeley: University of California Press, 1968), Frank Lentricchia is one of the few major critics to try to incorporate *Ideas of Good and Evil* into a reading of Yeats's poetics. Paul de Man is another; see his "Image and Emblem in Yeats," 145–238. Coincidentally, both Lentricchia and de Man were writing their works as doctoral dissertations about the same time, yet both reached almost opposite conclusions regarding similar essays such as "Symbolism and Painting." According to Zwerdling, Yeats's decisive first reading of Nietzsche occurred one year before *Ideas of Good and Evil*, in 1902: "we must remember . . . the ideas which we might think were actually derived from the philosopher can in fact be seen in Yeats' own work before 1902" (*Yeats and the Heroic Ideal*, 21).

23. Yeats, *Ideas of Good and Evil*, 288–89.

24. It is Buck Mulligan's statement to Stephen Dedalus to give up his "moody brooding" that triggers the allusion to "Who Goes with Fergus?" (Joyce, *Ulysses*, 11).

25. Freud's most famous discussion of this disorder is in "Mourning and Melancholia," but the larger implications of civilization as inherently "melancholic" are found throughout Freud's writings. See chapter 4 in this book.

26. Yeats, *Ideas of Good and Evil*, 285–86.

27. Ibid., 289.

28. Ibid., 279–80 (emphasis added).

29. Adding to the confusion is the fact that "Who Goes with Fergus?" first appeared in yet another context, Yeats's "first important play," *Countess Cathleen*, which precedes *The Rose* (Bloom, *Yeats*, 118). Although it may be unlikely that Yeats would have put "Who Goes with Fergus?" after "Fergus and the Druid" if he had intended it to precede the latter, it is by no means certain that this was not his intention. As Empson points out in *Seven Types of Ambiguity*, "Fergus and the Druid" does not necessarily precede the events described in "Who Goes with Fergus?" (188–89).

30. Yeats, *Collected Poems*, 43.

31. At one point, Bloom states that "only the poetic failure . . . mattered to

Yeats, as the Fergus poems in *The Rose* continued to demonstrate" (*Yeats*, 110); but two pages later, he says of "Who Goes with Fergus?": "This is not the defeated Fergus of *Fergus and the Druid*, but a poet-king of wish fulfillment who has pierced the woods' mystery and danced upon the shore" (112).

32. Empson, *Seven Types of Ambiguity*, 188–89.

33. Yeats, *Collected Poems*, 19.

34. Ibid., 18.

35. Ibid., 191. In *Yeats: A Psychoanalytic Study* (Stanford, Calif.: Stanford University Press, 1973), Brenda S. Webster's attempt to read this poem in a less ambiguous manner results in too reductive an antithesis: "In 'Sailing to Byzantium' Yeats, in order to banish sadness, makes use of both a good object that banishes bad objects—the precious golden bird—and a good feeling . . . gaiety, that banishes bad feelings" (220).

36. The sinister implications of these lines are not lost on M. L. Rosenthal, one of the most famous editors of Yeats's poems: "in 'Who Goes with Fergus?,' the impersonal sea and stars, for example, are made to seem distraught and erotically perturbed by the figurative language that associates them with white breasts and 'dishevelled wandering' lovers" (*Selected Poems of Yeats* [New York: Macmillan, 1962], xxii).

37. Empson, *Seven Types of Ambiguity*, 189.

38. Yeats, *Collected Poems*, 184.

39. Bloom, *Yeats*, 322, 325.

40. Ibid., 321.

41. Yeats, *Collected Poems*, 185.

42. Longinus, *On the Sublime*, 227. Longinus's work and the relation of tragedy to sublimity are discussed in chapter 4.

43. For example, Yeats notes that the "tragic generation" of his youth "followed more than any other I know of in the way of the mighty poets their miserable end" (qtd. in *Yeats and the Theatre*, ed. Robert O'Driscoll and Lrona Reynolds [London: Macmillan, 1975], 80).

44. See, for example, Yeats's "Faery Song": "We who are old, old and gay / O so old! / Thousands of years, thousands of years, / If all were told" (*Collected Poems*, 38).

45. Ibid., 291.

46. This is not of course the only time Nietzsche uses this image of metallic, stonelike hardening. In *Ecce Homo* (New York: Penguin, 1979), he demonstrates his continued allegiance to Dionysus when, discussing his book *Thus Spoke Zarathustra*, he writes: "Among the decisive preconditions for a dionysian task is the hardness of the hammer, joy even in destruction. The imperative 'become hard,' the deepest certainty that all creators are hard, is the actual mark of a Dionysian nature" (111).

47. See Bloom, *Yeats*, 318 and passim.

48. Compare the following passage from "Certain Noble Plays of Japan," in Yeats's *Essays and Introductions* (New York: Macmillan, 1967): "A mask will enable me to substitute for the face of some commonplace player . . . the fine invention of a sculpture, and to bring the audience close enough to the play to hear every inflection of the voice" (226).

49. Qtd. in Brunner, *Tragic Victory*, 49.

50. Ibid., 42, 52.

51. For example, see "Faery Song": "We who are old, old and gay, / O so old! / Thousands of years, thousands of years, / If all were told" (Yeats, *Collected Poems*, 38).

Chapter 4: Tragedy and Psychoanalysis

1. Sigmund Freud, *Jenseits des Lustprinzips* (1920), in *Gesammelte Werke*, 17 vols. (London: Imago, 1940–[52]), 13:3–69; Freud, *Beyond the Pleasure Principle* (New York: Liveright, 1961).

2. See my essay "Misogyny, Dionysianism, and a New Model of Greek Tragedy."

3. This is the only extant tragedy about the god of tragedy; but, it should be pointed out, there are numerous important yet often overlooked choral odes about Dionysus in such plays as Sophocles' *Oedipus Tyrannus* and *Antigone*.

4. In *The Birth of Tragedy*, Nietzsche unfortunately adopts the typical "party line" regarding Euripides' "rationalistic" inadequacies as voiced by Hegel and numerous others before and since (secs. xii, xiv, and xvii).

5. Sophocles, *Antigone*, 179.

6. Recall that Greek tragedies were always performed in Dionysus's honor, during his biannual "holidays" and with his surrogate priest in attendance as overseer.

7. The general Freudian view of art as evident in such essays as "The Poet and Daydreaming" is as a "return of the repressed" desires of civilized society (*Standard Edition*, 9:143).

8. The term "conflict of two rights" is Bradley's ("Hegel's Theory of Tragedy," in *Oxford Lectures in Poetry* [London: Macmillan, 1950], 69–95), but the *idea* is definitely Hegel's, as elaborated in his *Philosophy of Fine Art*, 4 vols. (London: Bell and Sons, 1920).

9. Sigmund Freud, *Civilization and Its Discontents* (New York: Dover, 1994), 77–78 (emphasis added).

10. Ibid., 75.

11. Ibid., 77.

12. It is for this reason that Nietzsche's frequent vilifications of this "golden rule" do not preclude his endorsing it when understood, as in *Thus Spoke Zarathustra*, as a way of loving oneself.

13. Freud, *Civilization and Its Discontents*, 76.

14. In "Freud's *'Über den Gegensinn der Urworte'*: Psychoanalysis, Art, and the Antithetical Senses," *Style* 24.2 (1990): 167–86, I argue for the importance of this idea in psychoanalytic theory.

15. In *Civilizations and Its Discontents*, Freud writes: "at bottom the sense of guilt is nothing but a topographical variety of anxiety" (69).

16. Sewall argues in *Vision of Tragedy* that "Aeschylus . . . was the first to subject the idea of justice to the full dialectic of action. It became a recurrent theme in all Greek tragedy, from *Prometheus* and the *Oresteia* to *Medea* and the *Bacchae*" (29). But if, as Sewall argues, justice is the essential theme of tragedy, that does not explain, as the theory of tragic rapture proffered here explains, why we enjoy plays where injustice inevitably prevails.

17. Freud, *Civilization and Its Discontents*, 71.

18. Ibid., 47. In *Freud's Odyssey* (New Haven, Conn.: Yale University Press, 1982), Stan Draenos writes: "None of Freud's works is so tortuously argued as *Beyond the Pleasure Principle*" (133). For example, as Freud writes in *Civilization and Its Discontents*, the death-drive is opposed to the libido but is identifiable with sadism (53).

19. Freud, *Beyond the Pleasure Principle*, 49. For Freud's earlier theory of sadomasochism see his *Three Essays on the Theory of Sexuality* in *Standard Edition*, 7:157ff.

20. Freud, "Sexual Life of Human Beings," in *Introductory Lectures on Psychoanalysis*, 303–19.

21. Freud, *Beyond the Pleasure Principle*, 54, 47.

22. Ibid., 32–35, 49.

23. In "The Theme of the Three Caskets," written prior to *Beyond the Pleasure Principle*, Freud is unclear whether the desire for death (Portia's leaden casket) is simply a structural reversal (the choice of a beautiful woman being the opposite of being chosen by death) or a desire in its own right, whereas the later work offers a different explanation of the "ancient theme" (in Freud, *Writings on Art and Literature* [rpt., Stanford: Stanford University Press, 1997], 109–21).

24. This is Nietzsche's term for pessimism, which is not based on a "strong" indifference to life's misfortunes (*Birth of Tragedy*, 1887 preface).

25. Michael Jameson writes: "The god himself [Dionysus] is represented to a surprising degree as detached and unconcerned with sex" ("Asexuality of Dionysus," in *Masks of Dionysus*, ed. Thomas H. Carpenter and Christopher A. Faraone [Ithaca, N.Y.: Cornell University Press, 1993], 44).

26. Freud, *Beyond the Pleasure Principle*, 34 (emphasis added). A footnote in the original added "1923" after the penultimate sentence quoted here.

27. There are seven references by five different authors (Diels A19–21) that attribute the notion that "everything is true." See Hermann Diels, *Die Fragmente der Vorsokratiker.* Zweiter Band (Berlin, 1952).

28. This idea is firmly established in Nietzsche's early unpublished essay, "Truth and Lies in an Extra-moral Sense" (1872), included in *Philosophy and Truth*, 77–91.

29. Freud, *Beyond the Pleasure Principle*, 34.

30. Ibid., 22. Nietzsche, too, discusses this "tragic" notion of Kant's in *The Birth of Tragedy* (xvii, 111).

31. Freud, *Beyond the Pleasure Principle*, 4.

32. Ibid., 50 (emphasis added).

33. Compare the German *Leid* and *Lied*, of which there is apparently no etymological connection.

34. Nietzsche's "will-to-power" is a force that, unlike "resolve" or "striving," "wills itself outside itself" (*über-sich-hinaus-wollen*) (Heidegger, *Nietzsche* 1:50–51). See my discussion of this in chapter 1.

35. Freud, *Beyond the Pleasure Principle*, 56–57.

36. Ibid., 56.

37. Ibid. (emphasis added).

38. Nietzsche writes in *The Birth of Tragedy* that "it is Apollo who tranquilizes the individual by drawing boundary lines, and who, by enjoining again and

again the practice of self-knowledge, reminds him of the holy, universal norms. But lest the Apollonian tendency to freeze all form into Egyptian rigidity" (ix, 65).

39. Sigmund Freud, *The Origins of Psychoanalysis* (New York: Basic Books, 1954).

40. In *The Birth of Tragedy*, Nietzsche writes: "So stirred, the individual forgets himself completely . . . the gospel of universal harmony is sounded, each individual becomes not only reconciled to his fellow but actually at one with him—as though the veil of Maya had been torn apart and there remained only shreds floating before the vision of mystical Oneness" (i, 22–23).

41. Freud, *Beyond the Pleasure Principle*, 56 (emphasis added).

42. Draenos makes the same point about the ultimate convergence of the life and death instincts (both of which he relates—correctly—to the development of Freud's theory of narcissism) most eloquently: "Here the Nothing that stands beyond life in death and the Everything that stands beyond life's longing for itself in the consummation of desire show themselves to be identical" (*Freud's Odyssey*, 138).

43. Freud, *Beyond the Pleasure Principle*, 11.

Chapter 5: The Life of Tragedy

1. In *The Birth of Tragedy*, Nietzsche writes: "Indeed, my friends, believe with me in this Dionysiac life and in the rebirth of tragedy!" (xx, 124). Cf. xvi, 96 and *Ecce Homo*, 78–83.

2. Steiner, *Death of Tragedy*, 194.

3. Many, such as Hegel, have followed Aristotle's initial declaration in the *Poetics* of tragedy as the most important of the literary genres ("If, then, tragedy is superior on all these counts" [xxvi, 115]). In his powerful essay "The Death of Tragedy Myth" (*Journal of Dramatic Theory and Criticism* 5.2 [Spring 1991]: 5–31), Thomas F. Van Laan notes that the idea that tragedy is dead is too "often accepted as dogma": "The writers most responsible for the formulation and dissemination of this myth are, in addition to Abel, Joseph Wood Krutch . . . and George Steiner, but numerous others have helped to spread the gospel, including several whose studies of tragedy do not explicitly assert the notion but implicitly support it by their definitions and their treatments of post-Racinian plays" (6). Unfortunately, Van Laan fails to support his otherwise valuable argument that tragedy is "alive and well" with any better theory of the genre than the ones he derides. His statement that "the relation between affirmation and tragedy has not been adequately discussed" (12) ignores one of the fundamental tenets of *The Birth of Tragedy*.

4. In Van Laan's discussion of the most important proponents of the "death-of-tragedy myth" Steiner's reliance on Hegelian concepts is obvious. According to Van Laan, Krutch argues that the "mechanistic, materialistic, and deterministic conclusions of science have destroyed our 'tragic faith,'" Abel notes that classical tragedy was made possible by a "lack of self-consciousness," and, finally, "Steiner insists (most of the time) that the changes in social life and thought that he delineates were uniform, universal, and irreversible, as opposed to their being, as is more likely the case, challenged in various ways by various thinkers" ("Death of Tragedy Myth," 21). In a Hegelian vein in *The Death of Tragedy*, Steiner him-

self writes: "As we have seen, the decline of tragedy is inseparably related to the decline of the organic world view and of its attendant context of mythological, symbolic, and ritual reference" (292).

5. G. W. Hegel, *The Philosophy of Fine Art* (New York: Hachet, 1975), 382–86.

6. Lest this seem too harsh, I found, after writing this, that Van Laan had already registered the same complaint in "The Death of Tragedy Myth": "To the extent that my speculation [about the survival of tragedy in the twentieth century] is true, it makes Steiner's formulation of the myth [of the 'death of tragedy'] even more suspect, makes it not merely the fiction the book's counter-argument reduces it to, but a fiction that even its author may not have genuinely believed" (23).

7. Although the French edition of Robbe-Grillet's *For a New Novel* only pre-dates *The Death of Tragedy* by a few years, I find Steiner's total lack of reference to this work, which contains an essay explicitly about the death of tragedy, most surprising in light of Steiner's intimate familiarity with European literature.

8. In "The Death of Tragedy Myth," Van Laan notes "the odd, loose structure of the book" (23).

9. Steiner, *Death of Tragedy*, 238 and passim. In "The Death of Tragedy Myth," Van Laan comments that Steiner "also tries to show, though without using the word, that verse is the natural medium of tragedy" (21).

10. Steiner, *Death of Tragedy*, 9, 5.

11. Ibid., 129. There are numerous examples of this contrast between Diony-sian flux and Apollonian stability; among them is the reference to Apollonian "sunspots" that soothe the eye after a look into the Dionysian abyss (Nietzsche, *Birth of Tragedy* ix, 59–60).

12. Nietzsche, *Thus Spoke Zarathustra*, 41–42.

13. Steiner, *Death of Tragedy*, 10.

14. Van Laan, "Death of Tragedy Myth," 23.

15. In *The Birth of Tragedy*, Nietzsche writes: "How can ugliness and dishar-mony, which are the content of tragic myth, inspire an esthetic delight? . . . of all the strange effects of tragedy this double claim—the need to look and at the same time to go beyond that look—is the most peculiar" (xxiv, 141–42).

16. Steiner endorses the widely held view that tragedy is distinctly Western (*Death of Tragedy*, 3). Here, too, I think Hegel's influence has resulted in too much faith in definitions. Although Nietzsche also considers the Hellenic manifesta-tions of tragedy, he does not need to restrict his definition to origins, periods, or geographical boundaries.

17. Van Laan, "Death of Tragedy Myth," 23.

18. Steiner states that "any realistic notion of tragic drama must start from the fact of catastrophe. Tragedies end badly" (*Death of Tragedy*, 8).

19. Ibid., 289, 355. Steiner writes: "*Woyzeck* is the first real tragedy of low life: That is Woyzeck's tragedy . . . One of the earliest and most enduring laments over the tragic condition of man is Cassandra's outcry in the courtyard of the house of Atreus. In the final, fragmentary scene of *Woyzeck* there are implications of grief no less universal" (274, 281).

20. Ibid., 247.

21. Ibid., 236.

22. Ibid., 293–94.

23. See chapter 4.

24. Steiner, *Death of Tragedy*, 295.

25. See chapter 3.

26. See my essay "Misogyny, Dionysianism, and a New Model of Greek Tragedy."

27. In *Aristotle's Poetics*, Else writes that "the *spoudaioi* are serious men, and many, perhaps most, of them will also be good, but the most important connotation of Aristotle's term ('spoudaios,' 'serious') is that they are noble characters, men of high seriousness" (83). I discuss Longinus's *On the Sublime* as a theory of tragedy in chapter 2.

28. Steiner, *Death of Tragedy*, 302.

29. Ibid., 300–301 (emphasis added).

30. Zarathustra's "tragedy" is discussed in chapter 8.

31. Steiner talks about the voices of the aristocrats (and Trofimov) "performing a quintet" (*Death of Tragedy*, 301). It is Mme. Ranevsky who hires the Jewish orchestra to play while the orchard is being sold to Lopakhin.

32. Ibid., 302 (emphasis added).

33. It would be interesting to consider the implications of such a "death sentence" in academic discourse; that is, what does it mean to declare an idea, a movement, a period, a style "dead"? And why is this particular figure necessary?

34. Albert Camus, *The Myth of Sisyphus*, trans. Justin O'Brien (New York: Vintage, 1955), 10–11.

35. Steiner, *Death of Tragedy*, 11.

36. Camus, *Myth of Sisyphus*, 16.

37. As has already been argued in chapter 1, this is where I would both agree and disagree with Cavell's notion of tragic recognition in *Claim of Reason*. Yes, tragedy involves learning—"the obvious scene for the learning is the moment of recognition" (389)—such as Oedipus's coming to know who he is or Lear's coming to know his folly. But such learning must always come after a life of "rapturous superabundance" in which such knowledge was expressly denied—for Don Juan just as it had been for Oedipus and Lear. As such, this knowledge must be seen, as Camus sees it in *The Myth of Sisyphus*, as paradoxical, as absurd knowledge that knows, as Oedipus and Macbeth know, that the answers to all riddles are also riddles themselves.

38. Camus, *Myth of Sisyphus*, 15–16.

39. I discuss the principle behind and the implications of aesthetic/rhetorical discourse of Camus's "thought which negates itself as soon as it is asserted" in *The Critical Double*. I have since argued, in this study and elsewhere, for the importance of humanistic grounding in such experiences as tragic rapture as adding a necessary element of referentiality to this model.

40. Camus, *Myth of Sisyphus*, 15–16.

41. Ibid., 53.

42. Ibid., 52, 56–57.

43. Ibid., 88, 89.

44. Ibid., 89–91 (emphasis added).

45. Nietzsche's *Thus Spoke Zarathustra* is discussed as a continuation of his earlier theory of tragedy in chapter 8.

46. Robbe-Grillet, "Nature, Humanism, Tragedy," 49.

47. Ibid., 53.

48. Robbe-Grillet's screenplay for *Last Year at Marienbad*, as well obvious stylistic similarities and admissions of indebtedness, attests to the enormous influence of the Czech author.

49. See my essay "Romanticism, Figuration, and Comparative Literature," *Neohelicon* 15.2 (1988): 239–59.

50. This is Aristotle's definition of metaphor: "Metaphor is the introduction [*epiphora*] of a word which belongs to something else [*onomatos allotriou*]" (*Poetics*, sec. xxi).

51. In Kafka's *Tagebücher* (ed. Max Brod [Frankfurt: S. Fischer, 1967]), the diary entry for December 6, 1921, states: "From a letter: 'I warm myself . . . in this sad winter.' Metaphors are one of the many things which cause me to despair [*verzweifeln*] of writing. The dependence of writing on the serving girl who heats the stove; on the cat which warms itself by the oven; even on the poor old man who warms himself; all these are self-sufficient actions, whereas writing is helpless, wanders outside itself, is a joke and despair" (550–51).

52. Paul Ricoeur, *La métaphore vive* (Paris: Editions du Seuil, 1975).

53. Dylan Thomas, *Collected Poems* (New York: New Directions, 1971), 52.

54. Robbe-Grillet, "Nature, Humanism, Tragedy," 51.

55. The nouveau roman and the theoretical positions laid out in Robbe-Grillet's defense of it are of course closely related to the popularity of phenomenology in France at the time.

56. Ibid., 63–64 (emphasis added).

57. Ibid., 59.

58. This is not meant as an attack on the nouveau roman but on certain of the positions laid out in Robbe-Grillet's theoretical manifesto.

Chapter 6: Nietzsche Sings the Blues

1. W. C. Handy, qtd. in William Ferris, *Blues from the Delta* (Garden City, N.Y.: Anchor/Doubleday, 1978), 36. The song is not a classical reference to the Dog Star but to the place where the Southern and Yazoo Delta Railroads intersect in the Delta (184n).

2. In *Blues and the Poetic Spirit*, Garon laments this realistic reductivism and lack of theoretical sophistication, writing that "the authors of earlier studies inevitably succumb, to a greater or lesser degree, to a sterile schematism or, at best, to a merely descriptive mode of apprehension which settles for an array of facts rather than seeking out the underlying meaning and movement. One would think, from the works of even the best of the blues critics, that such figures as Hegel, Fourier, Marx, Lautreamont, Blood, Freud, Roheim, Breton, Teige and Peret had never existed" (18). Although his approach is at times too emotional and too confident in the powers of the Marxist dialectic, and his attempt to understand the blues from a surrealistic perspective is vitiated from the outset, Garon's goal of going beyond the sociological clichés of earlier writers and analyzing the "poetic spirit" of the blues is similar to the goal here.

3. Paul Oliver, *The Story of the Blues* (Radnor, Pa.: Chilton, 1969), 13.

4. Bruce Cook, *Listen to the Blues* (New York: Scribners, 1973), 46–47 (emphasis added).

5. Ibid., 49.

6. For example, in *The Story of the Blues,* Oliver writes: "Yet, in the shifting rhythms of their playing, in the use of the flattened notes and the falling vocal phrases there remains *a glimpse* of Africa" (25; emphasis added).

7. Garon, *Blues and the Poetic Spirit,* 8.

8. I am not saying that blues artists do not sometimes refer to actual or contemporary events, although such references, in listening to the blues, are relatively scarce. When, for example, Charley Patton sings about the devastating Delta Flood of 1927 in "High Water Everywhere" ("Lord the whole roun' country Lord, river is overflowed / Lord the whole roun' country, man it's overflowed, / I would go to the hilly country, but they got me barred" [qtd. in Oliver, *Story of the Blues,* 31]), the topical reference is to be derived from what I talk about in this study as the general "metaphysical" nihilism of the blues, not the reverse. It is also interesting to note, in passing, that Oliver's analysis misses the reference in Patton's lyric to the internment of blacks to keep them from fleeing the devastation of 1927.

9. Garon, *Blues and the Poetic Spirit,* 36. Garon admits that this is precisely what previous studies of the blues, including his own, need to but always fail to address. Compare this more direct statement by Nick Perls: "'Country blues lyrics are meant to be coy—make people laugh with it or at it. The whole sadness thing about country blues is white publicity bullshit'" (qtd. in Jeff Todd Titon, *Early Downhome Blues* [Urbana: University of Illinois Press, 1977], 59). Titon goes on to argue, in much the same vein as I do in this chapter, that the blues is more aesthetic and less socially or politically relevant than realized: "The social function of the downhome musician was, outwardly, to provide entertainment. . . . a number of blues scholars recently have stressed the 'pure' entertainment quality in the downhome blues, denying claims that the music expressed deep sadness and that performances were social rituals purging sadness from singer and audience alike" (58–59).

10. In *Blues and the Poetic Spirit,* Garon asks: "How is it that we gain definite pleasure by identifying with the singer's sadness? . . . A clarification of this problem is essential if we are to understand how and why we enjoy the blues" (37). Unfortunately, he begs the question by falling back on the idea, as old as Aristotle, that the imitation of displeasure can be artistically pleasurable. This is right but leads one to ask "Why?"

11. "Seine Subjektivität hat der Künstler bereits in dem dionysischen Prozess aufgegeben" (Nietzsche, *Werke,* 1:37).

12. It is interesting to note, in this regard, the study of the noted psychologist Heinz Kohut (see "The Psychological Functions of Music," *Journal of the American Psychological Association* 3 [July 1957]: 389–407). In Garon's words, Kohut "provides us with a great service when he observes that words and their meaning are comparatively superficial and related to the secondary processes; tone, he continues, is a more primitive quality and more related to primary process activity" (*Blues and the Poetic Spirit,* 35).

13. In chapter 1 I discuss, in Heideggerian terms, Nietzsche's theory of rapture as the origin of art.

14. Garon, *Blues and the Poetic Spirit,* 37.

15. In light of the profound connection in Nietzsche's text between music and

suffering, it is tempting, although etymologically uncertain, to suggest a connection between the German root-words *Lied* and *Leid.*

16. See chapter 1 for a discussion of the two different kinds of suffering.

17. I am referring, of course, to the hybrid form of tragedy and to the considerable role of the choral ode in fifth-century Athenian drama.

18. In the *Poetics*, Aristotle ranks music as next to last among the six elements of tragedy (plot—*muthos*—being the "most important"). He also fails to discuss at any length the chorus, which is, of course, closer, by his own accounts, to the origin and "birth" of tragedy. See my discussion of Aristotle's "structuration" (pace Ricoeur) in "Enigma of Aristotelian Metaphor."

19. Society, according to Nietzsche, is actually based on the *principium individuationis* (*Birth of Tragedy* xxi, 124–25).

20. It is interesting in this respect that the first, and still most important, discussion of metaphor occurs in Aristotle's treatise on tragedy. It is thus worthwhile considering the parallels between a theory of linguistic transgression and a theory of tragic flaws. See my discussion of this in *The Critical Double,* 62–73.

21. The rending of Dionysus, and the ritualistic dismembering and ingestion of live animals, is discussed by Dodds ("Introduction," xi–lix).

22. The similarities between Nietzsche's model of the Apollonian/Dionysian and Freud's later model of the conscious/unconscious are addressed in chapter 4.

23. "Die einzige überhaupt wahrhaft seiende und ewige, im Grunde der Dinge ruhende Ichheit, durch deren Abbilder der lyrische Genius bis auf den Grund der Dinge hindurchsieht" (Nietzsche, *Werke,* 1:38).

24. It is remarkable, and a good example of what Garon means by the "indefensible premises" of most analyses of the blues, that some critics continue to insist on the idea of the blues as a direct representation of the artist's personal life, despite all the evidence to the contrary (*Blues and the Poetic Spirit,* 17). For example, the great blues historian Paul Oliver describes such lyrics as these by Robert Johnson as "autobiographical" solely because of the contemporary geographical references:

> If your man get personal, want to have some fun
> If your man get personal, want to have some fun
> Best come on back to Friars Point mama, barrelhouse all night long.
> I got women's in Vicksburg, clean on into Tennessee
> I got women's in Vicksburg, clean on into Tennessee
> But my Friars Point rider hops all over me.
> (qtd. in Oliver, *Story of the Blues,* 119)

25. Sophocles, *Oedipus the King,* 64.

26. As one might expect, the so-called twelve-bar progression is often noted, while the less quantifiable "choking," which I maintain here is even more important, is frequently ignored.

27. Confirmation of this definition of the two defining characteristics of the blues can be found in Oliver's *Story of the Blues:* "Though the influences on the blues are complex, the two major roots were the hollers of the field hands, *freely structured and modal* in character, and the [European] ballads with their more *disciplined* eight and twelve-bar forms and conventional harmonic progression" (25). Oliver goes on to explain that the "freer," "modal" melody is synonymous with the "tendency to flatten the 3rd and 7th in the major scale" that I describe.

Although I add the "choked" fifth as one of the essential flattened tones, I would not argue with his notion that the third and seventh are the most important.

28. There are none by Robert Johnson, and precious few are to be found among the recordings of other classic blues artists such as Muddy Waters, Blind Lemon, and others.

29. In *The Story of the Blues*, Oliver writes that the early blues songs "took the simple chord progression of the English popular ballads: tonic, subdominant, dominant . . . the basic progression" (24).

30. Although I am perhaps stressing the importance of the flattened third, fifth, and seventh more than most, my emphasis on the importance of this characteristic of the blues is hardly unique. As Oliver writes in *The Story of the Blues*, "it has been argued that the tendency to flatten the 3rd and 7th in the major scale which is characteristic of jazz and blues has resulted from the indecision that the Negro has encountered in attempting to relate an African pentatonic scale to the European diatonic. . . . this is too facile an explanation (24–25).

31. This essential Nietzschean doctrine of the creative "eternal return" is discussed in chapter 8. It is also elaborated poetically by Yeats throughout his oeuvre, most explicitly in the famous "Lapis Lazuli": "All things fall and are built again / And those that build them again are gay" (*Collected Poems*, 292).

32. The links between Nietzsche's and Freud's notions of the Dionysian and the unconscious (respectively) are discussed in chapter 4.

33. Of course, there are many studies, such as Alan Lomax's *Land Where the Blues Began* (New York: Pantheon, 1993), that read their theses of the blues as originating in the socioeconomic conditions of such artists as Son House, Robert Johnson, and Muddy Waters back into their "historical" accounts. But if one approaches these great artists less condescendingly, one would see that, at the very least, such conditions are no more significant in the creation of their art than they were in the lives of Mozart, Beethoven, Van Gogh, or Picasso.

34. In *The Birth of Tragedy*, Nietzsche writes: "In the Dionysian dithyramb man is incited to . . . sink back into the original oneness of nature" (ii, 27).

35. The same point is made, without any explanation, by Garon in his brilliant, iconoclastic *Blues and the Poetic Spirit*: "Matters are confused by the fact that the listener often tries to concretize his emotional response to the music by displacing the affect associated with the music on to the lyrics" (29).

Chapter 7: On the Kindness of Strangers

1. For example, see George Steiner, *Language and Silence* (London: Penguin, 1969), who nonetheless writes eloquently and at length about this silence.

2. Aeschylus, *Aeschylus*, ed. and trans. Richmond Lattimore, vol. 1 (Chicago: University of Chicago Press, 1953), 78.

3. Adorno, *Negative Dialectics*, 361.

4. Ibid., 364.

5. Ibid., 365. Frederic Jameson writes in *Postmodernism* (Durham, N.C.: Duke University Press, 1992) that the postmodern, schizophrenic "experience suggests the following": "first, the breakdown of temporality suddenly releases the present of time from all the activities and intentionalities that might focus it and make it a space of praxis; thereby isolated, that present suddenly engulfs the subject with

undescribable vividness, a *materiality* of perception properly overwhelming, which effectively dramatizes the power of the *material*—or better still, the literal—signifier in isolation" (27 [emphasis added]). In "De Man and Guilt," Allan Stoekl writes: "This [de Manian] performative aspect of language is 'anti-grav' (one imagines a word processor on autopilot drifting off into the void of space), operating like a grammar, with no necessary links to 'human' purpose or intention, but also 'entirely ruthless in its inability to modify its own structural design for nonstructural reasons' . . . . on this point he [de Man] never wavered; near the end of his life, in 'The Return to Philology,' he was still maintaining, as the most basic gesture of his approach, the refusal of a criticism that would play an ethical, moral, or 'religious' role" (in *Responses to Paul de Man's Wartime Journalism,* ed. Warner Hamacher et al. [Lincoln: University of Nebraska Press, 1989], 380, 384).

6. Robbe-Grillet, "Nature, Humanism, Tragedy," 51–53.

7. See chapter 5.

8. Although Resnais did not actually work with Robbe-Grillet until some five years after *Nuit et brouillard,* his obvious affinities with the experimental narrative techniques of the nouveau roman school, of which Robbe-Grillet's treatise is the representative manifesto, are noted by all his critics (Ward, Benayoun, Sweet, and others). Of Jean Cayrol, the screenwriter of *Nuit et brouillard,* John Ward writes in *Alain Resnais* (Garden City, N.Y.: Doubleday, 1968): "Cayrol's script [for Resnais's *Muriel*], *in common with the work of Robbe-Grillet,* owes its technique to Husserl's phenomenology" (65 [emphasis added]). Nonetheless, it is curious that the same writers who note the emphasis on "thingness" and objectivity in Resnais's films in general also interpret *Nuit et brouillard* as a protest against the very same materialistic immanence.

9. In *Alain Resnais,* Ward writes that "*Nuit et brouillard* is an exercise in artistic restraint. Resnais allows actual photographs and films to speak for him: in the few scenes he shot especially for the film points are made visually, and, in Cayrol's script, with infinite sadness rather than anger. A shot of the outside of the camp hospital bathed in red light says all that needs to be said about its purpose. . . . the result is an unbearably painful film. . . . Such restraint makes *Nuit et brouillard* unique among films about the camps: it succeeds in treating its subject with dignity" (142–43).

10. Robbe-Grillet, "Nature, Humanism, Tragedy," 58–59.

11. The barber (Abraham Bomba), qtd. in Claude Lanzmann, *Shoah* (New York: Pantheon, 1985), 117.

12. In *Negative Dialectics* (New York: Continuum, 1987), Theodor Adorno writes: "The inhuman part of it, the ability to keep one's distance as a spectator and to rise above things, is in the final analysis the human part, the very part resisted by its ideologists" (363).

13. Richard Rorty, *Contigency, Irony, and Solidarity* (Cambridge: Cambridge University Press, 1989), 16.

14. Yet there is a significant difference between these two "realists" regarding *metaphor.* In *Contingency, Irony, and Solidarity,* Rorty praises metaphor as a way out of abstract, dogmatic thinking (39), whereas Robbe-Grillet condemns the trope as an idealistic falsification of the literal reality—a view he shares with his artistic mentor Kafka (*For a New Novel* 53–54). Like Adorno, Rorty does not see the "negative dialectics" of a materially immanent world as sustaining objective truth,

a fact that explains why Robbe-Grillet—and not Adorno and Rorty—condemns tragedy.

15. Rorty, *Contingency, Irony, and Solidarity*, 39–40.

16. Ibid., 41.

17. Adorno, *Negative Dialectics*, 363.

18. Rorty, *Contingency, Irony, and Solidarity*, 40 (emphasis added).

19. Adorno, *Negative Dialectics*, 363.

20. Robbe-Grillet explicitly condemns irony, along with nature, humanism, and tragedy, in *For a New Novel* (49–75), while Rorty's *Contingency, Irony, and Solidarity* allows for the recuperation of meaninglessness that irony affords.

21 Roland Barthes, qtd. in Robbe-Grillet, "Nature, Humanism, Tragedy," 49.

22. See chapter 5.

23. Aristotle, *Poetics*, in *Classical Literary Criticism*, trans. T. S. Dorsch (Middlesex, U.K.: Penguin, 1965), 31–75.

24. "Spiel . . . welches der Wille, *in der ewigen Fülle seiner Lust*, mit sich selbst spielt" (Nietzsche, *Werke*, 1:131).

25. Freud, one will recall, expressly makes the point in "The Poet and Daydreaming" that play is not opposed to seriousness, but rather to the "reality principle" of everyday life (143).

26. This mockery of understanding is of course the theme, if not the very name, of *Oedipus*. Recall Gilles Deleuze's suggestive comment in *Nietzsche and Philosophy* (New York: Columbia University Press, 1983) about the misunderstood relationship between Nietzsche and Kant: "we believe that there is, in Nietzsche, not only a Kantian heritage, but a half-avowed, half-hidden rivalry" (52).

Chapter 8: The Birth of Zarathustra from the Spirit of Tragedy

1. Sallis's 1991 book *Crossings* is one attempt to reread *The Birth of Tragedy* (without, however, arguing for the connections analyzed here).

2. Friedrich Nietzsche, *Ecco Homo*, trans. W. Kaufmann (New York: Vintage, 1974), 80.

3. Heidegger, *Nietzsche*, 2:28–29 (emphasis added).

4. This is not to ignore the fact that Nietzsche omits the Latin phrase from the beginning of *Thus Spoke Zarathustra* (for which references appear parenthetically in the text). Stylistically, the title format is common only in *Fröhliche Wissenschaft*.

5. Heidegger, *Nietzsche*, 2:28 (emphasis added).

6. Sophocles, *Oedipus the King*, 64.

7. Deleuze's *Nietzsche and Philosophy* has a great deal of importance to say about the "eternal return" that is completely consistent with, although stated very differently from, the interpretation offered here: "How does the thought of pure becoming serve as a foundation for the eternal return? All we need to do to think this thought is to stop believing in being as distinct from and opposed to becoming or to believe in the being of becoming itself" (48).

8. Friedrich Nietzsche, *The Gay Science*, trans. W. Kaufmann (New York: Vintage, 1974), 273–74.

9. Heidegger, *Nietzsche*, 2:25.

10. This despite acknowledging that "the doctrine [of the eternal return] is so significant to Nietzsche's project in Zarathustra" (160). See Kathleen Marie Higgins, *Nietzsche's Zarathustra* (Philadelphia: Temple University Press, 1987).

11. See chapter 3.

12. Dionysus has a particularly compelling role in this regard; for, unlike the other Greek gods, he (like Christ) is known by his earthly incarnation.

13. Heidegger's analysis of Nietzschean "rapture as form-engendering" is discussed in chapter 1.

14. Jacques Sojcher (qtd. in Gérard Genette, *Figures of Literary Discourse* [New York: Columbia University Press, 1982]) says: "Metaphor is no longer a figure among others, but the figure, the trope of tropes" (115).

15. See *Friedrich Nietzsche on Rhetoric and Language*, ed. Gilman et al.

16. There have been numerous occasions to repeat Nietzsche's repetition of Schopenhauer's image of the "gently rocking rowboat" as an image of the Apollonian object versus the oceanic Dionysian (Nietzsche, *Birth of Tragedy* i, 22). The most famous reference to the sea is doubtless from *The Gay Science* (180–81), which precedes the famous "God is dead" aphorism.

17. In *Aesthetics*, Hegel writes: "Oedipus discovered the simple answer that it was man himself, and hurled the sphinx from the rocks . . . just as the famous Greek inscription cries out to mankind: 'Know thyself'" (2:83–84).

18. Metaphor, which Aristotle describes as a "transgression" of proper language, is also cognate with impurity and "incest." Despite numerous attempts to resolve the enigma of metaphor, it remains a "living" denial of rational meaning. See Ricoeur, *La métaphor vive*.

19. Heidegger, *Nietzsche*, 1:5 (emphasis added).

20. Arguing against the traditional view of tragic catharsis, Nietzsche insists that the affirmation of tragedy is "not so as to get rid of pity and fear, not so as to purify oneself of a dangerous emotion through its vehement discharge—it was thus Aristotle misunderstood it—but, beyond pity and fear, to realize in oneself the eternal joy of becoming" (*Ecce Homo*, 81).

21. In *The Birth of Tragedy*, Nietzsche asks: "What is the relation of the Olympian gods to this [Silenus's] popular wisdom?" (iii, 29).

22. In *Nietzsche and Philosophy*, Deleuze interprets the shepherd scene in similar terms as revealing the relationship between the eternal superhuman and its "disgust" with the stifling sameness of the human: "This condition of man is of the greatest importance for the eternal return. It seems to compromise or contaminate it so gravely that it becomes an object of anguish, repulsion and disgust. Even if active forces return they will again become reactive" (65).

23. See Nietzsche, *Ecce Homo*, 81–82.

Index

PAUL GORDON, an associate professor and chair of comparative literature/humanities at the University of Colorado at Boulder, is the author of *The Critical Double: Figurative Meaning in Aesthetic Discourse* and numerous essays on film, literature, and literary theory. He is working on a study entitled "Art and the Absolute" from Schelling through Heidegger, as well as a psychoanalytic study of the films of Alfred Hitchcock.

Typeset in 9.5/12.5 Trump Medieval
with Trump Italic display
Composed at the University of Illinois Press
Manufactured by Thomson-Shore, Inc.

University of Illinois Press
1325 South Oak Street
Champaign, IL 61820-6903
www.press.uillinois.edu